STUART HALL'S VOICE

David Scott

STUART HALL'S
VOICE

INTIMATIONS *of an*
ETHICS *of* RECEPTIVE
GENEROSITY

DUKE UNIVERSITY PRESS
Durham and London 2017

© 2017 Duke University Press
All rights reserved
Printed in the United States of America on acid-free paper ∞
Designed by Heather Hensley
Typeset in Chaparral Pro by Westchester Publishing Services

Library of Congress Cataloging-in-Publication Data
Names: Scott, David, [date] author.
Title: Stuart Hall's voice : intimations of an ethics of
receptive generosity / David Scott.
Description: Durham : Duke University Press, 2017. |
Includes bibliographical references and index.
Identifiers: LCCN 2016045050 (print)
LCCN 2016047430 (ebook)
ISBN 9780822363637 (hardcover : alk. paper)
ISBN 9780822373025 (e-book)
Subjects: LCSH: Hall, Stuart, 1932–2014—Criticism and
interpretation. | Culture—Philosophy. | Political sociology. |
Sociologists—Great Britain.
Classification: LCC HM479.H35S36 2017 (print) |
LCC HM479.H35 (ebook) |
DDC 301.092—dc23
LC record available at https://lccn.loc.gov/2016045050

Front and back cover art: Chris Ofili, *Afromuses (Couple)*,
1995–2005, Diptych; watercolor and pencil on paper; each:
9 5/8 × 6 1/8 in., © Chris Ofili, Private Collection.
Photo: Joshua White/JWPictures.com.

The greatness of a man is to be found not in his acts but in his style. Existence does not resemble a steadily rising curve, but a slow, and sometimes sad, series of ups and downs.

—Frantz Fanon

CONTENTS

Apology

On Intellectual Friendship

———

DEAR STUART,

I begin with an apology in advance for what follows, an apology for insisting on continuing our conversations in this *epistolary* form. I know it's an imposition, possibly an impolite one, certainly unsolicited; but with these letters I hope at least to be able to *clarify*—this is a word I'll use a lot throughout—something of what I've found so compelling in your way of being the intellectual you've been, or, I guess, the intellectual you *were*. (I have to admit straight off that I'm a little confused about the grammatical *tense* in which to address you, so I hope you'll allow me a certain ambiguity; it arises, I suppose, from my persisting inability to release you into a final past.) As you know, for me it's not been your views in themselves as much as your *way* of having views—how you've gone about having views, and again having *other* and further views—that has intrigued me. And in what follows this is what I want to talk with you about, to continue worrying you about—a little.

I saw you last in early December 2013 when I was passing through London on my way back to New York from Cape Town where I'd delivered three lectures under the general title "Stuart Hall's Voice" at the University of the Western Cape.[1] That was a very stimulating occasion, rich in innumerable intellectual ways. These lectures were an attempt to expand and elaborate an intuition about you that I'd been harboring for a while and that I'd tried to articulate in a short essay ambitiously called "Stuart Hall's Ethics," first presented, you may remember, at a conference in your honor at the University of the West Indies, Mona, in 2004, and subsequently published in *Small Axe*.[2] That essay had always seemed to me lamentably underdeveloped, scarcely finished, actually, and I'd always wanted to give its central concern—namely, to connect your explicit voice to your implicit ethics—another go. So, then, returning from Cape Town, and sitting as we often did at your dining table at Ulysses Road, under the blank gaze of a pair of Chris Ofili's sardonic *Afro Muses* (the ones that now grace the front and back covers of this book), we talked about my interest in the idea of *voice*, both in its literal and in its extended, metaphorical dimensions, and of the possible general relation between voice and the *ethos* of an intellectual style. And we talked in this context too about my exploration of the question of *your* voice specifically, and why your voice seemed to me so necessarily an integral part of who you've been, who you were, as an intellectual. Your voice, I suggested to you, might be thought of as sounding the *content of the form* of your ethos of intellectual style. Remarkably, you seemed to find this line of thinking of mine altogether unexceptional. Modestly, as usual, you wondered whether I wasn't making too much of it; but you also volunteered a number of personal anecdotes that suggested your self-conscious awareness of voice—including your own voice—and the possible implications of taking voice seriously for understanding your practice of the intellectual vocation. I couldn't, of course, set out for you the whole of what I wanted to say about voice and style and ethics in the couple of days we had to ourselves in London, but, needless to say, I was very pleased that you found what I was aiming to do in the Cape Town lectures an at least plausible and intelligible way of *approaching* you. That's all I needed.

But then, alas, Stuart, you died one morning early the following year: 10 February 2014. Not entirely unexpectedly, that's true. Not unreasonably, either, given the amount of your pain and discomfort, the sheer fatigu-

APOLOGY

ing difficulty of simply going on with the ordinary cares and duties and pleasures of living. Selfishly, though, greedily too, I guess, there were those of us remaining who'd hoped to have a little more of you, for a little longer. It's just that this nonnegotiable fact of death is so precipitous, so vertical in its irreversibly absolute finality. So much is left suspended in the sudden, unlit absence. It's what makes death so radical and so unforgiving an interruption, I suppose, so impossible to really prepare for. Finitude's wake is made up of ellipses . . . an infinite number of them. They mark out the soundless rhythm of eternal *aftermaths*. And what only yesterday had seemed so tangible in our conversations, so concrete, so here and now, however fragile and unreliable the languages of communication, must now depend almost entirely on the even more fragile and even more unreliable figurations of memory to order and shape with meaning and purpose our living sense of loss.

And so, Stuart, having barely set about the task, I found myself unable to revise the lectures for publication in the straightforward discursive form in which I had—perhaps naively, in retrospect—composed and delivered them to my indulgent audiences in Cape Town. That familiar form now seemed to me dismally inappropriate, hopelessly inadequate as a way of rendering to myself, and to others, what I felt I'd been learning from your voice and the intellectual style it sounded. Above all, I found I could not quite detach what I was trying to say in the lectures from the dialogical and exploratory texture of the conversations out of which they had originally grown, around your dining table, and especially from the implicit address and extended duration of those living conversations. Somehow the lectures, delivered while you were still alive, now seemed merely didactic, drained of the presence—and, moreover, the assumption of *continuing* presence—that had animated and driven them in the first place.

Indeed, I was on the point of altogether abandoning the task of revising them when it struck me that perhaps all was not completely lost, that something might yet be salvageable from what I'd written and spoken about you. Because, as it happened, I'd already, tentatively, it's true, begun to explore a mode of communication with you that was seeking, in the face of absence, to preserve and even extend some aspects at least of the character of our prolonged dialogue: the mode of communication of *letters*. I'd already written two of them, experimentally—one on the occasion of your eightieth birthday (about which you whispered to me an unspeakable comment), and the other in the immediate aftermath of your lamented passing.[3] For some reason, I can't exactly say why, the epistolary form had slowly begun to assert a certain claim on my way of thinking *about* you, and thinking *with* you. It came to me out of the blue, almost, as I was carrying on one of my interminable imagined conversations with you, as I was casting about for the best language in which to clarify our similarities and differences, where I thought our paths intersected and diverged, what we shared and what we didn't.

I suppose, though, that in some way my inchoate attraction to the letter-form grew out of my preoccupation with another somewhat hybrid form, namely, the *interview*, with which I'd been experimenting for many years, including, inaugurally, with *you*, you'll remember.[4] Hardly what connoisseurs would deem literature—too workmanlike, too clunky—still, for me, the interviews I've conducted have always been more than ways to convey the content of new information about my interlocutors; they have been explorations of form—as much as anything else. Like you, Stuart, I've always been provoked by the problem of *form*, by form *as a problem*, by the relationship between representation and the content of intellectual and political and artistic thinking, by the nontransparency and noncorrespondence of that relationship specifically. And these days I feel more and more provoked by it as we confront the inert cynicism of institutional authority toward conventional (realist no more than antirealist) modes of dissenting or nonconforming intellectual and political and artistic activity. (To me, Stuart, one way of understanding the "cultural studies" you invented is that it is less an experiment with new content, though there was plenty of that too, than an experiment with a novel thinking-form.) Therefore, to me, as I think also for you, form is an ever-present *question* rather than something we should take for granted as decided once and for all by the orthodoxies of doctrines and disciplines. Indeed, it is partly my worry about the adequateness or appropriateness or usefulness of "critical" discourses to their besetting challenges—their contexts of articulation, their problem-spaces—that brought me to the interviews and that has now prompted me down this epistolary path with you. In some measure, at least, I share the doubts of those like Rita Felski who urge that what has been called "critique" in various guises of method and mood stands in need of a good deal of rethinking.[5] In my view, as I've said elsewhere, part of the issue turns on the overbearing conceits of omniscience that critique seems unable (even where allegedly willing) to cast off.[6] Like an indulgent sovereign, critique seems invariably to stand, knowing and aloof, outside the community for whom it claims to speak, needing from its object of scrutiny nothing more than a passive, mute acquiescence. I know you had your doubts about certain tendencies in critique, Stuart (about "critical theory" most especially, its reflexive will-to-truth), but given your commitments as an actively engaged intellectual, perhaps you wouldn't have quite agreed with the formulation of my objections here. Still, persisting, in the following letter I will offer you a contrast between a "critical self" who is an agent of critique, and a "listening self" who is an agent of attunement and receptivity, and suggest that you, Stuart, were as much the latter as the former, possibly even *more so* the latter than the former.

As I have tried to use it, the interview has been precisely a way of evading critique while nevertheless practicing discerning and engaged thinking-with-others; specifically, it's been an experiment with the relation between form and historical-biographical-generational knowledge. And as I've said before (perhaps also to you, though I don't remember if I put it quite this way), what has especially interested me about the craft of the interview, so to call it, about its partly performative and partly contemplative craft, is the constitutive relation to dialogue and time it organizes. In a special way, the interview embodies (or, at any rate, *potentially* embodies) the *temporality* of dialogue. Its dynamic hermeneutic structure is that of the unfolding of question-and-answer; its motivation is more tentatively exploratory, clarifying, and reconstructive than explicitly critical or even analytical; and its medium is first and foremost that of *voice*—voice lived unevenly and somewhat asymmetrically, it is true, but nevertheless plurally and cooperatively, in a temporally open and recursive dialectic of speaking and listening.[7] Proximity and provisionality are therefore part of the very weaving of an interview—at least, such as I've tried to make use of the form in the many long inter-views I've conducted with Caribbean intellectuals and writers over the years.

And so now, Stuart, I want to speculate, even wager, that perhaps the letter-form might share at least some of these dialogical and temporal virtues, and might potentially disclose others distinctly its own that will help me clarify to us both what I think is going on with your voice in your style. You'd know better than me, I'm sure, that the letter-form is an old and almost legendary literary device for narrative fictions—from Samuel Richardson's *Pamela* (1740) and *Clarissa* (1748) to Alice Walker's *The Color Purple* (1970) or C. L. R. James's *The Nobbie Stories for Children and Adults* (2006), to cite some obvious (if not always juxtaposed) exam-ples. But more interestingly to me, in this context, anyway, the letter-form has also inspired such diverse and differently motivated instances as Georg Lukács's "On the Nature and Form of the Essay: A Letter to Leo Popper" and Françoise Sagan's "Lettre d'amour à Jean-Paul Sartre," in which an epistolary technique blurs the boundaries between the fictive and the nonfictive, between essay and story, between the philosophic and the literary, and offers me therefore a hybrid genre in which to con-sider, however preliminarily, some otherwise obscured questions about voice and style and ethos.[8] For like the interview, the letter, notably, is an explicitly *speaking* form. It is alive, almost. A letter dispatched is always an act of *address*; a letter received is always someone *heard* from. As with the interview, the letter is enacted in the register of voice—or the *mimesis* of voice—in such a way as to call into being, to activate, the dialogical presence of a specific interlocutor. In the case of the episto-lary interlocutor, however, this presence of the other, my putative corre-spondent, is a *physically* absent one. We are not copresent to each other's discourse. Indeed, as we write, we live suspended in the temporal delay between the letter's dispatch and the anticipated arrival of the returning voice. *Waiting*, I'd say, marks the letter's poetics of time, the projected duration that orients its shared imagination of dialogical possibility and expectation. My correspondent's reply, the letter's arrival, however belated, however postponed, completes—provisionally, for the time

APOLOGY

—

6

being—a *hermeneutic* circle of sorts. This perhaps is the implicit, minimum plurality that constitutes a *correspondence*. But alas, Stuart, what if, like you, my interlocutor has passed on—is now dead? How will I henceforth animate my expectation of our conversation's futurity? How much waiting can I endure? How will I anticipate the give-and-take of clarifying response that not only enlivens real dialogue, real exchange, but enables real learning and real unlearning as well? What mortal handicap, then, does this epistolary design augur? What act of imagination will my restorative desire to continue speaking to you in this way solicit? What grammatological fiction—or forgery—must I participate in if now I'm speaking to a ghost? You can see I'm full of uncertainties here. I'm already at sea. Now that you're no longer here, Stuart, I will be obliged to guess at what your reactions might be to what I'm saying to you, *about* you, and I'll have to hope that you won't mind if here and there I falter or misstep, or inadvertently take liberties with you I might not otherwise take. Here, maybe, are some of the privileges and hazards of presuming to converse with the dead.

But, to continue my wager, the letter-form potentially does something *more* than merely preserve and enlarge the dialogical voice in its temporal experience and in its elegiac mood—or, maybe it does something *else* in the course of doing these vital things. The interview, remember, though not a completely impersonal or detached form, is not exactly a solicitously familiar one either; its merit, it is true, is that it is not an abstractly critical interrogation like the monograph of an anthropological or philosophic treatise. But still it depends on relationships of proximity in which, generally speaking, nothing more than studied acquaintance is needed to drive the intellectual process forward. By contrast with this, Stuart, I want to suggest that the letter is potentially the literary embodiment of a quality of relationship that might be called, simply, *friendship*. As a way of keeping company with special others, the letter seems to me uniquely able to disclose, or, less passively, to enact, some of the relational sentiments and virtues we commonly think of as internal to friendship: among them (and in no particular order), affection, loyalty, indulgence, sympathy, complementarity, tolerance, equality, stability, candor, respect, truthfulness, liberality, trustworthiness. In this sense, more than any other literary form, I believe, the letter has the capacity to *honor* friendship—to give friendship its measure and its due. You'll begin to see what I mean, Stuart, if you think, for example, of the published correspondence between those legendary friends Karl Marx and Friedrich Engels. In the warmth and knowing familiarity and affection that saturates their epistolary exchange, you can see how their relationship (with all its itinerant, embattled uncertainties) sheltered their personal and intellectual lives, and even (to a very poignant degree, however precariously) enabled the very survival of their radical political projects.[9] Or, again, and perhaps more important to my considerations, think of the letters between Hannah Arendt and two very different long-lasting friends of hers from two very different literary-philosophic and geopolitical worlds: Mary McCarthy, on the one hand, and Karl Jaspers, on the other. In Arendt's correspondence with them you catch a glimpse of the contrasting tones of intimacy and concern and regard and rapport that nevertheless equally lit and enlivened the many years of their respective friendships.[10] You didn't much read Arendt, I know, Stuart (didn't quite see the point, you once told me). But I will hope to persuade you along the way—as I will with other thinkers you didn't much read—that she is useful to think with across many of the dimensions that mattered to us. And certainly in this respect, specifically, Arendt was a great, and more, an instructive, believer in the powers and promise of friendship, of what friendship potentially secures and enables in a relatively protected space that is neither exactly home nor world, neither exactly private nor public, but an unsystematic overlapping of both together.[11]

Anyway, Stuart, I'm sure you'll be relieved to know that while I do believe the letter *could* be a usefully didactic form I do not at this point intend to take you on an extended scholarly excursus through the great archive of writings in the history of Western literature about the value of friendship from, let's say, Plato and Aristotle and Cicero, among the ancients, to Michel de Montaigne and Immanuel Kant and Ralph Waldo Emerson and Maurice Blanchot and Michel Foucault and Derek Walcott, among the early and later moderns—a relentless parade, you'd have been sure to point out to me, of *men* fixated on men.[12] And indeed it is true, the literary-philosophic history of friendship is largely (if not entirely) the normative story of male homosociality, a point not unimportant to Foucault's brief but suggestive reflections on the privilege of friendship "as a way of life."[13] You will appreciate, though, I hope, Stuart, that while it will be Aristotle and Arendt (and Aristotle partly *through* Arendt) that stir much of my thinking here, I've also learned a lot from Cicero and Montaigne and Blanchot and Walcott especially, because their moving reflections on friendship (the first enacted, notably, as an imaginary dialogue, the other three as meditations) take the specific form of eloquent remembrances of a recently dead friend: in Cicero, Laelius remembering Scipio; in Montaigne, his remembrance of Etienne de la Boétie; in Blanchot, his memorialization of Georges Bataille; in Walcott, his evocation of Robert Lowell. This is where I find myself with you. To what extent friendship as a vivid idea is *retrospectively* called into being, to what extent it is largely if not only an effect of aftermaths, of looking back, and for this reason a value recalled principally in tones of *elegy*, I can't say. I have the sense, though, that part of what brings friendship's virtues into view, or better, into intimate experience, is precisely the irreversible vacancy that opens with the loss of friendship's company.

In recent decades, so it is said, there has been something of a revival of literary-philosophic interest in friendship.[14] You'll hesitantly ask me what has prompted this revival, and to tell the truth I'm not altogether sure. But it seems to me a very plausible and indeed attractive suggestion that it might have to do, at least in part, with some contemporary trends in approaches to normative ethics. I mean in particular the emergence of directions of ethical inquiry that are equidistant from, on the one hand, Kantian deontology (with its emphasis on rules and duties) and, on the other hand, utilitarianism (with its emphasis on the consequences of action), and that at the same time are more oriented toward varieties of Aristotelian virtue ethics (with its emphasis on the moral education of the excellences of character). As I've only just suggested, Kant himself didn't completely ignore friendship in his account of the doctrine of virtue, specifically moral friendship based on the union of love and respect, nor for that matter did John Stuart Mill, in his discussion of friendship in marriage, for example, in the last chapter of *The Subjection of Women*.[15] Still, Neera Badhwar is probably right to underline that on the whole both Kantianism and utilitarianism have largely neglected to treat friendship seriously as a generative ethical good.[16] You'll see, Stuart, as we proceed, why this turn in ethical inquiry toward

"virtue ethics" is of broad interest to me, how it connects to other preoccupations of mine—the idea of tragic conflict, among them—and in particular how it helps me frame a discussion about other excellences, such
as generosity, that I discern in your intellectual practice. Indeed, generosity is one of the cardinal virtues, and one that lives in the neighborhood
of "end friendships," as Aristotle understood those special relations that
disclose their own intrinsic values.[17]

Now, central to Aristotle's theory of friendship is his memorable idea
that a friend is essentially "another self." This is a frequently deliberated-
upon formulation, and I don't want to be waylaid by the thicket of ar-
cane philosophical discussion that surrounds it.[18] For my purposes, I
shall take Aristotle to be suggesting by this basically that friendship
with others is based, first and foremost, on friendship with oneself, or
more precisely with the other-in-oneself with whom one feels able to
carry on an inner dialogue.[19] We'll see later on, Stuart, that Arendt puts
this idea to very instructive use in *The Life of the Mind*, in describing the
"two-in-one" of the activity of thinking—thus making a link between
friendship and thinking that is very suggestive to me (even if I am not
going to be in entire sympathy with her formulation), because what
thinking was for you and how it connects to friendship are at the heart of
my preoccupations in these letters.[20] But for now it's enough to appreciate that a friend is best understood as a person who embodies those
qualities that make the externalization of the dialogue with oneself possible. If I can talk to you *as if* I'm talking to myself, in other words, *that*
is friendship. Put in a somewhat quotidian way, a friendship worthy of
the name is a *good* that grows voluntarily with time and familiarity out
of the rapport between individuals whose difference and similarity enable them to recognize something of value in each other, who treat each
other with constancy and respectful goodwill, and who (whether or not
they themselves are good) wish only for the good in the other.[21] Unlike kinship love and erotic love, friendship, which C. S. Lewis called in
his accommodating Christian way the "least natural of loves," the least
necessary, but also the least jealous, draws nevertheless from a mutual
recognition of something held in common, and is salted, seasoned, by a
reciprocal expectation for the kind of talk and company that meaningful
dialogue entails.[22] Not grace, then, exactly, that Lewis's charity maybe

brings, but something paradoxically at once nearer both the ordinary and the extraordinary.

At any rate, Stuart, considering friendship in this way helps me elaborate my intuitions about you because it reminds me of how much you yourself valued the company of friends, the fellowship, companionship, comradeship, they make possible—indeed, that with you, autonomous self-sufficiency was never a great aspiration, never an admired virtue. It reminds me that with you, speaking and listening (and therefore *voice*) were precisely organic modes of enlarging your self-awareness through your always-evolving awareness of others, the widening and deepening circle of others who could be thought of as dimensions of your extended self. But most of all, Stuart, it reminds me of some of the qualities of *our* friendship and offers me some conceptual resources with which to talk about it in the context of these letters. It helps me to talk, for example, about the familiarity-and-difference that animated our friendship, a familiarity-and-difference that, of course, was multidimensional but in defining ways was, I suppose, both generational and intellectual. I mean that we felt, I believe, a sense of kinship and recognition in displacement from Jamaica and all that that means symbolically and existentially, the sense of the loss of an assumed context of belonging. This is a Jamaica, moreover, that we knew from within a similar social and familial milieu and yet from different generational experiences and perspectives. It is not unimportant, for example, as I've said more than once, that we were shaped respectively by two especially volatile moments in Jamaica's modern political history: you by the decolonization of the 1940s, me by the socialism of the 1970s. But we lived our displacement from these Jamaicas through different metropolitan locations, in different political-historical conjunctures, and through different intellectual frames and commitments. Not surprisingly, then, our conceptual languages, though not necessarily at odds, were never identical to each other, were never seamlessly in harmony. Indeed, though I'd say they were sympathetic languages by and large, sharing some of the same sources and projects, they stood somewhat at an angle to each other, by turns converging and diverging in ways that, nevertheless, for better or worse, kept us talking to each other. And in this respect, one of the not-irrelevant things we talked about was our respective relation to "theory"—our senses of the discourses that constitute it, our senses of its role in the conduct of our intellectual lives. Or to put it another way, we read through different (if adjacent) archives—me often a philosophic and political-theoretical one, you a cultural-political one. Or to put it yet another way, but with a significant bearing on our styles of discourse, where you found yourself arguing with "essentialists" I find myself arguing with "anti-essentialists." These are not exact designations, of course, Stuart, but you know what I'm trying to get at; I'm saying only that our sense of familiarity-and-difference seasoned our friendship with an endless back-and-forth exchange and drew us to each other's work—less as a matter of adopting each other's perspectives (though, to be sure, we borrowed here and there) than as a matter of reciprocal learning and mutual clarification. I'll come back to this in a moment.

Now, for most writers who take up the theme of friendship, what matters principally is *personal* friendship, that is, expressly, the moral character of the bond of amity and pleasure and mutual goodwill and concord that secures and sustains the relationship between individual friends. Friendship is first and foremost a personal relationship, undergirded by passions and voluntarily assumed duties.[23] Undoubtedly this is the form of friendship that stands out most prominently in the canon, and rightly so. To this, of course, must immediately be added specifically *political* friendships, that is, friendships that are comradely solidarities and that have, as a consequence, a public, civic dimension. This is a form of friendship that resonates throughout the classical literature, in Aristotle and Cicero, for example; and it is certainly of explicit interest to Arendt.[24] What mostly interests me, by contrast, Stuart, is less our personal than our *intellectual* friendship, or what the former enables or implies (or *ought* to enable or imply) for the latter. By intellectual friendship I mean to focus on that dimension of friendship that offers a *dialogical context for thinking*. I'd tried to explain to you on one or two occasions, you'll remember, in between my other importunities, the sort of concern that gathers about this preoccupation with the relation friends might have to each other's intellectual work. Partly, this concern emerges out of the same doubt I've already articulated regarding critique, that is, what we do when we criticize the work of others.[25] Here I want to wonder what the implications of friendship are for the practice of criticism.

Let me ask it formally this way, Stuart: How should we approach the intellectual work of those we know well and, moreover, admire and honor? This is the general question about my relation to you that compels me. To put it slightly differently: What do friends *owe* each other intellectually? Are the obligations—say, of frankness, or of the offer of counsel—that obtain within the context of personal friendship central to the *intellectual* relationship between friends? When I read the work of my close friends, for example, should it provoke me into an attitude of "interpretation" or "explanation," or should it rather solicit from me some other mode or stance of intellectual consideration? I believe, Stuart, and I believe it more and more, that friendship might indeed have a bearing on how we should think about the intellectual work of those we know and admire and honor. It is, so it is said, one of the great consolations of personal friendship that not only is there a rough "harmony of interests" (Cicero) between friends but also, since friends are "ends" in themselves (Aristotle), this presumed convergence has always to be tempered by a measured "respect" (Cicero, Kant) for divergences and pluralities, and even irreducible conflicts (Arendt). So the question arises, if my friend is my "other self," what is the role of "disagreement" and "agreement" in *intellectual* friendship? Note, again, Stuart, that this is not a question about my *moral* attitude toward your views or behavior as such—whether they are, for example, "virtuous," as Plato and Aristotle and Cicero might have been keen to know (their idea being that friendship is only possible between people who are virtuous). I'm talking here about my *hermeneutic* relation to your intellectual work, and I'm asking whether agreement and disagreement are relevant to the vocabulary or to the virtues entailed in understanding each other. My working suggestion here is that these are at best minimally relevant. My suggestion is that what *is* relevant first and foremost to intellectual friendship is something more like an attitude of *attuned awareness* of the work of those we know and admire and honor—an attuned awareness, specifically, of something more than the substantive argumentative details of their intellectual contribution, an appreciative awareness, one might say, of something like the integrity of the ethos and style disclosed in their work.⌉

What intellectual friendship solicits, I believe, is an attitude of attentive receptivity, a readiness to appreciatively hear where the other is coming from. I believe this attitude comports with your intellectual intuitions, Stuart, your way of relating to the work of those who were significant to you. In my opinion, this attitude that intellectual friendship solicits does not depend on a necessary *convergence* between the respective views or perspectives or frameworks of relevant friends. To the contrary, an attitude of attentive awareness, such as I am commending here among intellectual friends, may well rely *more* on the resources of difference; it may well require sustaining a nonjudgmental and nonprescriptive *tension* between our views or perspectives or frameworks—a tension, the friction of a receptive resistance, that obliges some amount of *translation* to be constantly at play so as to enable each of us to gain some uptake on what the other is saying. This would be a continuous process, perhaps, of trying to evoke, or to *render* (that might be the better word), the ethos and style of the other's discourse in an idiom that is not necessarily or precisely their own. You can tell Stuart that such an attitude of receptivity does not aim at, or amount to, "explanation" in any respectable sense. But might it be a version of "interpretation"? I'm not completely sure. I'd say that the hermeneutic stance I'm gesturing at is one that aims more at *clarification* than at interpretation (or, if one were to insist, at interpretation understood as a *mode* of clarification).

You will immediately ask me what I mean by this, I know, Stuart, and rightly so, because for you too clarification was a term of art: I remember your use of it, for example, in your 1980 essay "Cultural Studies and the Centre: Some Problematics and Problems," in which you talk about the center's journal, *Working Papers in Cultural Studies*, being concerned not with a "descriptive definition or prescription of the field" of cultural studies but with a "sustained work of theoretical clarification."[26] Or again, later, in the famous 1988 "New Ethnicities" essay, you talk about a practice that aims to "clarify" rather than "pre-empt" issues.[27] So to me clarification is recognizably one of your own hermeneutic orientations. And I take my uses of it here to be allied to yours, if drawn from different sources and toward different concerns. As you already know, and as I've underlined earlier in talking about form, I'm not aiming at a critique of you or your work; I've no desire to get *beyond* you, wherever that would be. I am not even minimally trying to explain you to anyone (except maybe myself). I can't claim to be in command of the real Stuart Hall—whoever that might be (in fact, I wonder whether *you* were in command of him, whether, to the contrary, the absence of that command wasn't part of your point about "provisionality" and all that). And yet, Stuart, it is self-evidently true that I find myself talking with you, about you, here and elsewhere, and therefore tacitly at least invoking some "you" and some "aboutness" about you. I can't help it. There is therefore a hermeneutic at work in my relation to you that is not adequately covered by the term *interpretation* and that invites, rather, the more open, the more receptive, the more appreciative idea of clarification. I mean to suggest that clarification may be a better way to think about the internal goods to be derived from intellectual friendship. For clarification, notably, is not concerned principally with the truth as such of another's discourse. And consequently it doesn't present itself in an adversarial or combative attitude. Overcoming is not its ideal horizon. Rather, *learning* is what clarification seeks, encourages, more and better learning, and therefore what it aims at hermeneutically is that solicitous and receptive and dialogical attitude that cultivates the possibility of learning. Or again, clarification calls upon something already incipiently, discernibly, there in the ongoing dialogue, and calls for its amplification, elaboration. Clarification calls for a practice of reciprocity, but it need not be a reciprocity of a procedurally equal or symmetrical kind. Indeed, it is often an uneven or unequal or asymmetrical reciprocity—as I've said about intellectual friendship especially across generations, there is typically someone who seeks understanding and someone from whom understanding is sought.[28]

When I think of clarification, Stuart, I'm put in mind of something like the intellectual *attitude* one finds at work in the later Wittgenstein—again not exactly one of your go-to heroes, though I've known you to reference the idea of a "language game" at least once in the context of talking about language and its uses.[29] In any case, I have in mind the character of work such as *Philosophical Investigations*, or *Culture and Value*, or *On Certainty*, work in which we not only see Wittgenstein altering his very *idea* of what *thinking* is but also see him *carrying out, carrying on*, thinking, on the very page in a testing, exploratory way. Indeed, I confess I'm less interested in Wittgenstein's theory of language, however that might be defined, than the work his writing *does* in, about, and through language.[30] (I'm reminded of Susan Sontag's illuminating remark that Wittgenstein practiced philosophy as a kind of "art form.")[31] I'd say that the point for me of the approach to thinking exemplified in these works on the vagaries of ordinary language (even if Wittgenstein didn't himself explicitly say this) is precisely *clarification*: the putting to work of a recursive linguistic phenomenology, really only a practice of re-description, that seeks no more than to worry about, to elucidate, to draw out or make less inchoate or obscure, the assumptions and values and orientations already normatively at play in the discourse or text at hand. Clarification is a way of approaching thinking—and learning— that aims to make us more aware of what we are saying or doing. Thus you will recognize, Stuart, that on this view what clarification entails is not the tiresome drive for some final propositional truth, something beyond itself that will signal the authoritative end of the inquiry. Clarification is not a means to an end other than itself; it is its own end (perhaps, at once, its own cognitive and moral end). And, of course, as such it is an endless end. That is to say, clarification involves endlessly saying the *next* thing, never the last thing. Clarification therefore does not presume the possibility of resolution; on the contrary, there is no presumption of closure, only successive, provisional resting points along the way where we gather our thoughts for further dialogical probing.

It's obvious, Stuart, that I take you to be an exemplary intellectual, but in the sense that I find you good, that is, productive, to think with, to think through. If I repeat that this has less to do with the content of your thought than with the style of your thinking—what, in effect, I am calling your voice—it's only to underscore the paradoxical matrix of friendship that is the condition of these letters. I'm not drawn to you, for example, because I share (or even want to share) entirely your theoretical idiom or conceptual language—that, say, of "cultural studies." Nor is it because I share (or even want to share) entirely your substantive views about the various issues you've taken up over the course of a remarkable intellectual life—those concerning the Left, say, or British politics or the media or diaspora or race or visual art (the list is a long one). To the contrary, there is a sense in which it is precisely because I don't exactly share these, point for point, that there reflexively opens between us a potential hermeneutic space of overlapping difference. This, to my mind, is the space of our intellectual friendship. It is the space of the give-and-take of clarifying dialogue. Note once more that the hermeneutic idiom or figure that presents itself to me, that calls upon me—that summons me—is that of voice. I am, above all, interested in bending my ear to your resonant voice, Stuart. Even as I want to think of you as a responsive listener, I too am aiming to learn a mode of listening to what you have to say, and above all to the way in which you say it. I am aiming, in other words, to learn my own version of what I will shortly call your ethics of receptivity and reciprocal attunement. This, too, perhaps, is part of what it must mean to try to understand the friends we know and admire and honor. Listening, we will see, is the hermeneutic attitude, par excellence, of intellectual friendship. And what listening enables is the work of clarification.

So I'd say that the challenge that intellectual friendship calls us to is a reciprocal clarifying exploration, a process of gradually expanding, enlarging the cognitive circle, the space of intelligibility, that provokes and shelters the ongoing dialogue among friends who are not only personally friendly with each other but also engaged interlocutors. And my wager, Stuart, is that the epistolary form, tentative and provisional and familiar, as it should be, might allow me some dialogical room for just this kind of exercise with you. I should like to think of this gesture as having both Wittgensteinian and Emersonian inflections.[32] And my hope is that by addressing you in this way I can prolong our intellectual friendship.

———

I'll come back briefly to the matter of friendship in the last of these letters, Stuart, less to say more about it (since I don't know what that *more* could be) than to simply reiterate in other words how much of a gift ours has been to me. But you can discern, I hope, in what I've already said, why friendship has come to orient the way I think about you and your work. And I hope too that you are persuaded that the letter-form is the most appropriate for my address to you. Still, Stuart, I might as well admit that I'm well aware that in speaking to you in this fashion—I mean, in letters meant for publication—I've probably enmeshed myself in a paradox of sorts. Personal letters are principally a private form, clearly. They enact a distinctive intimacy and familiarity. They constitute their own world, without need for justification. But here I am addressing you with the full intention of exposing aspects of our friendship to a wider public—experimentally, it's true, but not innocent for that fact. I'm formally facing you, speaking to you, with my back turned to my readers. And yet I'm tacitly speaking to my readers too. Or else, I'm actually speaking to them in fictively speaking to you. I want to maintain this charade, though, if you don't mind, Stuart, because as I've already suggested, it helps me formulate more comfortably what I want to talk to you about, and how. So it may be helpful at this point, if only as a way of trying to mitigate this unavoidable conundrum, to forecast briefly what I aim to do in the letters that follow. This will allow me at least to orient you (and my potential readers) to the itinerary I aim to pursue.

To begin with, Stuart, I've decided to write you a series of separate letters rather than several installments of a single, interminable one. This is largely because although the letters are all interconnected I don't want to lose a sense of thematic variation between the different ones— they each do slightly different clarifying work for me. In the letter that follows this one, I will try to evoke for you both what I think is important in general about considering voice as a conceptual register, and how I think an ethos of style is disclosed in the singularity of your intellectual voice. I am going to dwell awhile on some of the virtues—principally dialogical virtues—that voice suggests against the hegemony of vision as the noblest of the senses and the exemplary model of reason and knowledge. In this respect, the work of Adriana Cavarero will be especially helpful to me because she wonderfully captures how voice subtends an ethical stance that I find in you.[33] In that letter, too, I will say a bit more than I have been able to do here about what, hermeneutically,

I'm trying to do with you, and in particular why *listening* is so integral to the process of clarification and elucidation as I understand them. If speaking is the expressive activity articulated in the register of voice, listening is the receptive attitude that corresponds to it. Leaning especially on some instructive work by Gemma Fiumara and David Levin, I am going to suggest that you, Stuart, were a "listening self"—perhaps as much as, sometimes more than, a critical one.[34] This contrast between a listening self and a critical self, no more than a heuristic, really, no more than a rough guide, will help me draw out both your doubts about some aspects of the practice of critique and the thoughtful dialogical bearing toward others you cultivated. Moreover, a large part of what friendship entails, I believe, is precisely this: learning to learn how to listen.

The two letters that follow that one have perhaps a slightly different tone and character than the first two. In them I take up aspects of your theoretical work and try to connect them to what I'm saying about voice and style—in the first instance, "contingency"; in the second, "identity." Why these two, you may well ask; after all, there are plenty of potential candidates to choose from. True enough. However, I will suggest that these—contingency and identity—were distinctly aspects of your theoretical preoccupation, that, in some way, they *belonged* to you. They were not merely elements of method or external objects of analysis; they were *exemplary* aspects of your *mode* or *style* of intellectual being. They were precritical, you might say: you seemed to know them *before* you had a conceptual language to give them theoretical definition and rhetorical-political force. You *lived* them—contingency and identity— in a manner of speaking. And once you had that formal idiom within your mastery, your attention to them always *sounded* natural, organic, as though *as concepts* they were made for you, speaking as you often did as much *of* them as *through* them. You will see then, Stuart, that in neither case am I very interested directly in your *theory*—your theory of contingency or your theory of identity. Indeed, throughout these letters I am not really interested in your theory of *anything*. As I've already hinted, and as I will repeat in one way or another throughout these letters, what is most compelling to me about you is precisely *not* the conceptual substance of any theory you've held of anything. What is compelling to me is your style of thinking and the ethos that animated and drove that style of always "going on" thinking.

At the same time, part of what makes contingency and identity especially intriguing for me to think with and through you is that they are concepts with a certain ambiguity built into them. What they do as concepts depends on how they are being put to work, and to what ends. Both should be on the list of W. B. Gallie's "essentially contested concepts."[35] But what I mean is something more specific, Stuart, something that orients us toward the connection and difference between us. Take the idea of contingency, for example. As we will see, you would maintain that contingency was your way of thinking determinations without a closed form of determinism. In a certain sense, Stuart, contingency was a way of freeing yourself from the intolerable conceit that Marxism (or dominant versions of it, anyway) guaranteed a direction and an outcome for politics. Most people would read your commitment to contingency along these lines, and they would of course be right. But I believe that there is another aspect of the idea of contingency, one that you were very much aware of, though to my knowledge it was never emphasized in your work, and one to which, as you know, I have been very much drawn to. This is an idea of contingency as comprehending what cannot be entirely known in advance about the course of an initiated action, the risks and collisions to which they are vulnerable, and therefore the unintended consequences they potentially suffer. This is less the dimension of contingency that speaks to the autonomy of agency than the dimension of it that comprehends tragedy. You place the emphasis along one vector of understanding, me along the other. You will see something similar where the question of identity is concerned—how in your accounts the emphasis is often (though not always) more on what we can *make* of ourselves with what we have found, whereas in my accounts the emphasis often falls on how what we have *found* of ourselves shapes or constrains what we can make. These are differences that I find intriguing.

In the fourth letter, the penultimate one, Stuart, I promise, I come at last to trying to elaborate and clarify something about the ethics that seasons your dialogical style, your voice. To my mind, generosity is the name of the virtue that most comports with your ethics. But it is a generosity of a very special sort, one that, borrowing from the work of Romand Coles, I will call "receptive generosity."[36] You will see, Stuart, that Coles has offered a suggestive reorientation of the conventional profile of the virtue of generosity, urging us to recognize a conjoined relationship between *giving* and *receiving*. On his view, receptive generosity is the ethical stance of someone for whom the act of giving and the act of receiving are not divorced from each other but are sides of the same coin, dimensions of the same dense gesture of generosity. Receptive generosity is a mode of giving that is at the same time a mode of receiving or, to render it in the register of voice, a mode of speaking that is at once a mode of listening. *This*, I believe, is Stuart Hall's ethics. But here, too, Stuart, I will want to press you a bit in a direction I believe already intimated in your thinking, though not quite, or fully, elaborated in it. Specifically, I want to wonder out loud with you about the role of the idea of "tradition" in figuring the Other whose reception might be at stake in any ethical (and political) relation. It is of course the idea of "culture" and not "tradition" that has animated your way of thinking difference in a historical and political frame. Indeed, some of your admirers might suggest that your ethical stance was antipathetic toward the idea of a tradition—given the supposedly conservative connotations that seem to stick to it. But again, considering you from the angles that preoccupy me, I think this would be too hasty a conclusion to draw about you and your intellectual style. In this letter I will wonder whether a conception of a tradition borrowed from the work of Alasdair MacIntyre mightn't indeed comport with your intuitions about the work of identity and difference, and deepen the scope of the receptive generosity we already discern in your ethics.

I close, following that, with a short, and finally *final*, letter of farewell in which I return fleetingly to some of the matters of friendship with which I began.

This is the arc of my epistolary preoccupations here, Stuart. My hope in all this is not to burden you further than I already have over the years with my constant questions, but, rather, to speak *with* you once more (however fictively) about the things that mattered in our discussions so as to enact one last episode in our intellectual friendship. This, to me anyway, will be enough.

With warm wishes,
DAVID

A Listening Self

Voice and the Ethos of Style

DEAR STUART,

In the wake of the 1996 publication of the edited volume *Stuart Hall: Critical Dialogues in Cultural Studies*, the Marxist literary critic Terry Eagleton wrote an ostensible discussion of it that appeared in the *London Review of Books* that same year.[1] Your editors, David Morley and Kuan-Hsing Chen, had aimed at a collection of writings, including some of your own key texts, that would capture the eloquent, dialogical spirit in which you had contributed to the shaping of the cultural studies project now associated with your name. The very image on the book's cover, a still from Isaac Julien's 1993 short avant-garde film *The Attendant*, in which you make a memorable cameo appearance as a visitor to a museum with a slavery exhibit, seemed an essential part of Morley and Chen's desire to evoke what is undeniably distinctive about your intellectual style, namely, the practice of making yourself tangibly—embodiedly, attentively—*present* in any particular situation in which you're involved. This style— and indeed this *question* of style—wasn't entirely lost on Eagleton, of course, sharp and witty critic that he famously is, but for him it pointed not to a dimension of moral-intellectual virtue but rather to a special kind of fraudulence or a special kind of betrayal, inviting mockery rather than dialogue. Indeed, the title of his essay, "The Hippest," was evidently meant to sum up his assessment of you as little more than a trendy recycler of intellectual fashions. Remember, this is how he begins:

> Anyone writing a novel about the British intellectual Left, who began looking around for some exemplary fictional figure to link its various trends and phases, would find themselves spontaneously reinventing Stuart Hall. Since he arrived in Britain from Jamaica in 1951, Hall has been the sort of radical they might have dispatched from Central Casting. Charming, charismatic, formidably bright and probably the most electrifying public speaker in the country, he is a kind of walking chronicle of everything from the New Left to New Times, Leavis to Lyotard, Aldermaston to ethnicity. He is also a Marxian version of Dorian Gray, a preternaturally youthful character whose personal style evokes a range of faded American epithets: hip, neat, cool, right-on. (3)

I have to say, Stuart (shake your head and shrug your shoulders, as you may, because it was all par for the course for you—merely Eagleton's mischief), that for many years, and perhaps perversely, I've been fascinated with this text because although, as we can already glean from the tone and perspective of this passage, it was meant to ridicule and disparage and trivialize rather than seriously engage you, it nevertheless has the paradoxical, unintended virtue of vividly calling to our attention a number of notable and valuable aspects of your way of being an intellectual, of carrying on an intellectual vocation. I would say that these include, one, your *responsiveness*, over the arc of your life, to a mobile diversity of cultural-political moments and theoretical orientations, your refusal to be confined to any single attachment or commitment; two, the way this responsiveness to political and theoretical pluralities is connected not simply to the content of ideas but also, perhaps principally, to an intellectual *style* or *ethos*, that is, to the cultivation not merely of doctrines but of alert modes of intellectual *presence*, or being-with-others; and, three, the connections between these—your responsiveness, your style and ethos of presencing—and the register of your *voice* (in literal and metaphorical senses) as a public intellectual.

ONE

—

For Eagleton, clearly, the most damning thing about you is precisely this mobile intellectual attitude of responsiveness, this refusal to stand still, to be arrested by conformity, this attentive *voice* of receptivity. Change, Stuart, including changing your mind about matters concerning change, is the signature of your style. Indeed, what has remained *unchanging* about you throughout the years is this "open-endedness," this ceaseless flexibility, this *willingness*—one might even say, this *courage*—to *not* stay the same. But for Eagleton this commitment to self-reflexive change only solicits an unflattering, sarcasm-saturated comparison with other prominent leftist intellectuals in postwar Britain who'd cultivated a rather more settled sense of intellectual identity. Listen again:

> Far more than Raymond Williams or Perry Anderson, and more persistently than E. P. Thompson, Hall has been the Left's finest instance of the strategic intellectual, the theorist as mediator and interventionist, broker and communicator, bringing the more arcane flights of Frankfurtian or Post-Structuralist theory to bear on questions of voting patterns and televisual imagery, racism and youth culture. Nimble, mercurial, and timelessly up-to-date, he has nipped from one burningly topical issue to another, turning up wherever the action is, like a cross between a father figure and Mr. Fixit. (3)

Your intellectual dexterousness and strategic sensibility, your idea of theoretical work as bound to a practice of intervention, serve here to merely underline your evident scholarly deficiencies. "In some forty years of ceaseless intellectual production," Eagleton writes with peculiar, gatekeeping zeal, "Hall has never authored a monograph" (3). It is, apparently, the final, shocking evidence of your lack of the right sort of intellectual value or credentials. But since when, we might ask—and on what disciplining criteria or convention—is the *monograph* the measure of intellectual (or even scholarly) merit? Are Eagleton's numberless little books monographs? Do they have—or lack—merit *because* they are monographs (if this is what they are)? Yet, interesting to me is the fact that Eagleton recognizes the importance to your intellectual style of the form of the *essay*—your "elective genre," he calls it—and offers that you've fashioned it with a "rare blend of metaphorical flourish and polemical punch" (3). *This* is an insight, I think, with important, if un-explored, implications. I return to it in my next letter, but the trouble is that, even here, Eagleton's intention is only to mock your irreverence for the conceit of originality, your indifference toward disciplines and the conventional criteria for what constitutes theory.

Let us listen one last time:

> If he theorizes himself, he gives off the air of doing so on the hoof, en route from one meeting to another, a prodigious improviser who can effortlessly churn out a sort of intellectual equivalent of rap. If he is sometimes a bit thin on the ground, with the odd bald patch peeping through his densely tressed conceptualisations, he compensates for this with a striking versatility, leaping from discourse to the diaspora, Rastafarianism to post-Fordism, with all the disdain for traditional academic demarcations of the classical left-wing intellectual. (4)

I've quoted enough, I think, to make the point I want to make.[3]

Implicit in Eagleton's characterization of you here, Stuart, is a very different ideal of the intellectual self than you cultivated, than abides with you. His is a familiar version of the "critical self." Now, I take it that the critical self is a resolutely theoretical and methodological con-sistent agent of dissenting inquiry whose analytics and rationalities and techniques and principles are put to systematic work on objects, conditions, events, situations, conundrums, in order to demonstrate the contrast between what they presume to be (in their hegemonic or fetishistic or normalized autobiography) and what they really are (in some epistemologically relevant sense of "really are"). The critical self is a courageous pursuer of truth who assigns itself the task of confronting and confounding and unmasking the semblance of the world as it is given to us in the ideological forms of its appearance. Certainly, Stuart, you, too, if in a qualified way, were a critical self in some such sense. But your intellectual sin, apparently, was your cavalier unfaithfulness to this cherished model and its authoritative ethos, your unshakable suspicion that it wasn't always easy for critical selves, such as those Eagleton admires (indeed, perhaps, such as Eagleton himself), to entirely abjure the conceits and pre-sumptions of enlightenment, the deceptive seductions and consolations of mastery, the studied air of condescension, sometimes supercilious arrogance and prideful abstraction, the willfully unexamined whiteness. By contrast, Stuart, what we find in you is a certain attachment to an ethos of intellectual being that, in working to temper the conscious and unconscious excesses and hubris of critique, sought to honor the contingent, unpredictable instability of the world, and endeavored to cultivate an attuned ethos of self-revision and recurrent readjustment to it and its possibilities. I'd like to call this posture of attunement the attitude of a "listening self." As we will see in what follows, I'm going to spend some time extolling the virtues of listening against the persistent deafness at work in much contemporary critical practice preoccupied as it is with its powers of pronouncement and argument. Thinking with listening may open us toward novel possibilities of being and acting. I will suggest that a listening self is one that, like you, Stuart, practices a style of intellectual being animated by the dialogical ethos of *voice*. Like you, a listening self is one that cultivates an intellectual habitus of voice driven less by the acquisition of more and better apparatuses of critique, less by *doxas* underpinned by metaphysics, than by a mobile responsiveness to marginalization and exclusion and by the moral-political prospect of being not only expressively but also *receptively* present to others.

In a broad sense, then, Stuart, these letters to you are going to be concerned with style, ethos, and voice—the connections among them, the company they keep with each other—in your intellectual practice. With you, I believe, *style* is everything—or very nearly everything. What do I mean by this? It's not easy to say with methodological precision. Style scarcely commends itself to propositional analysis. You might have said this yourself.[4] It's an intuition, yes? It *compels* you or it doesn't. And when it does compel you it does so as a moral-aesthetic whole, like a compound or a *gestalt*. By style, clearly, then, I don't mean to imply something merely decorative or ornamental, like a mannerism or a flourish, something exterior and thus detachable from the substantive core of your intellectual work. In a moody inscription dedicating a copy of his 1951 medical thesis to his brother, Félix, Frantz Fanon wrote, "The greatness of a man is to be found not in his acts but in his style. Existence does not resemble a steadily rising curve but a slow and sometimes sad series of ups and downs."[5] Susan Sontag might have disputed the value of the distinction here (between an act and its style), thinking it just another modernist fallacy.[6] But that would be a mistake. For while neither exactly an aesthete nor a moralist, Fanon is making a point that is really not very far from her (modernist) concerns. Like Sontag, arguably, Fanon is reacting against the familiar contempt for style, the insensitivity to style as a serious and worthy dimension of human conduct. Indeed, Fanon seems to share Sontag's insight (overstated, some might have complained) that style possesses its own kind of moral content, its own excellence or virtue—here, "greatness." He would, I think, have agreed with her invocation of Jean Cocteau's remark that "style is the soul of an act."[7] You'd have agreed too, Stuart, I imagine. I know that for you (and we'll come back to this in a later letter) Fanon had an almost *figurative* or maybe *emblematic* quality about him, something anyway that exceeded the mere facts of his biography or the mere details of his theories of black alienation and anticolonial violence—something that, to stay with Sontag for the moment, embodied his particular "style of radical will."[8] I've always found the pathos of phrasing in Fanon's remark unusual (the contrast between the progressivism of the "steadily rising curve" and the tragic sense of the "slow and sometimes sad series of ups and downs"), pointing, I think, to his often unnoticed or unappreciated depth of sensibility for paradox.

In any case, your friend the novelist and essayist George Lamming (you might have known him as a poet, too, in the early days in London) brooded on a very similar theme of style, you may remember, in an essay about his strange relationship to that inaugural and enigmatic and frustrated West Indian writer Edgar Mittelholzer, who immolated himself in England in May 1965. The essay, "But Alas Edgar," was first published in the Guyana Independence issue of *New World Quarterly* the following year, an issue I gather you worked on with its indefatigable and unforgettable editor, Lloyd Best.[9] (I wish I'd known more about your friendship with Lloyd—he was to me a most singular individual, at once absorbing and absorbed, someone else I might think of less in relation to his acts than his style.) In his inimitable way with poetic language, Lamming is trying in this essay to evoke what he intuitively recognized, painfully

but luminously, in the obscure figure of Mittelholzer, namely, a courageous "aristocracy of the will" that sheltered his absolute commitment
against all odds (against the pettiness and spiritual squalor of the colonial Caribbean and racist philistinism of colonial Britain) to the precarious life of the writer. And the only word that Lamming could summon to
capture the meaning he discerned in Mittelholzer, even in the manner
of his death, was *style*:

> Nothing matters more than a man's discovery of his *style*, a discov-
> ery which is also part of his own creation, and style—not a style—
> but *style* as the aura and essence, the recognized example of being in
> which and out of which a man's life assumes its shape. The flavour
> of his thinking, the furious silences that fill his heart, and finally his
> function, the work that chooses him and for which there is no alter-
> native; no other instruments he can select to fulfill that choice: these
> constitute the style of a man.[10]

I don't know of a more poignant, or a more profound, way of putting this
elusive matter of style. Fanon and Sontag would surely have approved.
Lamming here could just as well have been talking about *you*, not Mittelholzer. And indeed, Stuart, here is the *center* of what I too am reaching
for with you—your discovery-creation of the "aura and essence" out of
which your intellectual vocation took shape.

Indeed, in your case, Stuart, I believe that you cannot separate the
content of your thought from your style, because this style, itself a kind
of embodied action, a mobile mode of intelligence, is a *constitutive*—
not merely a contingent—element of the *content of the form* of your
practice of thinking itself. Or to put this another way, I take you to be
an intellectual or social critic (we may argue about the relative merits
of these terms) whose style is exemplary in the sense that whether or
not one agrees with the substantive content of what you have to say on
any given subject, from liberalism to race, there is something distinctive
about, and therefore something to be learned from, your way of *taking
your bearings* in relation to the topic at hand. I think of you as forever taking your bearings, forever orienting and reorienting yourself in relation
to the world around you. Such, one might say, is the instinctive gesture
of the listening self. Style, therefore, in the sense in which I'm going to

use it here, is connected to *ethos*, by which I want to evoke the general *character* or *disposition* of your mode of being an intellectual. Ethos, one might say, discloses an order of shaping values; it is concerned less with specific ideas or practices than with the animating spirit that motivates and moves—and moves *within*—ideas and practices, that finds expression in them. So what interests me, Stuart, is the ethos of style that composes and drives your characteristic way of carrying on an engaged intellectual life, the generative and orienting *tendency*, so to say, that establishes your inimitable *presence* as an embodied intellectual.

———

More specifically, though, Stuart, I am going to suggest that part of what establishes this presence and the style it vivifies is your *voice*. Your style, so to put it, has a *sonic*, an *acoustic* character, that renders the experience of your intellectual presence, however one encounters it, in print or in person, *audible*—we are listening to you. As I indicated in my first letter, this habitation of voice was by no means naive; you were not unaware of the ways you used your voice in your intellectual life. At any rate, I want to suggest that there are several *exemplary* dimensions that constitute the register of what I'm calling the listening self that is disclosed in your voice.

To begin with, and setting aside the semiotic *content* of your speech, the meaning, if you like, of your verbal utterances, there is the very literal *sound* of your voice, its audible materiality. I won't be alone, I think, in saying that for those of us who have heard it this voice is unforgettable—in its timbre and modulation and color, in its rhythms and accents and seawater sounds. But this is not all; there is *more* to it than these acoustically shaping features, something embodied in but that nevertheless exceeds the registration of the mere materiality of vocal sound in your voice and that renders it intelligibly *hearable*, in a specifically *hermeneutic* way. I mean, Stuart, that there is in your speaking voice that vital but elusive element that Roland Barthes famously called "grain," the texture that marks the specific phenomenological facticity of *this*—rather than some other—singular speaking presence. Barthes, whose work I know you became very familiar with in the 1970s (especially *Mythologies* and *Elements of Semiology*), had an uncanny way of putting his finger on the soul of certain dimensions of language and experience. Grain, he memorably said, is "the body in the voice."[11] Your voice, I think undeniably, Stuart, has a certain "signifying weight" that imparts an intelligible volume to your embodied presence and lends it altogether and at once a very recognizable inflected sense of *proximity* and *gravity* and *intimacy*. Erving Goffman would have had something useful to say about the "forms of talk" your voice disclosed.[12] Anyone who listens, for example, to any of the numberless audio recordings of your addresses or lectures or interviews (take, as one especially affecting instance, the Mike Dibb-directed and Maya Jaggi-conducted *Personally Speaking: A Long Conversation with Stuart Hall*) will immediately appreciate this *acoustic* dimension, the way the sonorous materiality of your voice establishes your concrete *being here* in the context of others, the way its measure as eloquent sound almost precedes, but certainly envelops and saturates, the conventional dimensions of your verbal meaning.[13] I don't, of course, mean to be obscure here. Think of John Akomfrah's three-screen film installation *The Unfinished Conversation*, and the documentary film *The Stuart Hall Project* that followed it. Clearly part of what makes them so captivating, part of what renders the succession of biographical images so arresting, is simply the *resonant* immediacy of the voice through which the story verbally unfolds.[14] You will remind me here, Stuart, I'm sure, that you've been a *public* intellectual all your adult life (from the Suez and Hungary crises in 1956 that led into the first New Left and Campaign for Nuclear Disarmament in the late 1950s, through the public broadcasts for the Open University much later), and therefore your voice is widely known—you are widely known *through* your voice. True, but what especially interests me is that quality in your voice of always being *turned* out toward an audience, however small. There is a relation therefore between voice and *action*—voice and *political* action, specifically—that I believe is central to you, and to which I will return, perhaps often, in these letters. Anyway, this is the first thing I want to say about your voice, Stuart, namely, that it literally *lives* in the world beyond you; and, having once *heard* you speak it is almost impossible to *not* go on hearing your voice, whatever the verbal register of the encounter with your work. Undoubtedly, every voice is inimitable, unique. I want, however, to urge that you are one of those rare intellectuals whose voice *all but coincides with*—and therefore is almost inseparable from—his person and his presence, and the content of his ideas and his work.

Besides the resonant, material sound of your voice, however, I mean as well to acknowledge and dwell on the sense in which *speaking* is literally a crucial dimension of your practice of *thinking*. For you, that is to say, speaking is not merely the *aftereffect* of thinking, the end result or product of prior thinking, what thinking might occasionally lead to—how a thought, once thought, vocally articulates itself, finds its way from inside your head into the world at large. Rather, for you, *speaking is a mode of thinking itself*. Would you agree with this way of putting it? Speech for you is not the simple *outside* of thought, its mechanical conveyor, its linguistic medium. I'd say that you are forever thinking *aloud* in the course of speaking. That's what your speaking *is*, thinking-out-loud. And part of what is important to appreciate about this thinking-as-speaking (or, alternatively, speaking-as-thinking-aloud) is, I believe, that it is congenitally, constitutively, a *social* or *relational* practice. Thinking-as-speaking is conducted with interactive *others*; it depends upon their collaborative presence through speaking and listening—it depends, in other words, upon *dialogue*. Here I think we are very close to the heart of the ethos of your work. Surely, for example, the entire project of the Centre for Contemporary Cultural Studies under your leadership has to be understood in relation to the ethos of this practice of dialogue; the idea of collaboration that produced work such as *Resistance through Rituals* and, above all, *Policing the Crisis* (whatever one makes of the substantive arguments that shape their respective content), are embodiments of this intellectual style.[15] Indeed, you will say, won't you, Stuart, that you have always thought of yourself as a *teacher*, above all; and that, for you, the classroom constitutes an exemplary pedagogical space in which voice, in the reciprocal exchange of speaking-and-listening, is the explicit register for a social practice of thinking.[16] Again, I am reminded that Barthes had something instructive to say about this inexhaustible relation between teaching and speaking—specifically about the classroom as a theater for the *provisionality* and *contingency* of voice. In particular, you will remember, Stuart, his observation about the unfolding, irreversible process of the speech of the teacher in which nothing can be amended or retracted *except*, precisely, by *saying* that it is amended or retracted—except, in other words, by *multiplying* speech, saying something *more*. "To cross out here is to add," Barthes remarks with characteristic economy. "All one can do in the case of a spoken utterance is to tack on another utterance."[17] For you too, Stuart, the teacher's speech, by which thinking appears in a *dialogical* space of learning, in a rhetorical space of pedagogical persuasion, is always partly open, partly provisional, partly vulnerable to error, to objection, to rethinking, and is therefore in principle never concluded but always in transition, always *to-be-continued*.

Furthermore, if speaking is an internal, constitutive dimension of your practice of critical thinking, Stuart, this is also evident in your *writing*. I mean not only that your writing is a mode of inscription of your thinking (that is obvious enough) but also that this writing itself has about it what might be best called an *audible* or *spoken* character. One can *hear* you in your writing. I hope you won't mind my putting it this way, Stuart, but in my view the undoubted expressiveness of your writing is perhaps not the result of its elegant "writerliness," strictly speaking, the self-conscious display of literariness, the carefully crafted arrangement of the words on the page. I've never thought of you as a writer whose writing was highly wrought, possessively worked over. Rather than elegance it is *eloquence* that marks your writing, and specifically the vivid sense one has in your writing that you are *speaking*, and speaking to *someone*, namely, the reader. Writing may well appear to start where speaking ends, as Barthes suggestively remarks, but your writing is carried on *as if* it were an organically seamless *extension* of your speaking.[18] And therefore your writing has an *aural*—a spoken—dimension. Your essays (as we know, the typical, almost exclusive, form your writing takes) carry the vibrant trace of your embodied vocal presentness. Your voice inhabits, *saturates* them. These essays are *addresses*, literally. What they *do* is verbally attend to others—this is what their linguistic action is. They presume—or perhaps more properly, they mimetically reconstruct—the *relationality* of your spoken discourse. In other words, there is always an imagined *addressee* who is to hear (and hopefully be persuaded by) what is being said; there is an implied audience toward which what is being said is being projected. In fact, as you said to me more than once, in

what seems to me a curious but revealing reversal of conventional practice, your published essays from talks you've verbally delivered are very
often "written up" *after* the fact. Certainly they are often texts initially
prepared *to be spoken* in public. And even when such talks are published
as written essays, they typically retain the grammatical and syntactical
marks of their origins in spoken discourse—the rhythms of punctuation,
the syncopated recursive flow of idiosyncratic phrasing and allusion and
metaphor that indicates that someone, *someone in particular*, is speaking
here in a relational context. There is about your writing, then, Stuart, the
sense of a *dialogue* being initiated, or being joined, or perhaps (in certain
circumstances) even a polemical *argument* being engaged. Moreover, especially given their typical origins in spoken discourse, your essays have
an *occasional—occasioned*—quality to them, the sense of being situated,
or *contextually* driven. Indeed, one of the virtues of your writings, it seems
to me, is the sense they give of being *precipitated*, of emerging out of—
and carrying with them—the concrete circumstances that brought them
about. They are *conjunctural*. It is partly this, of course, that imparts the
impression that there is something of *moment* about your written work,
and therefore something *at stake* in their execution. They are, in other
words, *interventions*. I'm going to return to this in my next letter.

———

Can you now begin to hear what I'm after, Stuart, where your voice is
concerned? I hope so. I want to speak more generally for a moment, and
to begin to pull you into a dialogue with work on voice that seems to me
resonant with what is disclosed in your own voice. With a few notable
exceptions, such as (in one direction) Don Ihde's *Listening and Voice*
and (in another) Jonathan Rée's *I See a Voice*, thinking through voice has
remained a somewhat minor department of intellectual discussion.[19]
Curiously, voice has seemed at once familiar and obscure, at once background and foreground, even where absent, silent, an ambiguous sort
of presence. We recognize in voice at once the ineluctable sign of our
sociality and the unique stamp of our *individuality*. If the voice is the axis
of our social bonds, the very texture of the social, it is also, as Mladen

Dolar suggests, "like a fingerprint, instantly recognizable and identifiable."[20] And yet, paradoxically, the voice appears to resist intelligibility, to fade from our conceptual hearing the moment we try to appreciate its theoretical implications. Part of the reason for this recalcitrance, Dolar suggests, is that, at least conventionally, the voice gives the impression of what, simultaneously, *supports* meaning and *disappears* in the moment of the production of meaning. As he puts it sardonically in a telling analogy: "The voice itself is like a Wittgensteinian ladder to be discarded when we have successfully climbed to the top—that is, when we have made our ascent to the peak of meaning. The voice is the instrument, the vehicle, the medium, and the meaning is the goal."[21] This conventional view gives rise to the assumption of an idea of voice understood as the merely empty, voided materiality through which the cognitive—that is, *real*—meaning is expressed.

It is in some sense this conventional conception of voice as nothing more than the helpmate of meaning that Adriana Cavarero wants to address and challenge, partly speculatively, partly deconstructively, in her admirable book *For More Than One Voice*, published some years ago.[22] I don't of course mean to be overly pedantic in these letters, Stuart, forgive me if that suspicion is growing on you, but it will be useful to spell out aspects of her argument and concerns in this provocative book because they will help to orient me in saying what I want to say about *your* voice. I think that had you had the opportunity to read it, you too would have found her work very suggestive on many levels.[23] Now, as I read it, Cavarero's central concern is with a consideration of voice as the *content of the form* of a social ontology that is at the same time the sonorous ground, so to speak, of a social phenomenology of human relationality and political community. Her overall theoretical aim is to reverse what she sees as the tendency in the tradition of Western philosophy to subordinate voice (and thus, by extension, speech) to that mute order of signification we call "thought," and in so doing to radically rethink the very role of voice in relation to being and *logos* (understood as reasoned speech)—and, ultimately, politics. Cavarero thinks of this effort as the project of an antimetaphysical and relational ontology variously inspired by Jean-Luc Nancy's idea of human being as constitutively "singular plural"; Emmanuel Levinas's idea of the ethical content of the face-to-face relation between self and other; and, above all, Hannah Arendt's idea of the human condition as a plurality of unique speaking-thinking subjects.[24] Once again, Stuart, these are not necessarily thinkers with whom you have ever expressed any particular intellectual kinship. But the contrast-effect might well be illuminating. In any case you will see in a moment that I am only partially persuaded that Arendt—at least the later Arendt—does the work Cavarero hopes for, that some of her considerations concerning thinking run counter to the dialogical implications of Cavarero's idea of voice, and counter, moreover, to what I take to be your own uses of it.

In the Western philosophic tradition, Cavarero argues, the silencing of voice has meant that speech has suffered what she calls a process of *devocalization*, in which speech is separated from its speakers, and this abstracted speech is relegated to the soundless dimension of thought, a purely "mental signified." As she recognizes, one reason why voice has suffered this devocalization is that it is connected to *hearing*; and hearing has long been overshadowed by sight as the most privileged dimension of our sensorium. Interestingly, though, in sketching her argument Cavarero makes no significant contact with the work of Walter Ong, and in particular his early and not-often-read account of the career of the obscure Renaissance logician Peter Ramus (Pierre de la Ramée), whose campaign against Aristotelianism initiated a gradual shift away from dialogical modes of thinking.[25] In any event, what she does take up is Hans Jonas's famous essay "The Nobility of Sight" in order to discern the contrasting dispositions of the cognitive senses of seeing and hearing.[26] For Jonas, remember, sight is the sense, above all, of simultaneity, detachment, and *therefore* objectivity. Sight, he tells us, is the basis for neutrality and mastery and timelessness, and consequently for *theoria*, or theoretical truth. By contrast, hearing is bound to the unstable passage of time, the contingent, uncertain experience of temporality. What sound discloses, Jonas eloquently observes, is not an object per se but a "dynamic event" of unfolding, surrounding. Hearing therefore is not only inherently a sense of *becoming* rather than being but also a sensuously *gathering*, *enveloping* mode of experience. Consequently, unlike with sight, which is the sense of sovereign intellectual control, with hearing there is always a fundamental experience of *exposure* and *vulnerability* and *susceptibility*. Our ears are continuously *open* to the world around us.

We cannot as easily shield ourselves from sound as we can from sight; we cannot simply choose to hear or not hear. Rée has some splendid reflections on this contrast in his book.[27] Now, admittedly, Jonas is not a critic of this hierarchy of the senses, of the privilege of vision; he believes himself to be merely underscoring the great intuition of the ancient Greeks, as well as *showing*, in a phenomenological way, how the other senses might supplement and even enhance the incomparable, indisputable nobility of sight. He is no particular enemy of "ocular modernity."[28] Needless to say, this is not satisfactory to Cavarero; her intention is fundamental, revolutionary. For her, inasmuch as the ocularcentrism of the Western tradition is intimately tied to the subjugation of hearing, what is required is not merely to reference it, acknowledge it, but to *overturn* it, so as to reverse the historical silencing of voice.

Speech, as Cavarero tells it, the living sound of the voice in dialogical motion, has been reduced to being merely the material or acoustic sign of inner thought, nothing more than its audible expression. This silencing, Cavarero says, is a symptom of the affinity within the Western tradition for an abstract, disembodied universality—its affinity, as she puts it, for "the domain of a word that does not come out of any throat of flesh."[29] By contrast, voice for her is always already *corporeal*; it rises out of the body and always retains a granular trace of embodiment. Moreover, for Cavarero voice is an antidote not only for the abstractions of Western metaphysics but also for its *individualism*. Voice, she argues, is the central human phenomenon through which a social ontology of difference and plurality can be conceived. In company with Dolar, she argues that what voice discloses are the common singularities of embodied being, or rather, embodied becoming. Cavarero seeks to affirm the priority of voice as embodied sound "whose human destiny" is speech—speech moreover that is fundamentally relational. As she says, "There is speech *because* there are speakers."[30] Speech in short is always potentially *dialogical*. (Here, it seems to me, Cavarero's work connects suggestively with that of Dmitri Nikulin, who, though inspired more by Mikhail Bakhtin than by Nancy or Levinas or Arendt, agrees that however seemingly ubiquitous it appears to be within contemporary theoretical debates, dialogue remains curiously misapprehended, given the persistence of modernity's "monological" conceit concerning the ultimate source of meaning and reference. Like Cavarero, too, Nikulin finds the implications of the constitutive polyphony of voice in the fundamentally relational ontology of the human condition.)[31] But Cavarero's point is that what is communicated in speech, first and foremost, is *not* the specific semiotic content of the words employed but, as she puts it, the "acoustic, empirical, material relationality of singular voices"—that is to say, the fact of speaking voices establishing and (implicitly) registering a *human* relationship.[32] As Rée puts the same point: "There is something peculiarly sociable about sounds: they only come into their own in each other's company."[33]

In the modern Western metaphysical tradition, Cavarero argues (whether Descartes or Kant serves as the point of departure), thought does not speak. Thought *cogitates*.[34] However verbally constituted the process of thinking is acknowledged to be, thinking nevertheless lives in silence. It inhabits the mute, inward-facing interiority of subjectivity. In this tradition, therefore, thinking and speaking are two very distinct and separate activities. But they are not only distinct and separate—they are also *unequal*. Thinking is understood to be unrivaled in its cognitive superiority. This is because thinking is presumed to have access to Truth. Thinking potentially *knows* Truth, the one, singular Truth, which is always the same. Thinking despises difference; it seeks to overcome otherness. And because Truth, in this sense of it, is eternal, timeless, abstract, and absolute, so too are the silent cognitive powers and processes that lead the way to it through the immense darkness of ignorance. Thus the sovereignty of Truth as eternal Sameness is the aim of thought; it is the result of the mastering labor of the possessive individual. In this tradition, thinking is ideally a solitary activity, depending only on the self-absorbed *autonomy* of the unencumbered self. Auguste Rodin's *Le Penseur* offers the paradigmatic modern image of this figure, self-possessed, detached, resolute—*sovereign*.

By contrast with this idea and ideal of thinking, speaking is a very different sort of activity, less precious, more concrete, more rough-and-ready, more worldly—in a word, more you, Stuart. Notably, speaking is always *temporal*; it takes place in time, and over the course of time, and is therefore always in—and saturated by—a *particular* time. Speaking is always situated, contextually *generated*, and contextually *animated*.

Consequently, its relation to the idea and ideal of Truth is necessarily more tenuous, less assured. Indeed, situated as it is in concrete time and space, speaking is always vulnerable to *contingency*, to chance; it is always exposed to *fallibility*. A speaker, once having begun to speak in the always unreliable company of other speakers, cannot ever know in advance how the speaking is going to turn out, how it will be heard, and what the implications will be for the ongoing dialogue. Much depends upon the situation and disposition of the interlocutors who are themselves not typically or consistently or universally predictable. Speaking, in this sense, is a mode of *acting* in the world. As all great tragedians know, it is speaking, not thinking, that precipitates tragedy because speaking exposes us to forces that, once set in motion, cannot be perfectly controlled, taken back, erased. Unlike thought, therefore, speech is fundamentally *relational*, even conflicted, action. Speaking lives, as Cavarero puts it, in and through the lives of others.[35] It depends upon plurality; it thrives on difference. To speak is to speak to *someone*, a precise and not an abstract someone. Speaking, then, is always an *interlocution*. It requires something that thinking doesn't, namely, *reciprocity*, or at least the *anticipation* of reciprocity. Consequently, as its obverse but complementary side, speaking requires *listening* to sustain it. Indeed, the two together—speaking and listening—constitute a kind of hermeneutic pair. On this view, speaking is not merely thinking that expresses itself aloud; it is not merely vocalized thought. *Speaking is thought in embodied motion.*

Now, to my mind, Stuart, Cavarero's argument about voice and the dialogical speaking-thinking it works through implies not merely an engagement with, or an extension of, Arendt's argument, in *The Human Condition*, about plurality, action, and appearance but also, in important ways, a departure from, if not a critique of, her argument about thinking in *The Life of the Mind*. I grant, of course, that Cavarero does not see it quite this way. It's true that, in the latter book, in the section "Metaphor and the Ineffable" in the chapter "Mental Activities in a World of Appearances," Arendt notes by way of the same Hans Jonas essay Cavarero engages, the age-old privilege accorded to sight.[36] But frankly, while she is clearly not unmindful of the conceits and exclusions that attend this ocularcentric tradition, I do not detect in her account any serious dissent or disagreement. Or to put this another way, however much Arendt may have been skeptical of the hegemony of seeing as a metaphor for the activity of thinking, unlike Cavarero her project doesn't seem to me to be explicitly directed at releasing voice from the prison-house of devocalization. Rather, the direction of her argument is to show how thinking emerges from, and remains constitutively tethered to, Plato's idea of the "soundless dialogue" I carry on with myself. For Arendt, although the activity of thinking may indeed move *toward* the world, its first impulse in fact is *withdrawal* from worldly appearance. Thinking, she repeats, depends upon a Socratic "solitude" in which I keep company with myself, in which I am both the one who asks questions and the one who answers them.[37] This, memorably, is the idea of the "two-in-one" that, for Arendt, as we have already seen, is rooted in and routed through her profound considerations on friendship: I think first and foremost with the friend I have in myself—the friend who is my other self.

So notably, Stuart, in Arendt's discussion we don't get much beyond our own plural constitution—our constitutive duality. Thinking for her doesn't really live (except derivatively, by extension) in speaking-with-others, at least not in the manner that Cavarero is pushing us to imagine. When Arendt asks the profound question, "Where are we when we think?," her answer is almost invariably, "By ourselves." I don't think this would have been your answer, Stuart, not exactly. You could just as easily have said, "In the company of others," meaning literal not only metaphorical others. Again, it's true that in her praise elsewhere of the example of her friend and mentor, Karl Jaspers, she demonstrates a pronounced admiration precisely for someone who, she says, refused to think of thinking as a purely solitary activity but rather as one enacted dialogically *between* human beings (the implied contrast here, of course, being Martin Heidegger, for whom thinking allegedly turned ever inward, away from appearance).[38] But curiously Arendt does not think the question of thinking *from* here, from this social-dialogical point of departure; the center of her concerns, to which she is never-not returning, remains that soundless dialogue one conducts with oneself. This is why in her discussion the Socratic dialogues appear less as themselves dialogical exemplifications of the activity of thinking with others than as the aftereffects of that silent exchange with myself *as* another.[39]

By contrast, Stuart, it strikes me that the full implication of Cavarero's argument about the sociality of voice, together with the force of your intellectual example, is to think of the dialogical itself as a worldly space of thinking, of questioning and answering. None of this is to diminish the general significance of that soundless dialogue, or even to undermine its ontological predominance (if that is what it is). I would obviously not say that you did not also think with yourself-as-another in the way that Arendt discusses. I am only suggesting that this is not what is most *distinctive* about the way you practiced thinking in your vocation as an intellectual. What is most particular about you is the speaking-thinking you conducted with real, living others beyond yourself.

––––––––

I hope it's a little clearer now, Stuart, what it is about the conceptual register of voice that strikes me as compelling (and even necessary) in talking about you. I now want to turn, more specifically, to one aspect or dimension of voice that, as I have already indicated, is especially pertinent for talking about the particular ethos of your intellectual style, namely *listening*. I've said earlier that you are consummately and above all a listening self as opposed to a critical self, and some of the rationale for that distinction has been further elucidated through the thought-provoking work of Cavarero. What, though, is listening? What is the perspective that it brings to thinking and acting? Why might listening be so significant for, say, altering our pervasively deaf ways of talking about our life-worlds and the powers and relations and understandings that constitute it?

In a little book published some years ago, *À l'écoute*, Jean-Luc Nancy raised the following questions: "Is listening something of which philosophy is capable? Or . . . hasn't philosophy superimposed upon listening, beforehand and of necessity, or else substituted for listening, something else that might be more on the order of *understanding*?"[40] These seem to me profound and provocative questions to which Nancy offers a wonderfully meandering meditation but no real answer. Maybe there isn't one. Especially notable, though, is the agonistic contrast Nancy suggests between *listening* and *understanding*—the sense that the latter may be a mode of appreciation that, in fact, stands in a hegemonic relation to the former, or indeed, that authoritatively precludes it. These are issues productively taken up by Gemma Fiumara in *The Other Side of Language*, an insightful book in which she seeks, as she puts it, to restore the "life-enhancing role of listening" to considerations of human coexistence.[41] Like her Italian compatriot Cavarero, she believes that the Western tradition has embraced an impoverished notion of *logos*, a merely "talking logos." In Fiumara's view, we have yet to develop a sufficiently capacious conception of *logos*, one that not only comprehends the present preoccupation with "saying," that is, with assertive, expressive language and cognition, but also equally comprehends the capacities and processes of listening, especially the "keeping," "gathering," "sheltering" dimensions of attentive, thoughtful listening. Of interest to me about Fiumara's reflections in this book is her critical appreciation of Hans-Georg Gadamer's "hermeneutics of the question" in relation to listening. I will return to Gadamer toward the end of this letter, Stuart, in a related connection, but you were aware of my near-obsession with R. G. Collingwood's formulation of the central role of the question, so here I want to share with you the way Fiumara raises an instructive issue regarding its assumed privilege, because I've learned something from it. On Gadamer's account, famously, hermeneutic consciousness is characterized by a fundamental attitude of *openness*. And for him a listening posture is a central element in maintaining this attitude. In this connection Fiumara quotes Gadamer from his *Truth and Method* as follows: "Anyone who listens is *fundamentally* open. Without this kind of openness to one another there is no genuine human relationship. Belonging together always also means being able to listen to one another."[42] This is very classic Gadamer. But here's Fiumara's doubt. The linguistic form of the question, she suggests, is one of the most "assertive and expressive" modes of language and may well restrict our ability to adopt an attitude of listening for the answer, may indeed prejudice or foreclose the answer. The question-form, in other words, is not always an invitation; it potentially discloses its own cognitive will-to-power. We might be able to

ONE

—

42

learn more, Fiumara urges, by suspending our inclination to question and simply "stopping to listen."[43] I'm going to have to think about this provocation.

Nancy and Fiumara have been important to my thinking, Stuart, and you can see why (they open the question and set the terms of a philosophy of listening in motion), but it is the work of David Levin that has particularly caught my attention, and it is indeed from him that I borrow the felicitous term "the listening self." It would be hard to exaggerate just how productive I've found this idea of his and the way he has sought to develop its resources and implications in the book devoted to its theoretical elaboration, *The Listening Self*.[44] For Levin, Stuart, as for you, listening is more than a hermeneutic method; it is a hermeneutic *attitude*—for it depends upon more than a calculative rationality or a research protocol. It depends upon the cultivation of a new *habitus* of listening—or what Lisbeth Lipari might call "listening-thinking-being" (as a kind of compound).[45] This is what I take you to have achieved, Stuart, this habitus of "listening-thinking-being." And what is at stake here for me, as I've already suggested, is to cultivate in turn a reciprocal listening responsiveness to your thinking-speaking voice. Levin is aware, of course, of the denigration of hearing and listening in the history of Western metaphysics, but he is encouraged by those who have from time to time pointed to, or even lamented and criticized, the constraints of the Cartesian conceit of ocularcentrism—among them, Søren Kierkegaard, John Dewey, and (again) Hannah Arendt. However, as with Fiumara, it is especially Martin Heidegger who inspires Levin's idea of *listening* and its possibilities. In a sense, Levin aims to take up what he sees as Heidegger's challenge (already adumbrated in *Being and Time*, but further articulated in the wake of the legendary "turn") to cultivate what he referred to as the "ear of our thinking"—that is, that we aim to develop an attitude toward listening-thinking-understanding that, on the one hand, abjures the speculative, representationalist reasoning characteristic of Western metaphysics, with its ocularcentric disposition toward masterful, controlling knowledge, and, on the other hand, strives to *let go* and *let be*, as a nonassimilationist orientation toward otherness and difference.[46] Many seem to have found Heidegger's ears perspicuously tuned—though with a more inward and passive (not to say conforming) orientation than you would have liked.[47] Indeed, Stuart, here is a conversation we oddly never had, though we should have done: the question of Heidegger. Why didn't we talk about him? No matter the instructive and interrogatory biographical repair he has undergone, Heidegger certainly wouldn't be an easy figure to integrate into your style and concerns—even though I can hear you mobilizing his idea of our "homelessness" in the world as a way of pointing to the constitutive discordance, for example, of diasporic experience.[48]

At any rate, for Levin our hearing is a gift of nature: "We receive it without having to ask for it," as he fittingly puts it.[49] We receive it as a capacity, an endowment, but one that is, as yet, *unrealized.* Such gifts of nature, Levin urges, make a moral claim on us to develop the possibilities they passively or latently harbor. However, the realization of the potential of these gifts is not in any sense guaranteed, but rather entails an existential labor on the self, the vigilant, deliberate *cultivation* of the gift of hearing into an attuned practice of listening. Much like you, Stuart, Levin wants us to change *ourselves* as well as change our world—he is as much concerned with social struggle as with personal growth—and therefore, not surprisingly, a number of emblematic theoretical perspectives inform his polyvalent endeavor: among them, phenomenological, Freudian, Foucauldian, and Marxist perspectives. But what Levin ultimately aims at (with the diverse tools he mobilizes against the pervasive nihilism of our age, and through the successive stages of learning and unlearning he encourages) is a Heideggerian attitude of "hearkening." Who today *hearkens,* Stuart? Who today gives heed? Who might we appropriately call a hearkener? In *Being and Time,* of course, Heidegger devoted a number of suggestive passages to listening as part of the larger discussion of attunement and understanding. For Heidegger, listening-hearing is one of the fundamental existential attitudes of being (as he says, with all the characteristic difficulties of his trying formulations: it "even constitutes the primary and authentic openness of Dasein for its ownmost possibility of being").[50] In his terms, understanding and listening (or "acoustic perception") are conjoined, coconstitutive, co-original. Listening does not, for example, *lead* to understanding; nor, vice versa, does understanding lead to better listening. Rather, understanding presupposes a listening self, and listening depends upon heedful understanding. This is why Heidegger says, paradoxically, "Only one who already understands is able to listen."[51] Certainly this is the case for "hearkening," an especially acute mode of listening. Hearkening has, as Heidegger puts it, the very "mode of being of a hearing that understands."[52] In a certain sense, one might say, hearkening constitutes a nonrepressive and nondismissive mode of hearing that encourages *heedfulness* to what is being said, a thoughtful, reticent attention that is receptive to otherness, or that is at least open to unlearning the ready-made conceits that disable our capacity to *let otherness be* in relation to ourselves.

Again, Stuart, I know this is decidedly not your language. Nor is it exactly mine, though I perhaps "hearken" to its resonances more readily than you do. But nevertheless, wouldn't you agree that it is suggestive of the intersubjective resources of voice, and of the possibility of cultivating a more richly dialogical sensibility, a more responsively nonrepressive and nonappropriative one? And it's suggestive too for my concern to cultivate my own capacity to listen to *you*, heedfully, in intellectual friendship—that is, to listen to you in such a way that yields enough to you (lets you *be*, enough) so that I can hear you in the idiom in which you are speaking, but that retains at the same time enough *contrast*, and enough *tension* (through the languages of my own preoccupations), to disable mere assimilation, mere absorption: to listen to you, so to speak, as another—but not identical—self. It is this doubling of attunement, Stuart, that seems to me vital to dialogue and dialogical learning, especially between friends.

———

Let me remind you, if only briefly, of one instance—now famous—when listening broke down, when a lack of heedfulness, and an absence perhaps of even a modicum of reciprocal friendship, disabled the work of clarification. It's an instructive example. I'm referring to the so-called Gadamer-Derrida encounter that took place in Paris in 1981. I wonder whether it made any impact on you (likely not, I suppose, given the intensity of the heady debates at the time in Britain around Thatcher and your work with *Marxism Today*—to which I am going to turn in the next letter). In a certain respect, the Gadamer-Derrida encounter turns on the implications to be drawn from the idea of voice and dialogue entailed in a hermeneutics of listening.[53] It's a useful event to consider not least because one way of thinking about listening as a hermeneutic attitude is as encouraging the kind of noncompetitive thinking-with-others that in *Truth and Method* Gadamer called a "fusion of horizons."[54] Who today, Stuart, remembers *that* idea—that aspiration? Indeed, as I've already noted, in that vast Heideggerian book *Truth and Method* (that, I know, wasn't your sort of reading), Gadamer urged the primacy of hearing as precisely the basis of a hermeneutical practice.[55] Now I don't think, of course, Stuart, that you or I should feel obliged to rigidly follow Gadamer in rehierarchizing the senses—in establishing a simple reversal of the standing privilege of sight.[56] And yet, at the same time, I don't believe either that we need to take Gadamer as advocating in his idea of a "fusion of horizons" a mere assimilation or incorporation of one viewpoint into another—even though the idea of "fusion" certainly lends itself to this kind of misunderstanding. I suspect, for example, that this is how Jacques Derrida read—or misread—Gadamer in their "improbable debate" (as it has been called).[57] It might well be true that Gadamer, who led off the debate, offers a model of dialogue that relies strongly upon an idea of understanding as tending in the direction of convergence, in the direction of overcoming differences and arriving at a kind of common agreement, even if all that is agreed on is clarification about what cannot be agreed on—in this instance, for example, the exact standing of the philosophy of Heidegger, the alleged common denominator between hermeneutics and deconstruction, between Gadamer and Derrida.[58] For Gadamer, evidently, debate and dialogue depend, minimally, on a practice of question and answer, and therefore on a communicative attitude of attentive willingness to being at least open to what the other is trying, whether successfully or unsuccessfully, to *say*—a listening stance, in other words. To my mind this doesn't necessarily imply metaphysical deafness to indeterminacy or undecidability or ambiguity, but only a commitment, at least in *living* dialogue, to holding oneself solicitously receptive to the otherness of the other. I take this to be your attitude, Stuart—it is the nonrepressive attitude of a listening self.

—

What Derrida's response to Gadamer amounted to—whether in fact it can, in the first place, even be called a "response"—has been open to widespread discussion.[59] For despite the fact that Derrida begins his presentation with a polite gesture of address and homage to his elder, he seemed really less interested in actually engaging Gadamer's text than in tuning it out—on the one hand, playfully, ironically, misreading Gadamer's Platonic expectation of dialogic participation as a dubious invocation of Kantian, and therefore *metaphysical*, goodwill; and, on the other, occupying himself with showing that, in the end, it is Friedrich Nietzsche rather than Heidegger who evades the philosophy of presence—and that, therefore, Gadamer's admiration for Heidegger is, precisely, misplaced. Now, arguably, Derrida's point may have implicitly been a version of Fiumara's, namely, that Gadamer's questioning attitude sought to stack the deck, so to speak, in order to preemptively shape the space of dialogue. But such, it seems to me, is in the very nature of questions—they are not neutral. So it's hard for me not to sympathize with those who discern in Derrida's performance on that occasion a sort of insouciant *inattentiveness* to what Gadamer was setting out to say, indeed a subversion of the very possibility of being on the way in dialogue with him. The deconstructive aim, if that is what Derrida's strategy embodied, seemed more concerned to *deflect* and *undermine* rather than to constructively *listen* and *learn*, to see in his potential interlocutor little more than an intellectual *adversary* from under whose feet the theoretical rug of presumed "presence" had to be pulled so as to reveal his complicit naiveté—and, by contrast, his own superior theoretical cleverness. It may be hard to altogether deny the "metaphysics of presence" that Derrida detects in the eagerness with which Gadamer imagines the *willing* basis of intellectually friendly interlocution (Gadamer himself strenuously denies being the prisoner of any such foolish philosophic innocence); but it may be equally hard to deny the repressed, unacknowledged labor of presence at work in Derrida's own antimetaphysical pronouncements. For it seems to me that at least *living* dialogue, face-to-face communication, as opposed to intertextual dialogue, reading one text in relation to another (and however much these may be entwined, they are not usefully thought of as *identical*), must depend on the construction of a kind of presence—one not necessarily thought of as realized or transparent or masterful, in which subjects are fully present to themselves, fully in tune with all facets of their multidimensional selves. Derrida showed up, after all, for the real-time dialogical occasion with Gadamer. To open one's mouth and speak to another living being, or even in the company of other living beings, Cavarero might say, is to *present* oneself in some form, however partially or obliquely or ironically. Indeed, it is the *absence* of this presumption of transparent self-presence in the very act of presencing that affords the always fallible, always provisional, basis for being on the way in dialogue in the first place.

Now it is true, Stuart, that both Gadamer and Derrida are here involved in a quarrel that is at once largely *philosophic* (in discursive design and structure) and *Eurocentric* (in the provenance of its presuppositions and presumptions), and in this sense I take it that neither you nor I could have any self-evident *affinity* with it, or deep *stake* in it. (Indeed, given the matters under discussion, Gadamer's and Derrida's obliviousness to this dimension of their "encounter" seems to me to speak volumes about the self-absorbed, navel-gazing solipsism of European philosophy—its unfriendliness, despite its pretense of cosmopolitanism.) I imagine, Stuart, that neither you nor I would much care which of the two—Gadamer or Derrida—has the best reading of Heidegger and Nietzsche, or of Heidegger's Nietzsche. To us, I think, from our perspective on the ambiguous creole edge of the West's traditions, inside its outside, so to say, or outside its inside, they are both reproducing the very same disciplines and gestures of the metaphysics of truth-seeking they are claiming to evade. From the seemingly secure withinness—or perhaps, more pointedly, *whiteness*—of the West's philosophic traditions, something appears, naturally and normatively, to stand or fall on the aptness or otherwise of one's reading of Heidegger (or indeed one's reading of any of the luminaries who, like Heidegger, represent that tradition). Not so, I think, for us, standing as we do somewhat askew to both Europe and philosophy, and merely eavesdropping on a debate that largely excludes us anyway. In a curious way, perhaps, Stuart, seen from our inside-outside perspective, Gadamer and Derrida represent only contrasting (even rival) styles of roughly the same language-game.

Still, I've wandered a bit into this rather abstruse domain with you, Stuart, partly because it's what you and I would occasionally do, wander into offbeat terrains, but also because I believe that the nature of the impasse in the Gadamer-Derrida encounter is germane to thinking about the hermeneutics of heedful listening, of hearkening, about what the reciprocal recognition involved in intellectual friendship entails for the endless ordinary work of clarification in dialogue. In some sense it goes to the very heart of the ethos of your style and the ethics of your vocation as an intellectual. What is disclosed, for example, in your navigation of, on the one hand, the Charybdis of the deconstructive impetus to think of language as an opacity, to always read against the grain of convention, and to read "doubly" or "under erasure," and, on the other hand, the Scylla of standing, proximately, provisionally, yes, but *standing* nevertheless, on the commitment to some convergence of positions (what you called an "arbitrary closure"), is precisely your idea of *politics*—and perhaps, too, at least implicitly, your idea of political friendship.[60] Thinking about *politics* rather than thinking about *thinking* as such (that is, philosophy) was almost always the direction in which your thinking-speaking-listening-understanding—in effect, your *voice*—tended to orient itself. Indeed, looked at from this angle, it may well be that the impasse between Gadamer and Derrida partly turns on the fact that what is at stake between them is less how to *act politically* (as friends) in some conjuncture than how to *think philosophically* (as rival *maîtres*) in matters concerning truth or principle. This is an important distinction to make, isn't it? A lot about who you were can be discerned through it; I think it's of enormous importance for how one considers the significance of your voice in your work. And I'd say that voice is a register of action, or that action draws us toward the domain—your intellectual-political comfort zone—of speaking-and-listening. And I'd further say that in the dialogical exchange that matters to this practice of speaking-and-listening (of which intellectual friendship is a model) it is the luminous work of clarification that is primarily at stake.

A LISTENING SELF

—

49

So, Stuart, provisionally and tentatively as usual, I've been offering you the suggestion that there may be important contrasts to draw between listening selves and critical selves, that the two are not, necessarily, synonymous or even adjacent—that listening selves may not be critical, in any of the standard senses of that modern term, and that critical selves are very often not listening selves at all, in the senses in which it is relevant to me. And I believe that conjuring this contrast potentially illuminates something vital about your way of being the intellectual you are.

You live and work in the realm of voice in literal and metaphorical senses. Where critical selves often inhabit an abstract and rarefied world of sometimes-obscure formulations and sometimes-obscurer sentences, you live and work in and through the sound and sense of your voice. And it is a very particular voice—in both sonic and social aspects. In tone and accent and color and measure it is altogether distinct, activating and establishing the embodied presence that is our experience of you. Resonance, I might say, is the proper name of your special register of intellectual presence. Your voice has a round, enveloping warmth and everyday modesty and cordiality about it that has always put me at my ease, that has always had the demeanor of an invitation to join you in some conversation or other, that has always made me feel that it was me and not you who was saying something intelligent. Your voice, sonically, is like your fingerprint. It identifies you materially in a singular and unmistakable way. But voice invariably also identifies you as an individuated presence within an ongoing social, often public, dialogue. Here, for sure, is a truism about you, Stuart—you are committed to the practice and process of dialogue, and not as a specific element of any theory but as the overall ethos of your style of carrying on the intellectual life. The distinctiveness and sometimes the authority of your voice affirms itself within the endless back and forth that constitutes the ebb and flow of dialogical situations, whether pedagogical or political. And dialogue, obviously, is made up of speaking as well as listening, not as discrete activities but as bound together constitutively and dialectically as porous sides of an integrated if not unified whole. Though there is a convention of valuing speaking over listening, we learn from you that these are better thought of as forming a dialogical pair, the two together unevenly inseparable. In your style they come together as a kind of hermeneutic pair. What I mean is that for you, speaking and listening are not only inseparable from each other, they are inseparable from the practice of understanding you engage in—that is, from a form of practicing understanding that is less about the arrival at truth than about the endless recursive process of provisional clarification. Speaking and listening are inseparable, therefore, from the practice of thinking that makes understanding-as-clarification possible. Speaking and listening, or better, speaking-listening (to join them into the compound they properly are in ongoing dialogue), is the context in which you have practiced thinking. What thinking is for you, Stuart, I believe, is a living, exploratory exercise, that is never merely mental, never merely a matter of the private internal processes of cogitation, never merely internally self-referential.

To my mind this image of the listening self is one that gathers together in an especially amplifying and clarifying way a number of features of your ethos of intellectual style that might otherwise appear arbitrary, or anyway extraneous to the seemingly more substantive content of the many important things you said—by way of critique—about the many important things that have mattered to you: about, say, the dilemmas of the Left, or the conundrums of popular reason, or the antinomies of race, or the paradoxes of diaspora, or the enigmas of visual art, or whatever have you. What matters to me especially is less the theory of them than that organic fluency that animated and inflected how you approached them, and that, indeed, has animated and inflected virtually everything you ever approached. This embodied fluency is defined not so much by a rigorous structure of logical propositions, as by what I've been calling an attitude of attunement or a mode of responsiveness to the world you lived in. And this receptive awareness, I'm saying, is most effectively activated in the communicative register of your voice, as it expressed itself in literal and extended senses. Further, I'm saying that your intellectual resonance is deliberatively articulated in the hermeneutic posture of a listening self, a dialogical self that cultivates the ability to constrain, where appropriate, the egocentric impulse to speak, so as to be able to better hear the voices of others.

Let me stop here, Stuart. I hope I've said enough, and in a way sufficiently persuasive, to allow you to see why the register of voice is so instructive to me—how it captures an important dimension of the ethos of your intellectual style, and how it helps me to think about what I'm seeking to learn from your listening self. In the next two letters—about contingency and identity, respectively—I am going to take up two substantive areas of your intellectual work and suggest how they reflect the play of voice in the articulation of your style. Bear with me.

Best wishes,
DAVID

Responsiveness to the Present

Thinking through Contingency

DEAR STUART,

You once said the following: "Contingency is a sign of [the] effort to think determinacy without a closed form of determination."[1] Do you remember this particular remark of yours? I especially like it because as with so much of your thinking-aloud it seems to want to overflow itself—it seems barely able to contain within itself, beneath its nonchalant and eloquent surface, the paradoxical tension within it between "determinacy" and "determination." Anyway, it issues an invitation—or a *provocation*—to consider with you the particular *sensibility* for contingency it articulates. Can we talk a bit, then, about the generative role the idea of contingency has in your thinking? Or rather, and perhaps more to my concerns, can we talk about the *ethos* this notion discloses and what perhaps it suggests about your intellectual *style*? Over the years, you and I have talked a great deal about contingency, coming at it perhaps from our different angles, different locations, different expectations, different theoretical archives and vocabularies, grappling with what certain attractive conceptions of it seem to enable and other less attractive ones to disable. Note the contrast between an *idea* and an *ethos* of contingency. I draw it because, as I've already suggested, I've come to think that your well-known *alertness* to moments of change, or to the "indeter-minate determinacy" that characterizes moments of change, that opens up new possibilities and closes off others, that rearranges the conditions of political action, registers more a mode of *attunement* than a *theory* as such—more an engaged and responsive *disposition* toward the concrete than an abstract set of formal propositions ready-to-hand. Contingency is a notion inseparable from the *habitus* of your moral imagination of time and historicity, politics and action, agency and identity, reason and desire, criticism and dissent; and therefore wherever else it belongs I mean to suggest that it belongs to the universe of your style—and, as such, the universe of your *voice*.

I'm going to try to persuade you that there is a worthwhile connec-tion to sound out (so to speak) between an ethos of contingency and what I've already said about an ethos of voice. Indeed, that voice and contingency conjugate each other reciprocally will roughly be the whole of my point here. There's no need to remind you of the dimensions of voice—your voice—that interest me, but I do want you to keep in mind something of the scope and spirit of my motivations and preoccupa-tions here, so you'll forgive me, I hope, if I belabor some of the lines of potential contact I want to draw together. Remember that my aim is not only to mark the materialities by which the grain of your richly textured voice lends to your intellectual style an intimate and resonant presence. My aim is also to suggest that thinking through voice—your voice—thought of in an extended sense as a hermeneutic register might, on the one hand, discourage some of the reifications and abstractions, and ethical and methodological individualisms associated with the West-ern philosophical tradition (even in and around its more critical edges), with its relentless drive toward empiricist or metaphysical truth, and might, on the other hand, encourage us to imagine and engage more re-lational, more worldly, more fallibilistic, more dialogical, more both/and modes of interpretation. Yours, I suggest, is a listening self that derives its practical form from the intellectual-political *thinking-aloud* you do in the collective, collaborative presence of others. For you, in other words, Stuart, speaking and listening form a sort of interwoven hermeneutic pair, one moreover that figures also in your writing, in the performative provisionality of formulation, the self-consciousness of address and of audience, the attention to the poetics and rhetoric of *persuasive* talk. Finally, and here I'm aware I may be pushing you a little bit, voice not only decenters the frigidities of sight's presumption of sovereignty and cultivates our sensibility for temporality and contingency; in doing so it also keeps us alert to the irreducible exposure and fragility that attends human action in the world—and therefore, I believe, helps us to keep attuned to human finitude and otherness and tragedy.

———

In this letter, Stuart, I want to think with you about what strikes me as a very prominent dimension of your style, one that distinctively discloses the role of voice in shaping an ethos of intellectual *presence*. I'm thinking of the sense in which you are, preeminently, a theorist of the *present*, or more precisely, a theorist of the *contingency* of the present. Your example of a listening self suggests that an ethos of receptive and responsive intellectual engagement ought to encourage a certain hearkening attunement to the present in its punctual particularity. But to begin with, what exactly is the present—or *when* is it? What is its time, its historicity? What are its logics or poetics of determination or overdetermination? What structure and dynamic defines its presence or absence, its arrival or departure? What temporal boundary separates it from past and future? What are its modes of specificity or difference as a phenomenological order of experience? These, I think, are not easy questions to answer, at least not definitively, conclusively, comprehensively. But for you, Stuart, my guess is that the present is not merely the one Michael Oakeshott once memorably described, namely, the "world upon which I open my eyes."[2] It may be *that* too in some important temporal senses, as we will see, but it's not *only* that, surely. Oakeshott, whom you once derided as the Conservative Party's "latter-day Bagehot," meant to underline the unmistakable immediacy of the present to experience: the world beheld.[3] Alertness, attentiveness, and responsiveness to that world unfolding before one's eyes are clearly indispensable for thinking about—and thinking through—the present. But the mere *presence* of the present, I take it, is *not* enough for what you're after.

The present that matters conceptually to you is not just any experience of temporal presentness but rather the *evental* present that constitutes what you would famously call a "conjuncture." *Here*, undoubtedly, is a category of enormous importance to your theoretical thinking. Stuart Hall, so it might be said, is inimitably a theorist of the conjuncture, or, more precisely, the present-as-a-conjuncture. Some close readers of your work would even cogently argue that it takes precedence over the idea of contingency that I wish to commend.[4] Indeed, Stuart, *you* might argue this yourself. Isn't that so?

A number of years ago, remember, in the course of reflecting on a conference in Kingston devoted to your work you remarked in the following sympathetic-yet-differentiating way with reference to my suggestion that what you were concerned with intellectually might best be termed the "contingency of the present":

> Now actually I would not quite put it that way myself although I understand perfectly well why he [David Scott] did so. I would say that the object of my intellectual work is "the present conjuncture." It is what Foucault called "the history of the present." It is, what are the circumstances in which we now find ourselves, how did they arise, what forces are sustaining them and what forces are available to us to change them?[5]

I have to say here, Stuart, that I have a doubt. Not a fatal one, to be sure, but, still, one I think important for discerning some usable conceptual distinctions between your thinking and that of others with whom you might bear comparison. My own view is that if, as you say here, your principal concern is with the "circumstances in which we now find ourselves" and the means available to change them, then Michel Foucault's idea of the "history of the present" (as the covering description of what his great genealogies are about) is not so apt an analogy—except maybe in only the very broadest and loosest of senses. The present with which Foucault was concerned, it seems to me, has a wider epistemic scope and structure, and belongs to a much more *macro* and a much more *long-run* conception of historical time than you are typically willing to traffic in. Foucault's historical sensibility was, I think, more *epochal* than yours. Does that make sense? What he aimed reiteratively to illuminate was the difference that constitutes something like the *modern age*, not an immediately contemporary political formation, such as the rise of Thatcherism. In *Discipline and Punish*, for example, one of the central texts in which his "history of the present" is worked up as a genealogical story, Foucault's aim is to re-describe the changes in dealing with criminals that occurred in Europe between the eighteenth and nineteenth centuries—dramatized in the contrast between the violent public dismemberment of Robert-François Damiens and the systematic regulation of the everyday life of inmates in a prison. His objective is to show how modern power is more concerned to *discipline* than to destroy the body and how it comes to depend upon formalized knowledges of the social and the subject.[6] So I can agree with you entirely, Stuart, that you share with Foucault a motivation to unsettle the conceit that the present is naturally (and therefore *properly*) what it is in order to subvert its *normative* hold on us. But I believe that the *temporality* relevant to your idea of a conjuncture has more concrete specificity, and more immediately consequential implications, than Foucault's—at least, *politically* speaking. Indeed, again, perhaps *this* is the crux of the difference that I'm reaching after. In his genealogies Foucault aimed at a more deep-structural level of historical difference between past and present than you ever did, but at the same time the *political* ramifications of these genealogies, while undoubtedly significant, were nevertheless more removed, or stood at a greater distance from *organized* possibility, than your sensibility of political commitment demanded. To my mind, in other words, as indeed I've already said, your idea of a conjuncture is inextricably connected to your idea of the circumstances and entailments of acting for political change. This is why, whatever the kinship between Foucault's ideas and yours might be, anyone familiar with the arc of your work will know that your idea of a conjuncture draws principally on your reading of Louis Althusser (especially *For Marx*) and, in a more sustained way, of Antonio Gramsci (especially *Prison Notebooks*).[7] However much knowledge and power was understood to shape its constitution, for both Althusser and Gramsci "conjuncture" named, first and foremost, a *political* concept and not an epistemological one; it named, in other words, the materiality (political, economic, ideological) in which possible action could take place. Do you agree?

Take, for example, your (and your colleagues') *Policing the Crisis*. It is an exemplary investigation of the idea of a conjuncture, and one, moreover, that offers a compelling contrast with the structure and project of Foucault's *Discipline and Punish*.[8] Notably both works (published within a few years of each other) are concerned with the knowledge/power nexus through which crime is constructed as a social problem, but the present that interests you is not articulated in the same register as Foucault's *epistemes*. The contrast-effects that you want to evoke are nearer-to-hand, indeed within the range of the everyday experience of the very people you are addressing. As everyone knows, *Policing the Crisis* sought to re-describe postwar Britain as a succession of historical conjunctures through which the "historical compromise" that constituted the emergence of the social-democratic welfare state (with its Keynesian project of full employment, wealth redistribution, public control of the "commanding heights" of the economy, health and social security systems, and so on) began to buckle and collapse, such that the politics of consensus gradually gave way to a more openly repressive politics of law and order. The rise of "mugging" and the public and judicial responses to it were symptoms of the emergence of a new conjuncture in which the *racialized* figure of black youth came to symbolize the crisis of the state and the need for a reconceived notion of authority.

Quite evidently, these are not the temporal rhythms of a Foucauldian present. As I understand you, the idea of a "conjuncture" designates a specific historical *moment* in the dynamic life of a social and political formation when the antagonisms and contradictions that have been unevenly unfolding begin, as you put it, to "condense" and "fuse" into a crisis configuration—what you call, again in your paradoxical language (drawn from Althusser), a "ruptural unity."[9] Thus the idea of a conjuncture animates a conception of historical temporality that comprehends the development of contradictions, their fusion into a crisis, and their resolution. These resolutions, of course, are not preordained; they can take many different forms: they might allow the existing historical project to continue, for example, or to be renewed, or, again, they might provoke a radical process of social and political *transformation*, such that something novel comes into being. Moreover, conjunctures have no fixed duration; rather, so long as the crisis and its underlying contradictions remain

TWO

—

58

unresolved, further crises are likely to proliferate throughout the various dimensions of the social and political formation. And so long as a period is dominated by roughly the same struggles and contradictions, and the same efforts to resolve them, it can be said to constitute the same conjuncture. Thus, in the sense of a conjuncture, a *present* can last a long or a short time, because although time is central to its duration, the passage of pure time itself (whatever that is) is not what governs the rhythms of its temporal presence or absence, its coming into being or passing away.

I don't mean to suggest that you, Stuart, are against abstractions. Don't get me wrong. I know you aren't. After all, as you understand them, conjunctures are never simply *given* transparently *as thought*. Rather, a conjuncture presents itself as what you call "a *chaos* of appearances" and has, consequently, to be *produced*, analytically as such, in theory. For you, in fact, this is the *only* reason for theory's existence. The work of theory, "the necessary moment of abstraction" in thinking the present, as you sometimes say, constitutes a reflexive "detour" through which the world of appearances is conceptually organized.[10] That analytical work consists of "breaking into" the series of congealed and opaque appearances that make up the world as given, reconstructing *conceptually* its various levels of "determination," and then, having made this "detour" through theory, returning to the surface phenomenon that was, to begin with, the matter in question, in order to come up with a practice for acting politically in the world. I'm sure many people will recall that you take this to be a key lesson derived from Marx, and that it forms the basis of your famous reading in the early 1970s of the 1857 introduction to the *Grundrisse*.[11]

In any case, Stuart, the idea of a "conjunctural" present for you is a way of thinking the political present as overdetermined, as the result of many overlapping determinations, and therefore as always remaining, as you say, "an open horizon, fundamentally unresolved, and in that sense open to 'the play of contingency.'"[12] Here, therefore, is where for you the idea of contingency *meets* the idea of a conjuncture. Listen to the way you pose and respond to the following questions:

> Why contingency? What is it that I have been wanting to say about contingency? I do not want to say, of course, that the world has no

pattern, no structure, no determinate shape, no determinacy. But I do want to say that its future is not already wrapped up in its past, that it is not part of an unfolding teleological narrative, whose end is known and given in its beginning. I do not believe, in that sense, in "the laws of history." There is no closure yet written into it. And to be absolutely honest, if you do not agree that there is a degree of openness or contingency to every historical conjuncture, you do not believe in politics, because you do not believe that anything can be done about it.[13]

Contingency, therefore, is a way of thinking with determinacy and indeterminacy without being trapped by a reductive idea—a closed form—of *determination*. It is contingency that calls into play the strategic necessity of political action. If you take contingency seriously you are always obliged to ask yourself—and others: Where are we now? What are the questions that present themselves? Are we in a new conjuncture, a new configuration of the present? If you take the idea of contingency seriously, you will be encouraged to think and act *politically*, as you famously say, "without guarantees."[14]

I'm going to return to this question at the end of this letter, Stuart, but I want to signal here a point of contrast between our perspectives that has seemed to me a productive dimension of our conversations and the friendship it animated, namely, between a sense of contingency attuned to openness (yours) and a sense of contingency attuned to finitude (mine). I think these may be sides of the same coin but they point perhaps to contrasting orientations, activated perhaps by different objectives, maybe different conjunctures, maybe different temperaments. I'm going to suggest that one direction (yours) oriented itself around a notion of *practice*, whereas the other direction (mine) oriented itself around a notion of *action* and a sense of the tragic. But more on this later.

―――――

To my mind, then, Stuart, you are above all a theorist of the contingency of the present—that is to say, a theorist attuned to the present-*as*-conjuncture. Contingency and conjuncture are, in this sense, aspects of the same conceptual phenomenon. But what is instructive about considering your moral imagination from the *side* of contingency (that is, thinking the significance of conjuncture as an *effect* of an attunement to the indeterminacy of contingency) is that it brings the idea of *intervention* into view as your signature style of intellectual action, your distinctive mode of critical responsiveness to the present. This is what interests me centrally here. As I never tire of repeating, Stuart (you must have heard me say it on half a dozen occasions by now), you are less the author of books than the author of interventions. But what exactly is an intervention? What is its relation to contingency and conjuncture? An intellectual intervention, I take it, is a discursive move in an ongoing argument that aims to engage, and perhaps to change, the terms of a debate and, by doing so, to alter the possibilities for acting differently. I know you are a reader of Kenneth Burke, or were, but do you remember his famous image (from *The Philosophy of Literary Form*) of the agonism that shapes and vivifies the dramatic give-and-take of argument conceived as an "unending conversation"? Especially suggestive in this image is its foregrounding of the dimension of voice.[15] For Burke an intervention is a mode of "verbal action" that responds to the unforeseen circumstances that bring about new "contexts of situation." As such they are always provisional, always occasional in their temporal and situational routing, always somewhat experimental and uncertain given the novelty that brings them about, always a way of thinking aloud toward a future that is not known in advance. This is exactly what your intellectual style has been all about, Stuart. Interventions are your modus operandi.

This being so, it seems perfectly unsurprising that it is the *essay* that is the generic form most conducive to your written work. The essay is precisely a nonfictive literary mode of writing into the present. I do not mean, of course, to imply, Stuart, that (*pace* Eagleton) your name isn't attached to significant monographs. One only has to think of the early *Popular Arts*, which you cowrote with Paddy Whannel in the period between leaving *New Left Review* in 1962 and joining Richard Hoggart in founding the Centre for Contemporary Cultural Studies at Birmingham University in 1964; or again, *Policing the Crisis*, which you cowrote with Chas Critcher, Tony Jefferson, John Clarke, and Brian Roberts, and which was published shortly before you left the center for the Open University at the end of the 1970s.[16] What there isn't, though, in the extensive archive of your writings, is a Big Book in which you will be able to read, once and for all, "Stuart Hall's Theory of Everything." This book does not exist. This is a good thing in my view. It would run counter to an ethos that sees virtue—not failing—in the *fragment*. Therefore, there is no book in which you have comprehensively wrapped up your topic, brought your thinking to an authoritative and exhaustive close, in which you have said the *last* word on the subject matter at hand. I believe that there is in your intellectual practice an implicit worry about the false unity of the monograph—the book's *illusion* of closure, you might have said. Rather than the book, the authorizing academic form of the treatise, it is the essay that is your métier. The essay is the literary vehicle par excellence for the ethos and style embodied in your voice; and as we know, you've written an almost uncountable number of them.[17]

What is it about the resources of the essay-form, we might ask, Stuart, that so comports with your moral imagination? Of course, in debates about criticism as a dimension of literary modernism, the question of the essay as a distinctive *form* of self-consciously engaged writing has had a privileged place. And one memorable site of this debate is that of the contrasting account of the form and function of the essay offered by those two giants of the Western Marxist or critical theory tradition, Georg Lukács and Theodor Adorno. I know there's no evidence that you ever read their respective reflections on the essay-form, that indeed both Lukács and Adorno embodied an ethos of critical thinking that you deliberately distanced yourself from, but, still, I think that aspects of their contributions are worth remembering at least as a way of locating how the essay-form generatively enabled the activation of your voice and your style, your way of being a listening more so than a critical self.

Readers of Lukács's early work from 1910, "The Nature and Form of the Essay" (written in the form of a letter, as I mentioned earlier), will recall his appeal to the essay as a "form of art" that expresses a certain longing for coherence and totality.[18] To be sure, Lukács underlined the "occasional" and "mediated" character of the essay, the fact that it was not an autonomous form, not sovereign, not originary, but always, in its way, *dependent*, concerned with something already formed, on which, or *against* which, or anyway in relation to which, it produced its meaning. Moreover, for Lukács the essay had a specifically *evaluative* dimension; it carried out, in this sense, a critical labor of *questioning*, of intervention. "The essay is a judgment," he wrote, "but the essential, the value-determining thing about it is not the verdict (as is the case with the system), but the process of judging."[19] Not the final judgment itself, but the process of discursive movement enabled by the essay—the essay as a platform for the verbal activity of *saying* rather than the substantive conclusions of the *said*. So far so good, yes?

At the same time, however, Lukács's overwhelming preoccupation with the idea that the essay expressed a luminous union of soul and form was bound to arouse skepticism. And, indeed, it was this quasi-mystical conception of the essay that Adorno famously took exception to in his own meditation, "The Essay as Form," published more than four decades later.[20] Adorno, of course, shared Lukács's sense of the essay's refusal, on the one hand, of the methodological strictures of organized science and, on the other, of the empty abstractions of academic philosophy. But for Adorno, the essay was precisely a literary form that, above all, resisted the drive toward the totality, universality, and permanence that motivated the young Lukács. The essay-form was necessarily fragmentary, partial, and as a consequence tended to evade doctrine, a dependence upon absolute principles, closure. For Adorno, the essay-form sheltered a *restless*, reiterative impulse, openness to contingency, to the recognition of life's ineluctable exposure to chance and to error: it sheltered, in other words, the unavoidable fact of human *finitude*. Moreover, as an intervention, Adorno understood the essay to have a *performative* dimension; it aimed, in saying, to also be *doing* something, which is why he underlined its close connection to *rhetoric*. As a self-conscious mode of language *use*, the essay seeks to breach the wall between form and content, the barrier between "presentation and what is presented." Thus for him the essay does not proceed by an abstract automaticity; rather at every turn it is propelled by a recursive self-consciousness and a speculative self-reflexiveness.[21]

Already we can recognize ourselves as inhabiting the force-field of your preoccupations, Stuart, however imprecisely. It is true that, as I've said, neither Lukács nor Adorno belong to the family of continental European thinkers that you have, from time to time, mobilized in your work. You've always resisted the self-referential grandiosity and pretentious elitism that saturates their work, even as they themselves sought to unsettle the metaphysical assumptions in their heritage of German idealism and historicism. By contrast, there is in your style a characteristic reserve, a quotidian modesty and discretion of tone, an attuned responsiveness and approachability and solicitousness, altogether absent from either Lukács or Adorno. And yet, there is much, especially in Adorno's sense of the essay's provisional and meditative character, its self-conscious occasionality and presentness, its alertness to itself as process, that are very much dimensions of your use of the form. In my view, moreover, and this is what your practice of the essay-form discloses so distinctly, the essay is the nonfictive written form that most approximates the *spoken* voice, the act of *thinking-aloud-as-writing*. In your eloquent hands, the essay is a textual expression of the dexterity and resonance of voice in all its open, recursive, and contingent articulation.

———

In this letter, Stuart, I want to talk to you specifically about one of your essays, a very famous one, "The Great Moving Right Show." This essay has always fascinated me, for its labor of contingency, voice, and performativity. It was first published in January 1979 in the British communist party's theoretical journal *Marxism Today*, edited at the time (and until its demise in 1991) by your friend Martin Jacques, and with which you were associated—not uncontroversially, I might add.[22] Indeed, Jacques commissioned the essay from you. Reflecting on your close friendship in the decade between 1978 and 1988, Jacques has described how you wrote it—how *in general* you wrote—in terms that are now so familiar to me:

> The way in which Stuart wrote was fascinating. Some, like Eric Hobsbawm, the other *Marxism Today* great, produced a perfect text

first time out. Stuart's first draft, in contrast, would arrive in an extremely incoherent and rambling form, as if trying to clear his throat. Over the next 10 days, one draft would follow another, in quick succession, like a game of ping-pong. His was a restless, inventive intellect, always pushing the envelope, at his best when working in some form of collaboration with others. His end result was always worth savouring, his articles hugely influential.[23]

I like that image very much of your writing as a gesture of "clearing your throat"—provisional, uncertain, trying to take your bearings, on the terrain on which you find yourself, and all of it embodied in the grain and register of voice.

As everybody knows, "The Great Moving Right Show" constitutes the first in a series of essays published between 1979 and 1988 (most of them initially published in *Marxism Today*) that sought to define the character and significance of Thatcherism, and the crisis of the British Left it both precipitated and disclosed.[24] As I mentioned earlier, this was a period that marked a new and distinctive *conjuncture*, a turning point in the cultural and political life of postwar Britain. The essays in this period, subsequently brought together in a single volume, *The Hard Road to Renewal*, were self-consciously conceived as a series of interventions aimed at polemically engaging other leftist positions in the ongoing debate about the rise of Margaret Thatcher and its implications for socialist thinking.[25] Each of the essays, to my mind, is an exemplary instance of your style and ethos—in their concrete immediacy, their self-conscious positionality and personality, their strategic openness to the rhetorical state of play of the questions at hand, and thus their reflexive attunement to themselves as *contingent* acts of persuasive language, as essayistic *interventions*. The focus in them is politics and ideology. Yet this was not because you believed that these dimensions were, abstractly, as a matter of first philosophy, foundational. To the contrary, for you this focus on ideology was part of a deliberate *strategy* of intervention, given the economic and class reductionism that, at the time, characterized the central dispositions of the Marxist debate in Britain. The Left, you argued, lacked a sufficiently nuanced sense of the specificity of the way in which the ideological and political "instances" shaped the emergence of the contemporary conjuncture. It was necessary, therefore, you claimed, to "'bend the stick' in this direction" (mobilizing here an Althusserian image you much admired), in order to make a more general point about the need to develop a theoretical and political language on the Left that would more carefully avoid the temptations of reductionism and teleology.[26] This by itself is notable for the reading I want to commend of you as a thinker responsive to the contingency of the present. You are almost never-not *gauging* the state of play of the Left debate, seeking to discern the relative strengths and weaknesses of the contending analytical perspectives at work, so as to be able to judge where, in what register, and in what conceptual idiom, to intervene. What theoretical contrast-effect will enable us to see something about the present that is not already inscribed in the conventions of Marxist analysis? What, if you like, is the new question that demands an answer?

"The Great Moving Right Show" is in many ways consummately *Stuart Hall* in its structure and movement, and above all in the lucid thinking-voice that animates it. The theatrical title, with its allusions to the populist idiom of the circus, alerts us not only to the "authoritarian populism" that you found at work in Thatcherism but also to the dramaturgical self-consciousness that frames and drives your deliberations, the performative or interventionist register in which your arguments are going to unfold. Memorably, Stuart, you open the essay this way:

> No one seriously concerned with political strategies in the current situation can now afford to ignore the "swing to the Right" which is taking place. We may not yet understand its extent and its limits, its specific character, its causes and effects. We have so far—with one or two notable exceptions—failed to find strategies capable of mobilizing social forces strong enough in depth to turn its flank. But the tendency is hard to deny. It no longer looks like a temporary swing in political fortunes, a short-term shift in the balance of forces. It has been well installed—a going concern—since the latter part of the 1960s. And though it has developed through a series of different stages, its dynamic and momentum appears to be sustained. We

need to discuss its parameters more fully and openly on the Left without inhibitions or built-in guarantees.[27]

The polemical note sounded here in your voice is unmistakable. A challenge is being issued—a gauntlet is being thrown down—to those on the Left who understand themselves to take seriously the need to develop an adequate grasp of the political present. There is a sound of urgency, too, in your voice; indeed, you can hear in it a certain ring of impatience. But the essay is not, notably, an intervention from some assumed *outside*; you are not exempting yourself from criticism (the nominative plural "we" announces this). The appeal is for a collective endeavor—a thinking-together. The state of knowledge of the situation, as you discern it, is admittedly fragmentary and provisional. The totality of the structure is still obscure because all its determinations have not yet been theoretically reconstructed. Yet, at the same time, there is enough already to suggest that what is at stake here is not merely a fleeting series of events, but the emergence of something settling into the shape of a new conjuncture, which, although still clearly developing and therefore unstable, is secure enough to sustain and reproduce itself. What is necessary, then, you seem to be suggesting to your comrades, is to engage in an agonistic dialogue about the present, a dialogue unconstrained by doctrine—taking the risk, in other words, of standing open to a horizon in which the analytical end is not already known in advance.

The problem with the Left is that it has been content to read the crisis of Thatcherism from "within well-defined and respectable 'common sense' positions." There are those on the Left, for example, who believe that "worse is better," for whom the "sharpening of the contradictions" is a good thing because it will result, so they say, in the "inevitable rising tempo of the class struggle and a guaranteed victory of the 'progressive forces everywhere.'" Or again there are those who interpret the "swing to the Right" as a simple expression of the economic crisis. For these, Thatcherism is merely the "political bedfellow" of capitalist recession—not a new political and ideological instance, but a mere variant of previous forms of "Tory philosophy."[28] For you, by contrast, Stuart, these positions neglect almost *everything* that is specific to the contingent nature of a historical conjuncture, namely, the particular condensation of distinct contradictions in multiple registers moving uncertainly according to different rationalities, and differently structuring temporalities. These leftists, in short, read history as mere *repetition*; by assuming that the character of the economic base would be—or could be—immediately and seamlessly translated into the political and ideological levels they assume what in fact needed to be put into question in the first place. For you, however, part of what was distinctive about the conjuncture of Thatcherism was precisely its resistance to this reductionism.

The bulk of the conceptual work of "The Great Moving Right Show" is taken up with a *re-description* of this conjuncture that aims to bring into view the way in which the new balance of forces cannot be understood as simply growing organically out of some deeper more fundamental level (the economic recession, say), but rather constitute a new "historical bloc" of alignments ideologically and politically *constructed* by the Right. What the Right was able to effectively do strategically, you argue (and this was a great insight), was to disarticulate the assumptions that had made up the old consensus of social democracy that governed political reason in postwar Britain—the assumptions about the role of the market, for example; the assumptions about the relation between state and society generally, or between moral values and political authority, more specifically; the assumptions about Englishness and immigration, and therefore race and belonging; and the assumptions about law and order—and to rearticulate them into a new configuration, that is to say, a new *hegemony*. In this sense, you argued, the swing to the Right is not merely a thoughtless reflection of the crisis, as the doctrinaire Left imagined, but a deliberately *constructive* political and ideological *response* to it. This is what made it distinctive, novel. Part of the problem with the Left was its arrogant refusal to read the Right as a form of intelligence.

In your view, Stuart, the importance of thinking through the political and ideological dimensions was to be able to identify what was specific about the new Right, the differences that marked it off from other variants of conservatism and authoritarianism that have flourished in postwar Britain—and to take them seriously. For, contrary to the consoling story retailed by the orthodox Left, the ability of the new Right, for example, to neutralize the contradictions between the people and the state (its populism, in other words), was no mere conjuring trick but had to be seen as operating on genuine grounds, on really altered circumstances. The Right's self-understanding wasn't empty; it exhibited what you called a "rational and material core."[29] Its populism worked on real problems and lived experiences, but it did so by representing them within a new logic that pulled them progressively into their own political and semantic orbit. The lesson for you, then, was that the political and ideological transformations were *reconstituting* the ground of already existing social practices and lived ideologies; and consequently if the Left was to have any hope of being able to influence real politics, it had to be able to think the hegemonic structure of the new conjuncture and contest the Right on precisely *this* terrain. (Maybe, Stuart, re-described in this way you can see the senses in which your "present" is not quite the same as Foucault's.)

To put all this another way, and in a different hermeneutic idiom (more mine than yours): to understand the present in its conjunctural specificity is to understand it in terms of the new "problem-space" of questions it poses for criticism, and the new possibilities it both lays open and shuts down. For, as I have explained elsewhere, one way of describing the temporal *discontinuity*, the historical *punctuation*, that constitutes a conjuncture, is as the reorganization of an existing cognitive-political problem-space, the reorganization of an existing configuration of questions and answers.[30] The conjuncture of any given present, on this view, is the outcome of a contingent historical interruption and conceptual reconfiguration in which one field of argument displaces another. As I read your uses of this idea, therefore, Stuart, to grasp a particular conjuncture it is not enough to seek to inquire whether a new answer (a new proposition) can be arrived at from the old questions; one must also seek to understand whether in fact a new question has been contingently *posed* by the present. This is exactly what is going on in "The Great Moving Right Show." What's becoming clear to you is that Thatcherism had effectively posed a fundamentally new question to the Left for which it had, as yet, no adequate answer. Read this way, a conjuncture is not merely a cognitive category in a social-historical reconstruction but a moral-political category in a strategic framework of intervention. For what is important in the theorization of any conjuncture of the present is not only whether it is possible to identify the question to which the proposition addresses itself as an answer but whether that question *continues* morally and politically to be one worth having answers to. As I've said to you more than once, one way of thinking about what you're saying about the conventional questions the Left was continuing to ask of the Thatcherite moment and the rise of the new Right is that they were, in effect, questions that could no longer *yield* politically useful answers.[31]

———

I never asked you this, Stuart, in all the years (it is one of many regrets), whether you think there is an internal connection (something at the level of style, ethos) between the essays of this period and those of twenty years earlier that mark the conjuncture of the first New Left.[32] For at least as I've come to understand it, your central concern in the immediate post-1956 period, building the New Left clubs and editing the newly minted *Universities and Left Review* with your comrades, was with trying to pry open cognitive-political space for a debate concerning what, in your view, the *new* or emerging Left did not seem to adequately appreciate about the novelty of the new conjuncture in postwar Britain. Yes? I'm thinking in particular of your essay "A Sense of Classlessness," published in 1958, that elicited, as I'm sure you can't *but* remember, some sharply critical response.[33] You were still a very young man then, Stuart, twenty-six or thereabouts, but there are in this essay what I would now call the recognizable figurations of "Stuart Hall's voice"—the thinking-aloud in the dialogical context of an ongoing argument; the attuned, speakerly character of a style of writing that offers a resonant sense of presence; the practice of intervention that, rather than repeating the old, familiar shibboleths, seeks to change or at least *expand* the state of play in the language game of Left theoretical-political discussion. Written, too, notably, out of your own learning-to-listen to what British working people are saying about their postwar lives (as you travel up and down the country), the essay already exudes a receptive sensibility—an aptitude for learning to unlearn conventional wisdoms—that only becomes more pronounced in your later work. In short "A Sense of Classlessness" has about it the same "throat clearing" quality that Jacques noted about "The Great Moving Right Show."

You discern, you say in the essay's opening, a "major shift in patterns of social life" in urban Britain that will have political implications for the Left and the question of socialism. The shift is as yet inchoate, so you are still uncertain how profoundly or fundamentally older conceptions of class, and the role of class in social life, will be affected. Indeed, *here* is the question that precisely prefigures your later idea of "reading the conjuncture." "Where," you ask, "does the old end and where does the new—the real not the superficially new—begin?"[34] Essentially the changes you perceive have to do with the emergence of consumer capitalism in Britain—on the one hand, changes in the rhythms and nature of industrial work in certain parts of the economy, and, on the other, a postwar prosperity that has made possible new habits of spending among working people and that therefore has implications for the Marxist notion of "class consciousness." The upshot of these changes, you venture, is the emergence of an uncanny "class confusion"—or, more provocatively, a *sense* of "classlessness"—in which some of the classical assumptions about working-class aspirations have been turned inside out. For you, Stuart, the sheer novelty of the situation demands not the reapplication of old forms of Marxist analysis but something new, exploratory, however uncertain the theoretical yield. This is of course why Richard Hoggart's *The Uses of Literacy* and Raymond Williams's *Culture and Society* (published within a year of each other, in 1957 and 1958, respectively) are so crucial to your attempt to redraw the portrait of the postwar "age of apathy" and to understand the new "attitudes" to social life, the new moral psychology at work among working people and young people.[35] But even more suggestive, I think, is that you are not only listening to the novel resonances at play in Hoggart and Williams, with their familiar Leavisite sensibility for the British literary-cultural heritage; you are also attuned to such work as William Whyte's *The Organization Man*, C. Wright Mills's *The Power Elite*, David Riesman's *The Lonely Crowd*, and John Kenneth Galbraith's *The Affluent Society*—that is, the new American sociology that was trying to get a handle on the novel social-psychological mechanisms by which late capitalism was creating a new kind of "mass man" (Riesman) or "mass society" (Mills).[36] It isn't of course that Marx and Engels have ceased to preoccupy you. To the contrary, but Marx and Engels understood *how*? That's your question. In your view, because what's at stake in the conjuncture that solicits your intervention here is a "changing pattern of life, attitudes and values—particular responses to a particular situation," reading the so-called ideological superstructure is all the more important; reading the rise of the new "mass media" or "communications industry" concerned to deliberately shape and manipulate opinions and attitudes as being inseparable from the new consumer-oriented capitalism.[37] With Engels's famous letter of 1890 to Joseph Bloch in mind, you recall for your readers that although Marx focused more and more on objective factors "as he elaborated the labour theory of value[,] . . . a reading of *Capital* will not reveal the clean separation of subjective from objective factors in the growth of the working class."[38] This is why for you there is an internal connection between the chapter on commodities in the first volume of *Capital* and the earlier conceptualization of "alienation" in the 1844 *Economic and Philosophical Manuscripts* (that you'd then just gotten your hands on).[39]

But, alas, as with the later "Great Moving Right Show," your intervention was not as productively received as you might have wished—isn't that so? Not Marxist enough? In the tellingly titled "The Big Swipe," one can detect your frustration with the responses, in particular those of your supposed comrades Edward Thompson and Ralph Samuel.[40] It's interesting because Samuel of course was one of your coeditors at *Universities and Left Review*, and Thompson was coeditor with John Saville at the *New Reasoner*—and both journals had, by then, recognized their overlapping concerns and would soon concretize the discussions that would merge them and bring the first *New Left Review* into existence.[41] So one might well have thought there'd be *some* synergy between you, some receptivity. But instead they "came back on the attack," as you put it, rather wearily.[42] Their respective criticisms of your essay were different in emphasis, but, as you lament, they had both missed your point entirely—the point that was quite clearly indicated by the register to which your title gestured: not the fact, but the *sense*, of classlessness. Your concern, you now underline again (in "The Big Swipe"), is with the "sense which many people have that they live in a more 'open' society, in which class consciousness tended to play a lesser role than it had done previously." That was your principal argument. "In other words," you clarify, "my piece was an admittedly impressionistic excursion into the field of working class *psychology*, and only more tentatively a discussion."[43] Now, Samuel gave you a long lecture in the historical sociology of class relations within British capitalism, which was benign enough in the circumstances.[44] But Thompson's response, "Commitment in Politics," must have irritated you some, I imagine.[45] Your relations with him, I know, had never been easy, given the "mixture of suspicion and stifled hope" (not to say arrogant *hauteur*) with which he treated the *Universities and Left Review* project, and *you* in particular.[46] But the odor of disingenuousness and resentment surprised me. Though he does not doubt, he says, your "integrity and commitment to the socialist cause" (the standards of which are, evidently, *his* to judge), he finds you (and your generation) lacking in a proper "sense of history," which, inevitably, will "lead on to attitudes that are both precious and self-isolating."[47] And in the same superior, admonishing tone he went on:

> These attitudes seem to me to stem from an ambiguity as to the place of the working-class in the struggle to create a new socialist society: a tendency to view working people as the *subjects* of history, as pliant *recipients* of the imprint of the mass media, as *victims* of alienation, as *data* for sociological enquiry: a tendency to under-estimate the tensions and conflicts of working-class life, and the creative potential—not in the remote future but here and now—of working people: a tendency to assert the absolute autonomy of cultural phenomena without reference to the context of class power: and a shame-faced evasion of that impolite historical concept—the class struggle.[48]

For Thompson there was just too much Williams and Hoggart in your intellectual system—not a "whole way of life" (the phrase you borrow from Williams), he insists, but a "whole way of struggle"; not the "uses of literacy" (the organizing phrase of Hoggart's book) but the "uses of history."[49] On my reading, anyway, it's clearly Thompson's essay that is the "big swipe." What else could one call it? And with remarkable restraint and maturity you refrain from engaging the attack frontally, sufficing to say, "In one sense, seen through the 'uses of history,' the development of the 'communications industry' can be understood as a gradual development. But we need the 'uses of literacy,' which Thompson under-rates, to explain the *qualitative divergence* between the 'self-help' ethic of the chapel preacher, and the techniques of public persuasion today."[50]

I don't want to go further with this comparison, Stuart, but do you see what I'm driving at here concerning the connection between this New Left moment and the later conjuncture of the late 1970s and 1980s? I'm sure that there is much that divides these historical moments, but the connection is suggestive.[51] When you respond to Bob Jessop and company's reading of "The Great Moving Right Show," there is a sense for me therefore of déjà vu.[52] For once again, you seem to find yourself not only oddly misread and misrecognized but misread and misrecognized by readers who, given their proximity to you and the debates of which you are a part, might have been expected to be better—more discerning—*listeners*. But alas, they are not—which, perhaps, only goes to show, as Fiumara and Levin might have cautioned, how difficult it is to cultivate a listening self. In your reply you seem struck precisely by their unreceptive deafness; you're not being *heard*. As with Samuel and Thompson in the earlier period, Jessop is someone who not only shared some, anyway, of your criticisms of the prevailing Marxist orthodoxies but also was, as you mentioned, a participant in the Hegemony Group in which, along with Ernesto Laclau, Chantal Mouffe, and others, you read and debated Gramsci. So it's strange, puzzling in fact, this misunderstanding of you, and once again you get the gloomy, uncanny feeling (or anyway *I* do) that the whole thing is overdetermined by factors not easy to pin down. Jessop and company have misunderstood your seminal idea of "authoritarian populism," the generative center of your critique of Thatcherism. To begin with, they miss crucial aspects of the genealogy of the concept itself. They miss not only how it builds organically out of the hard-earned insights of *Policing the Crisis* that (as I myself now more deeply understand) laid the groundwork for your work on Thatcher and the Left in the 1980s, but also how it builds out of your dialogue with Nicos Poulantzas's late idea of "authoritarian statism," on the one hand, and Laclau's thinking around "populism," on the other. So it's not simply the substantive conceptual matters as such that they misapprehend; they also miss the intrinsic relation your theory-work has to a dialogical mode of thinking-with-others, and therefore the implications this has for the structure and function of a concept like "authoritarian populism."

I'm going to come back to this issue, Stuart, but I want to pause a moment on the question of Poulantzas (who, it is not irrelevant to remember, you interviewed not long before his terrible death, and partly with Jessop's assistance),[53] because to my mind what his work discloses for you—what you discern in his last book in particular, *State, Power, Socialism*—is especially illuminating for precisely your conduct of Left intellectual practice. To begin with, as I've just mentioned, there is your substantive engagement with his political concept "authoritarian statism"—what you see it *enabling* in terms of its theorization of the specific register of the state, and the wider domain of the political in the context of the crisis of the democratic state and considerations of Euro-communism and socialist transition; and what you see as its *limits* in terms of obscuring the ideological struggle through which, from the base upward, a "popular consent-to-authority" is constructed (this is *your* insight about the authoritarian populist character of Thatcherism).[54] But there is also something else, I think, that *draws* you to Poulantzas, and that is your admiration for a thinker who is profoundly, even sometimes resolutely, dogmatically, committed to practical and theoretical struggle *but* who is not afraid of taking risks, of changing his mind, of opening his thought to challenges, of unlearning and learning again, in the pursuit of his ideals. For you, Stuart, it is *this* ethos that, above all, is disclosed in his last book. The closing passage of your tribute to him and his work, published in *New Left Review*, is worth quoting in full because it is as significant for *our* understanding of *you* as it is for your understanding of him:

> It should be clear, by now, that *State, Power, Socialism* is a profoundly unsettled, and therefore unsettling book. Its incompleteness throws up far more than Poulantzas was ready to secure within the framework of a coherent and integrated argument. The book opens up a series of Pandora's boxes. Often, there is a too-swift attempt to secure their lids again, before their untameable genies can escape. This produces a real theoretical unevenness in the book. Yet, this very unevenness also constitutes, by its reverse side, the stimulus of the book, its generative openness. Poulantzas's earlier books gained much of their

force precisely from their completeness and consistency: some would say from their straining after a consistency which contributes to a certain impression of premature closure, of dogmatism and ortho- doxy. He leaves us with a book which is, in many ways, clearly coming apart at the seams; where no single consistent theoretical framework is wide enough to embrace its internal diversity. It is strikingly *un-finished*. It offers us a picture of one of the most able and fluent of "orthodox" Marxist-structuralist thinkers putting himself and his ideas at risk. This is Poulantzas adventuring. . . . The example it leaves us—above all, in its determination, at the end, to address questions of the utmost and immediate political relevance—is, in a very special way, exemplary. The "perfectly complete and rigorous text" must wait for another moment. Given the way in which the search for correct- ness has systematically distorted Marxist intellectual work through its Althusserean, post-Althusserean, Lacanian and now Foucauldean deluges, this infinite delay may be no bad thing.[55]

A good deal of who you are as an intellectual, Stuart, is contained in this passage. The recognizable attunement to what is going on in the contingent margins of Poulantzas's text is precisely what I mean by your receptive listening. You detect a *rumble* in the uneven, disquieting voice you hear in his "unsettled" pages that is not reducible to the register of propositions arrayed in the theater of Marxist theoretical battle. It points rather to a tentative but genuine uncertainty, and therefore a real internal struggle, breaking occasionally out of the center of the text's thought and disabling, subverting, its presumed *will* to theoretical tidi- ness, the systemic illusion of a *last* word.

And this is what escapes Jessop and company about "The Great Mov- ing Right Show." Moreover, because they are deaf to the dialogical reso- nances in your thinking they also can't make out the *strategic* nature of your theory-work. For they are looking for putative *philosophic* concepts, that is, concepts that are rigorously and systematically constructed so as to be able to perform *general* if not comprehensive work. But as you say, the idea of "authoritarian populism" was generated "in the heat of conjunctural analysis," on the move, as you sought to grasp an unsta- ble target—namely, the historical shift toward Thatcherism unfolding chaotically around you.[56] Consequently the theorization is necessarily provisional, "rough and ready." It doesn't aspire to the elegant, abstract structure of a philosophic system, conjured Kant-like out of whole cloth and meant to work like a master key. But then again, surely *none* of your work embodies such aspirations. As you say, in a quite remarkable account of your own self-conscious ethos of theory-work, one of the things that separates you from the "fundamentalist" Marxists is that you do not hold the assumption that the concepts "advanced at the highest levels of abstraction" by Marx "can be transferred directly into the analysis of concrete historical conjunctures."[57] Concepts vary in their levels of abstraction depending upon their purposes. Against the fundamentalist view, you hold that concepts like Gramsci's "hegemony" and your own "authoritarian populism" are "of necessity somewhat 'descriptive,' historically more specific, time-bound, concrete in their reference."[58] Therefore the horizon of your essay is necessarily partial because it is only an endeavor to capture some of the shifts taking place in the given political-ideological conjuncture: changes in the balance of forces, in the modalities of the political and ideological relationship between the state, the ruling bloc, and the dominated classes. (Again the contrast with Foucault is as striking as the similarity.)

Finally, in their charge that you succumb to a kind of "ideologism," Jessop and company miss what informs the decisions you've made about the specific objects you take up or the specific domains you intervene in.[59] In finding yourself accused of suggesting that Thatcherism is *exclusively* an ideological phenomenon simply because you draw attention to features of its ideological strategy that are specific to its political form, you offer a penetrating reflection on precisely what thinking strategically entails for you:

> It seems well-nigh impossible on the left to affirm the importance and specificity of a particular level of analysis or arena of struggle without immediately being misunderstood as saying that, because it is important, it is the *only* one. I have tried in my own work not to make that easy slide. I work on the political/ideological dimension (a) because I happen to have some competence in that area, and (b) because it is often either neglected or reductively treated by the left generally and

by some Marxists. But the idea that, because one works at that level, one therefore assumes economic questions to be residual or unimportant is absurd. I think the ideological dimension of Thatcherism to be critical. I am certain the left neither understands it nor knows how to conduct this level of struggle—and is constantly misled by misreading its importance. Hence I was determined to bring out this level of analysis—and AP ["Authoritarian Populism"] in part served to do just that. But since AP was never advanced as a general or global explanation, it entailed no prescription whatsoever as to the other levels of analysis. The fact is that until these other dimensions are in place alongside the concept of AP, the analysis of Thatcherism remains partial and incomplete. But the "foregrounding" involved in AP was quite deliberate. "Bending the twig" toward the most neglected dimension, against the drift of discussion, Althusser once called it.[60]

What can there be to add to this, Stuart? It speaks so eloquently of the ethos of your style of responsiveness to the contingency of the present. The process is now familiar: There are intimations of a new conjuncture. You ask yourself what its *demand* is. What question does it pose that is not being engaged by others? You seek to elaborate and probe *that* dimension as a way of enlarging or shifting the way we conceive what is *distinctive* about the present, what is newly or differently contingent about the new conjuncture. And sometimes this involves rhetorically *bending* an argument away from the positions in which it has become congealed or stuck so as to open up cognitive room for alternative intellectual-political interventions. It is the mode of intervention of a listening self.

———

"The Great Moving Right Show" then, is undoubtedly a model of conjunctural analysis, that is, the practice of peeling back the layers of the present to show the varied determinations that constitute its distinctiveness. But it is, to my mind, Stuart, more than that, as I hope I've shown. For what it discloses is more than mere analytical technique. It discloses an *ethos* of responsiveness to the present, a *dispositional* attunement to the contingency through which the features of *difference* that constitute any new conjuncture come to be apprehended in the first place.

In my view, and in language perhaps more mine than yours, your work discloses the pragmatic or diminutive truth that to honor the contingency of the present is to be prepared to give up a certain metaphysical conception of history, namely, the idea of history-as-teleology: a progressively unfolding succession, driven by a built-in law or logic of temporality, carrying humanity forward from a determinate past in the direction of a specifiable future. In this view, as you suggest, the present can hardly have any theoretical significance, being merely a predetermined stage on a journey whose script is already written, whose end is already known. To give up this metaphysical notion of history and embrace the idea and vocabulary of contingency is to see the structural, institutional, and discursive shape of the present as nonnecessary, as, rather, the conjunctural effect of a multiplicity of articulations and determinations that cannot all be known in advance. It is to see that the present does not rest on a fixed and enduring foundation, the identification or uncovering of which will provide assurance that our moral and political practices are the best or right or certifiable ones. And if the present is not shaped by a predetermined past, neither of course is it governed by a preordained future, by an a priori horizon waiting for us, however far away that future and however long it might take to get there.

The main point about contingency, it seems to me, then, is not, strictly speaking, an *epistemological* one. At least as you use it, Stuart, contingency is not meant to be elevated into a new metaphysical first principle, an anti-essentialist theory of essential meanings. Consequently, it is never the absence of essence per se that matters to you (this is one of the senses in which you are not a "philosopher," properly speaking) but the implications of this refutation of foundations and teleology for how one thinks about moral judgment and political action. In this you separate yourself from a wide swath of contemporary anti-essentialism in which the critique of foundations only serves to reinscribe a surreptitious metaphysics.[61] You always expressed a worry about this *theoreticist* inclination. And in this one particular, Stuart, and perhaps surprisingly, I've always found you to share something with Richard Rorty, who, while applauding much in the strategies of "deconstruction"—in, for example,

Simon Critchley or Ernesto Laclau, or indeed Jacques Derrida—always deplored the hidden *metaphysical* drive that often reasserted itself as a sort of regulatory mechanism aiming to guarantee philosophic fidelity.[62] As I understand you, the idea of the contingency of determinations is important insofar as it helps to unsettle—indeed, subvert—a naturalized idea of politics as the mastering and instrumentalist practice of securing a preconceived community of the Good or the True or the Right. To hold open a space for contingency, to read the present conjuncturally, is to see in this conventional idea of politics an ideal of *antipolitics*, in other words a politics conceived to preempt and foreclose the possibility of an ethics of politics as such. The point you hold about contingency, then, is that it promotes a conception of politics understood as *strategic* practice, as always *earned* rather than derived, as always a matter of ideological struggle, as always (in the Gramscian language that you always have ready-to-hand) an ongoing "war of position."

I think it is important to bear in mind here, though, that for you the argument is not that politics is *therefore* groundless, that politics can be conceived *without any premises at all*. To turn down this road is, again, to *convert* politics into epistemology, into an endless game of Truth. If there are no Final Grounds for politics there have always to be *enough* grounds to give traction to a position, to give force to a claim, to give point and uptake to an argument. Such grounds, however, have always to be treated lightly, as provisional rather than fixed or hard-wired or ontological. "Let me put it this way," you once remarked, deploying a handy pedagogical instance so characteristic of your style, "you have to be sure about a position in order to teach a class, but you have to be open-ended enough to know that you are going to change your mind by the time you teach it next week. As a strategy, that means holding enough ground to be able to think a position but always putting it in a way which has a horizon toward open-ended theorization."[63] This, Stuart, is inimitably you—the speaking-listening way of thinking that shaped your ethos of contingency.

Finally, as we have already found in the work of Adriana Cavarero, the vocabulary of contingency commends itself to the vocabulary of voice, and vice versa, what the vocabulary of voice honors is precisely indeterminacy, plurality, worldliness, and provisionality. Voice and contingency,

I'm saying, are reciprocal dimensions of receptivity to a present without guarantees. Intertwined as they are in the essayistic, thinking-aloud, interventionist style you cultivated, they suggest one way of practicing a dialogical ethics of responsiveness to what you would call the present-as-conjuncture, in which priority is given to moral-political dispositions toward making provisional claims and negotiated settlements (constantly reopened and reimagined and reworked) over the epistemological or ontological aim of converging on a final Truth or sovereign Being. The intertwining reciprocity of voice and contingency that you embody aims to make us receptive to the given—and not always (not ever) transparent—circumstances in which we are obliged to act, receptive to the dialogical encounters of agonistic argument in which some positions are staked out and other positions undermined or subverted, and receptive, moreover, to the risk of failure to which any intervention (by dint of being without guarantees) is necessarily always exposed.

———

Perhaps by this point, Stuart, it should need no reinforcement that for you the idea of contingency does not license an ethical-political subject of sovereign agency. The idea that the present is contingently over-determined does not imply that it is simply constructed or invented by the sheer will of rational action, and therefore can simply be reconstructed or reinvented by a fresh application of radical agency. Liberal as well as postmodern subjects often perceive themselves to be agents of pure choice, ironizing agents who can stand back from themselves, so to speak, and revise and modify their ends at will. Richard Rorty, for instance, in work such as *Contingency, Irony, and Solidarity*, sometimes gave the impression of holding this position.[64] In this (by contrast with his instructive doubts about theoreticism) you two are conceptual miles apart. For you, Stuart (and I return to this in the next letter), part of the point of contingency is precisely that we are not simply the sovereign authors of ourselves and our worlds, that we are partly constituted by energies—desires, injuries, dispositions, pasts—flowing beneath the threshold of rational self-consciousness. These are subterranean contingencies that William Connolly felicitously calls "entrenched" or "branded" contingencies; they are contingencies (whether internal or external to us) that are not given, as he says, to easy modification or revision—or, however much they might be modified or revised cannot be *eliminated* altogether.[65] Such contingencies make us alert to the hubris of reason, to the plain and simple limits of sovereign agency.

Another way of saying this, Stuart, one though that begins to stray somewhat from the orientation of your language game (and Connolly's as well, I suspect), is that contingencies alert us to the forms of our *finitude*. I can see the skepticism forming in your eyes as I write this. I've said elsewhere, in a previously published letter reflecting on your lamented passing, that finitude is not an idea anyone would readily associate with you, with your turn of mind, your sensibility.[66] Finitude, I imagine, must seem too constricting an idea for you, to conjure up a realm of necessity, whereas so much of your life was devoted precisely to refusing constraints, overcoming them, strategically negotiating them, transforming them into possibilities. And yet I wonder, Stuart, and wondered again and again in what I've called your "last conjuncture," as you yourself wrestled with a certain kind of limit, whether finitude isn't, in some sense anyway, the name of the *other* side of your thinking about contingency, its photographic negative—there in the mirror, so to speak, a listening, brooding presence.

Let me develop this briefly in the following way, just as something provisional to consider and to close with: the *vector* of your thinking about contingency (not the sum of it, just the vector of it), as we've abundantly seen, is to encourage us to not feel trapped by determinations, by historical circumstances, by the present as a given arrangement of social and political forces. Contingency in this sense is meant to encourage us toward opportunity, new initiatives, the challenge of remaking our worlds. But I wonder whether there isn't another vector of thinking about contingency, one that follows from the fact of our finitude and that can sometimes be occluded by a focus on the first. This is the vector of thinking about contingency that connects it to the *tragic*. And as you know, Stuart, the idea of the tragic as an effect of contingency is one that has been animating me for some time. I've often thought that you and I followed the implications of contingency along these divergent vectors.

One dimension of the contrast between us that I want to draw turns on a distinction that grew out of a strand of my thinking in *Omens of Adversity*, namely, a distinction between a "practice" and an "action."[67] I put this distinction to you on a few occasions, though we never converged on a resolution of our differences. The two—a practice and an action—are obviously connected, but they are not identical. And they may have, I submit, different implications for thinking about contingency. You, of course, Stuart, were mainly interested in *practices*, whereas what has preoccupied me these last many years are *actions*. For my purposes here, I take a practice to be an informed organization of actions aimed at specific purposes. Practices seek to coordinate or harmonize actions, to give them solidity, regularity, repeatability, consciousness, direction. In this sense, and thinking about your work especially (the work that gave rise to "The Great Moving Right Show"), a practice is about how to break into the present, or how to break out of it; it is about how to intervene in the present as opposed to merely submitting to it. Practices, then, are about making history, or *remaking* it. They have a political pedigree; they are the source of our freedom. If our historical orders are known to be contingently put together (by determinations that are not reductively determinate), a practice, specifically a political one, aims to take advantage of this recognition in order to propel us beyond the mere repetition of the status quo. Actions, by contrast, though often constituents of practices, need not be; they need not be embodied in practices; they need not have met the threshold for practices. Actions can be more elemental, sometimes irrational, intuitive, in any case not necessarily thought-out in the way practices are. In this sense actions, while attached to beginnings (as Hannah Arendt famously suggests), often disclose our finitude, the *limits* of practices.[68] This is because actions inhabit a plural world of other actions that are not only not necessarily in harmony with each other but sometimes mutually contradictory. Actions sometimes inadvertently collide. And such collisions are sometimes fatal, irreversible. To think in terms of actions, therefore, is also to think about how the present sometimes breaks in on us, how it potentially unmakes our best hopes, our finest practice-driven intentions. This is because though we may self-consciously initiate an action we have no guarantee of how it will turn out.

I wonder, then, Stuart, whether thinking contingency in terms of actions instead of practices might give us a somewhat different orientation and allow other dimensions of experience to come into view. It might encourage us to dwell awhile with the consideration that we are not only contingent choosers but also contingently chosen; not only contingent actors but also contingently acted upon. We are also, in other words, sufferers of the indeterminate actions of others (whether our interior or exterior others). I believe that dwelling with this tragic fact can be beneficial for our thinking, not least the kind of thinking-with-others you gave us an example of. Although I'm now routinely accused of being a pessimist or a defeatist (or worse), this moralizing characterization of me, I believe, quite misses the point of thinking with and through the idea of the tragic. Part of the virtue of thinking contingency within the purview of tragic action is that it potentially brings into view the fact that our finitude is not a mere inert or passive limit waiting to be surpassed by our Promethean agency, but is itself a dynamic source of multiple, sometimes nameless, energies, that, unbidden, act upon us from within or from without, and to which, sometimes, we can do no better than yield. Recognizing this is not, to my mind, a sign of defeat or resignation; or, rather, it might be important to learn to think of defeat and resignation as dimensions of life that can teach us something valuable about how the past lives in the present. Recognizing this is its own form of realism, I'd say—a tragic realism, perhaps. My view, as I think you have understood better than most even if you didn't share it exactly, is that the tragic allows an openness to humility, an attunement to mystery, and a sense of proportion and measure that I know you value, and that, indeed, I have learned from our friendship.[69]

Would that there had been time enough to think further together about these matters, my friend. But let's leave it here for now.

Best wishes,
DAVID

——

Attunement to Identity

What We Make of What We Find

DEAR STUART,

I want to talk to you now about identity. I think of identity as another one of those distinctive terrains—like contingency—on which one can appreciatively hear the resonant grain in your thinking-aloud voice and its connection to the larger ethos of your dialogical style. As with your responsiveness to the present that we've just talked about, the question of identity draws us toward something essential, even vital, to your way of being an intellectual. Memorably, in the late 1980s and early 1990s, and in company with a number of other politically engaged intellectuals on the Left, you *turned* to thinking about—and thinking through—the concept of identity. It was a novel turn, wasn't it? It emerged in a new conjuncture, you'd probably say, one that may well now have passed, displaced as happens by new preoccupations—those, for example, that concern the "human" and its relation to politics: the so-called ontological turn that you've been spared. That itself might have been worth a separate conversation, this fading of identity as a contemporary conceptual concern. When *was* identity, we'd have had to ask? Are we now living in its aftermath?[1] But in any case identity hadn't quite organized your work before the late 1980s, not generatively anyway, not formally, not self-consciously. It's not really central to *Policing the Crisis*, for example.[2] And yet in a curious and profound way, once explicitly installed there as a central category of your preoccupations, it so easily seemed as though it must *always* have been a germane, constitutive part of your thinking. It seemed to very much *belong* there among the other ideas that have your personal stamp on them. I mean, you appeared in a way to inhabit the problematic of identity; or maybe the problematic of identity inhabited you. What is it, Stuart, this familiarity, this *intimacy*, between you and identity? I know you won't say exactly, directly, that wouldn't be you; only obliquely maybe, only, so to speak, sotto voce.

Still, this is what motivates me here, this intimate proximity that characterized your relation to identity—that uncanny sense of your attuned affinity with it. It's overdetermined, Stuart, undoubtedly, like everything else you touched, that touched you, but what brings this special rapport with identity home, at least to me, what especially alerts me to it, is that, as you make the *turn* toward it in the late 1980s, early 1990s, one has a palpable sense of you changing yourself once more, of you learning to learn once more who you are, where you belong, what you should be doing. One has the sense of you clearing your throat again, to borrow Martin Jacques's fitting phrase, thinking-aloud with new dialogical others, explaining something to yourself about the world and (what will be especially important to me) about your own lived experience of it, your own autobiographical location within it.

Identity, of course, is an old philosophic topic; whether in the style of Derek Parfit or Bernard Williams, say, or more recently Charles Taylor (your old friend) or Paul Ricoeur, the question specifically of personal identity—the nature of selfhood or personhood, the problem of continuity and discontinuity through time, the role of experience and memory and narrative, and so on—has not lacked contemporary, sometimes controversial, discussion.[3] Not surprisingly, while not unaware of these issues and debates in the high register of the philosophic discourse on identity, you were not significantly motivated by them in your thinking on the subject. At least as I've come to understand it, Stuart, and somewhat belatedly I'll admit, your turn to thinking about and thinking through the concept of identity is inseparable from a larger rethinking in which you were engaged at the end of the 1980s, namely, the rethinking that you (and Martin Jacques) called "New Times."[4]

This is certainly not the place to rehearse in any detail the whole scope of—and justification for—the New Times project, or to engage with its critical reception.[5] I know that at least some people on the Left believed you to have finally gone off the fellow-traveling deep end.[6] But be that as it may, part of the point of New Times as a political-theoretical intervention, I take it, was to offer, tentatively and provisionally, the description of a new conjuncture of late capitalism as well as to urge, again tentatively and provisionally, some new directions and some new languages (as always) for the "hard road" of *renewal* of Left politics. Advanced capitalist societies like Britain were undergoing a kind of transformation that seemed to you "epochal," in the sense that it registered a change in the character of the present that was "qualitative" and not merely "incremental" or incidental.[7] Something almost *tectonic* was at work such that, while the changes were by no means either comprehensive or complete, they were nevertheless generative and dynamic enough to fundamentally shift the very "centre of gravity" of capitalist societies in a new direction, altering the "tone" of these societies as well as their "dominant rhythm of cultural change."[8] "Post-Fordism" is what, with its Gramscian sources and allusions, you called this new conjuncture in order to mark an alteration both in the structure of capitalist economies (the rise of more flexible, decentralized labor processes; the decline of blue-collar relative to white-collar work; the multiplication of transnational capital flows; the greater role played by consumption; and so on) and in the relation between the economic and other domains—in particular, the cultural domain (the new, more seamless interpenetration of economic and cultural dimensions). What you were describing in the late 1980s is of course the escalating and ramifying unfolding of the "neoliberal revolution" whose outline you had already presciently observed in "The Great Moving Right Show" (though, interestingly, *neoliberal* is inserted only in the revised version of the essay published in *The Hard Road to Renewal* the year before *New Times*, as though you'd only lately learned to use it). In any case, in that essay you do remark incisively on the fact that Thatcherism had renovated the antistatism and anticollectivism of conservative philosophy, creating the conditions in which the "sacred orthodoxy" of Keynesianism could be displaced by the "possessive individualist and free market nostrums of Hayek and Friedman."[9] And indeed, Stuart, the catastrophic global dimensions and implications of this revolution in capitalist ideology and practice would haunt you for the rest of your life.[10]

Anyway, New Times is one problem-space in which identity acquired a particular prominence for you, because one pronounced feature of the post-Fordist transformation was a disintegration of the old, seemingly stable, and reliable relation between, so to say, "social consciousness" and "social being." Certainly it was becoming more and more evident to many that it was less and less plausible to speak in terms of a single subject-position—say, the classical collective class position—that could be depended upon to organize, or even hegemonize, the vanguard of a progressive political strategy. As the homogeneity and mass standardization of Fordism gave way to a relentless tendency toward diversity, fragmentation, and differentiation, potential sites of social antagonism—and consequently potential sites of resistance, around sex, around race, around gender—multiply, proliferate. New subjects, and new collective identities, emerge, making incompatible claims and expressing irreconcilable demands, and therefore undermining any notion of a unified collective will. This fundamentally alters how one can think about politics; it introduces an ineradicable element of contingency and sometimes contradiction and even incommensurability about political horizons and directions, as well as about who the privileged agents of political change ought to be, or *could* potentially be. And this both brings identity into view *and* puts it into question.[11]

———

So, Stuart, it seems to me enormously important to underline at the outset (especially because it's so often lost in reflections on your work and intellectual trajectory) the way for you the identity question is internally connected to your larger thinking about the Left and socialist change. For you, for example, identity is not an *anti*socialist category, let alone an anti-Marxist one; to the contrary, identity is sutured to the changing problem and problematic of Left politics. Not that what constitutes socialist change is somehow already known, is ready-made, and that identity has merely to fit itself into that given framework. For indeed nothing historical is given like that. Rather, it is precisely *because* the socialist project is now finally unhinged from its untenable foundationalist moorings that identity has become disembedded from naturalized invisibility or normalized essence, and therefore has emerged as contingently unavoidable to think about and indispensable to think with in the reconstruction of socialist possibility. In some sense identity emerges at the end of a long road of debate about the relation between "base" and "superstructure" that for you started in the 1950s.

And yet to be sure, Stuart, even this problem-space of late or post-Fordist capitalism, central though it may be, is not the whole or the only problem-space that shaped your turn toward identity. Something else, equally important, is going on in these years. You would be the first to remind us that identity is nothing if not incorrigibly paradoxical, at once *outside* as well as *inside* experience. What I mean is that if identity is a category you want to urge your socialist comrades to *learn* to think with, to learn to bring into their conceptual work, this is partly because one version of it is already being thought—and lived—by *you*, on precisely the ground of one of those new proliferating sites of antagonism and dissension, namely, *race* (or what you would call "ethnicity"). That is to say, part of the cultural-political problem-space of your turn to identity in these years was shaped by the emergence in postcolonial Britain of a new generation of black voices, in the expressive arts perhaps most dramatically, most poignantly, but not only, who were in the process of interrupting and revising the narrative of Englishness, nation, and empire, and thus telling a new story about what it meant to be *black*. I'm thinking especially of your association with David A. Bailey and the group around the journal *Ten.8* in the 1980s. I'm thinking of your movingly attentive little essay on Vanley Burke, a little older than this new generation, and of course born in Jamaica not in England, but whose photographic imagination documented black Birmingham from the 1970s with affecting sensitivity.[12] These eloquently assertive young people whose work you are discovering around you, and who are teaching you something new about being black in contemporary Britain are, by and large, *not* people connected to the New Left or any talk of socialism; but they are, nevertheless, Stuart, and in a very material way, people connected to *you*. They are an intimate part of *your* story. The age of New Times is simultaneously the age of Diaspora. There is a sense, therefore, in which while you offer identity as a new point of conceptual *departure* for your socialist comrades, it also emerges as a kind of *return* for you, an existential kind of coming home. I wonder what you make of this formulation? I've not put it to you in quite this way before. And, in fact, now that I think of it this way, I'm going to press this direction a bit more. So bear with me.

The view I'm groping toward, Stuart, is that from the beginning, identity came to you ineradicably marked by this paradox of departure and return, discovery and recovery. Is this, do you think, one reason why for you identity has never been merely a theoretical abstraction, nor a matter simply of social construction? For you, I think, however much identity was meant to be encountered somewhere along the famous "detour of theory," it was always nevertheless ensconced within a concrete mode of *personal* as well as political experience. It was as though it made no sense to you to talk about identity in purely schematic terms. Not that you never did, but only rarely so.[13] Again, to my mind, there's an instructive contrast to be drawn here between yourself and Ernesto Laclau (who, alas, followed you to the grave within a matter of months), a contrast more in terms of style and ethos, I think, than in terms of substantive theory-content or political purpose. Like you, of course, Laclau also began in this period to engage with identity as central to an anti-essentialist conceptualization of a post-Marxist politics. In some sense, the landmark book he coauthored with Chantal Mouffe, *Hegemony and Socialist Strategy*, deconstructing as it did the very grounds of a universal subject of revolutionary politics, set the stage for his theorization of identity from the 1990s onward.[14] But enormously valuable as this thinking is, what's notable I believe is that, like most other concepts in the exacting corpus of his work, identity always moved in a somewhat rarefied theoretical—some might say *theoreticist*—atmosphere.[15]

THREE

—

I mean that in Laclau's work identity is conceived and theorized at such a high level of generality and abstraction, almost purely in the register of the logical structure and internal movement of categories, that it barely has any discernible existential or sensual or experiential content, barely any recognizable *embodied* texture. It scarcely touches the "stony ground" of everyday life. The point may simply be that unlike you, Stuart, Laclau saw himself as a kind of political *philosopher* rather than a theorist of conjunctures. He was, preeminently, a *critical self* whose thinking, though allied in certain respects to yours, inhabited a different "intellectual universe."[16] Not surprisingly, in that intellectual universe identity functioned as an element in a rigorous philosophic *system*, as a dimension of an antifoundationalist *method*. Neither of these—neither system nor method—much interested you, right? You instinctively stood away from them, using them as sparingly as possible. Perhaps it's because as a *listening* self your suspicion was that one of the effects of such a relentless demand for system and method is that, however much it aims at a critique of hegemonic essence or of absolutist totalizations, its own theoreticist dynamic harbors a deaf yearning for yet new versions of the very sort of truth-effects it allegedly fears. I wonder parenthetically whether this was Frantz Fanon's worry too when he announced in a terse and peremptory remark in the introduction to *Black Skin, White Masks* that he would leave method to the mathematicians and botanists because there comes a moment when method makes itself irrelevant.[17]

By contrast, Stuart, I've always had the sense, listening to you talk about identity, listening above all to the uncanny *fluidity* with which you articulated its peculiar demands, that it is something profoundly if paradoxically familiar to you—as though you speak about identity from *within* the lived experience of its contradictory force-fields, its nuances, its ruses. One has the sense, Stuart, that for you identity is an "experience-near" concept rather than an "experience-distant" one, if I can draw on a somewhat abstruse but nevertheless helpful distinction I think you'd have liked (it's one that the psychoanalytic theorist of narcissism Heinz Kohut used in his discussion of the self and its modes of experience, and that the anthropologist Clifford Geertz later borrowed to contrast concepts people might use to talk about themselves or their

fellows, and those that a theorist, say, might use).[18] Now, I don't mean
to say anything as silly or meaningless as that identity was somehow
always the suppressed idiom of your intellectual vocation, one that only
revealed itself later—even though I admit that what I'm trying to say
may sound uncomfortably close to that. Rather, I'm trying to describe, or
maybe evoke, something about the character of concepts like identity
that seem to depend, as *concepts*, upon a certain proximity to *experience.*
And I'm wondering aloud whether the experience that "identity" comes
conceptually to name (or rename) from the late 1980s on was one that
you could, as it were, already identify with, call your own. It somehow fit
you. It is as though the story of the erosion of the seeming self-evidence
of the stable and homogeneous self of Western modernity—that is at
the same time the story of the eclipse of the idea of the universal subject
of revolutionary politics—has a special, perhaps personal, resonance
for you; as though the history that had come to meet you through this
new reflexivity about decentering and displacement and whatnot only
brought into sharper focus something you already had a vivid if inchoate experience of: as a black subject, as a colonial subject, as a diasporic
subject, or something like that. Do you sense what I'm reaching for?
Indeed, it is as though with the concept of identity in hand you now discovered yourself able to *retrospectively* re-describe forms of experience
that had not hitherto found a responsive reflexive vocabulary. I believe
that this movement in the activity of thinking suggests a complex, a
not self-evident (maybe not even a fully conscious), relation between our
concepts and our lived experience that's often missed in much of the high
theorization of identity that you characteristically eschew. How might one
describe the palpable intimacy of this subject-object relation that identity
names *for* you, or names *in* you? For in so much of the work of this period,
Stuart, you become, in part at least, your own autobiographical figuration
of identity. Or else, identity becomes a sort of Winnicottian or Lacanian
mirror in which you can recognize in outline the interior historicity of
who you are. That is to say, the story of who you're taking yourself to be
in these years—let's say, increasingly, a *diasporic* intellectual—could now
be folded into a larger, world-historical story that accompanied the very
making of the modern world: as though who you are and where you come
from—your specific Jamaican journey—was now not extraneous to the

grand political-theoretical issues of the moment (namely, New Times) with which you were engaged on the Left, but internal to them, an exemplification or even a magnification of them. Your historical particularity, so to put it, was now an *instance* of a recognizable universality.

———

Some of this sort of thinking about the distinctiveness of the concept of identity is at work, for example, Stuart, in one of the talks you gave in 1989, "Old and New Identities," as the second of two lectures in a symposium organized by Anthony King at State University of New York, Binghamton, around the theme of globalization and the contemporary conditions for the representation of identity. I don't know much about the symposium, but from the look of the published volume it seems it was tailor-made for your preoccupations and interventions. Now, one of the intriguing things to me about this talk is that, in the margins so to speak, one can hear you wrestling precisely with the fact of the paradox of concepts like identity, that are *both* old and new, both "experience-near" as well as "experience-distant," at one and the same time. And in the course of this wrestling one recognizes you saying something about the contingent historicity of concepts—something general, perhaps, but something that comes to you mediated through the specificity of identity—that seems to me enormously insightful and, moreover, true (or true enough). Early in the essay we hear you say,

> I return to the question of identity because the question of identity has returned to us; at any rate, it has returned to us in British politics and British cultural politics today. It has not returned in the same old place; it is not the traditional conception of identity. It is not going back to the old identity politics of the 1960s social movements. But it is, nevertheless, a kind of return to some of the ground which we used to think in that way.[19]

This is a startlingly recursive formulation, full of the allusive sense of anomaly and ambiguity that, you seem to suggest, should always inform our relation to the nuances of concepts. What is this *return* to a politics of identity that is nevertheless not a return to that *idea* of identity that undergirded such social movements as Black Power or national liberation or second-wave feminism in an earlier historical period?

Leaving aside the whole matter of the characteristically *spoken* character of this formulation, Stuart, in which we can clearly make out the rhythms and cadence of your speaking voice, what is arresting is the both/and conjunctural dimension of identity that you're pointing us to. You are obliged to return to identity, you suggest, not because it is, abstractly or self-evidently, a concept of the first importance, and that demands our attention on this basis, but rather because identity has, contingently, come back to you—from elsewhere, as it were, partly from an old incompletely resolved past and partly from the new dispensation of the present. It is as though you've rounded a corner and there it is, looking back at you, beckoning obligingly if a little obscurely, deliberately, seductively, resentfully. And yet, though in a certain sense recognizable (since, say, racism, colonialism, and sexism continue to exist in multiple, subjectifying forms, and continue, therefore, to condition varied modes of dissent and refusal), it isn't quite the same concept you knew before— it isn't exactly the same even if it isn't exactly different either; something has changed even as something has remained the same. I keep wondering, Stuart, whether part of what intrigues you about this both/and paradox of the "return" of identity is that it discloses something—perhaps something *intrinsic*—about the way theoretical work should conceive of at least certain kinds of concept formation, those of experience-near concepts: the way, as you vividly put it, theoretical-political work seems to "lose things on the one side and then recover them in another way from another side, and then have to think them out all over again." This, you suggest, is what theoretical work is made of—a never-ending process of "losing and regaining concepts" (42). I've always thought this a remarkable way of thinking the historicity of concept formation, Stuart, and it seems to me very characteristic of the ethos of your style, of always pointing us away from simple either/or binaries and toward the anomalous slippages, the enigmatic doublings, involved in intellectual work.

Now, what is the character of the concept of identity that we seem to have lost or anyway left behind, that concept of identity that you think shaped the demands of the great movements for social emancipation?

THREE

—

In this lecture (but elsewhere as well) the story you tell is that the old logic of identity, as familiar to us from Cartesian philosophy as from developmental psychology centers identity as the founding ground of subjectivity and personhood. It functions as the guarantee of a stable, continuous, authentic source of the sense of self—a class self, a gendered self, a nationalist self, a black self. It gives depth to our sense of meaningful interiority, and an assurance of integrity and validity. As you put it in a memorable passage that I've quoted once before: "Increasingly, I think that one of the main functions of concepts [like identity] is that they give us a good night's rest. Because what they tell us is that there is a stable, only very slowly changing ground inside the hectic upsets, discontinuities and ruptures of history. Around us history is constantly breaking in unpredictable ways but we, somehow, go on being the same" (43). I've always admired this formulation, again especially for what it discloses about your sense of the *intimacy* of concepts like identity, their connection to our embodied *selves* not only our abstract minds, their ability to organize our worlds not merely in experience-distant but also in experience-near ways. As you see it, such concepts function to stabilize the world for us; and in doing so they impose the illusion of changelessness upon a world of ceaseless change. And the virtue of this illusion is that it allows us a comforting sense of undisturbed continuity—a restful sleep.

However, even so, the conceit of this old logic of identity has now exhausted itself. That whole conception is, you say, "for good or ill, finished" (43). In your view, a number of world-historical "decenterings" in modern thought have made it more difficult to go on thinking about identity in this way—among them, Karl Marx's idea that we make history in circumstances we do not choose; Sigmund Freud's "discovery" of the continent of the unconscious; Ferdinand de Saussure's insight that meaning in language is shaped through difference; feminism's critique of masculinist assumptions concerning public and private; and the postcolonial critique of the West. These decenterings, you urge, are aspects of the self-questioning of identity that has gone hand-in-hand with the post-Fordist erosion of the conditions of those great modern collective social identities—class, race, nation, gender—that could be spoken of as though they were "singular actors in their own right," as though they "allowed us to understand and to read, almost as a code, the imperatives of the individual self" (44). These collective identities, you urge, have not disappeared from our world, but they are not quite what they used to be; they are no longer in the same "social, historical or epistemological place where they were in our conceptualizations of the world in the recent past." This is because, while something of them still persists, we cannot think of any of them any longer as homogeneous totalities, internally undifferentiated, undivided by contradiction or fragmentation. "If they have a relationship to our identities, cultural and individual," you explain, "they do not any longer have that suturing, structuring, or stabilizing force, so that we can know what we are simply by adding up the sum of our positions in relation to them" (45). In other words, they do not, as they did in the past, give us that good night's rest—quite the contrary they disruptively leave us without guarantees of just who we are, who we should be. It is the fracturing of this conception of identity that opens the way *not* for the end of identity but rather for its "return" in a transfigured form.

———

Of course, Stuart, there are a number of essays in which one could listen to you talk about identity. Certainly, one of these would be the well-known and enormously influential essay "New Ethnicities."[20] You and I talked quite a bit about this "somewhat notorious" essay (as you once referred to it), and as you know I've tried to write about some aspects of it.[21] Indeed, I've always thought that "New Ethnicities" (high-stakes intervention that it is) was much misunderstood inasmuch as the idea central to its concerns—of the "end of the innocent notion of the essential black subject"—has often been taken to authorize an uncomplicated (that is to say, an ahistorical and progressivist) anti-essentialism.[22] I mean that it has been often assumed to sanction a just-so story of identity according to which, whereas once upon a time, during the old social movements days of black liberation, we thought identities had singular and originary essences, now we know better, now we know that they are in fact socially constructed, and therefore that there are many ways to be black. Your use of "innocent" is bound to mislead, but I take it to be moral and political in implication rather than epistemological. Mistaking you to be the advocate of an unqualified methodological constructivism what has often been missed is the tentative and strategic character of the intervention you're making, the fact that you are *not* expounding a new sociological principle of identity formation but rather, and characteristically, reading in the just discernibly emerging conjuncture the contingent figuration of new possibilities of identity.[23] What is missed, in other words, is an appreciation of your sense of the "unguarded moment," as you put it, in which you are thinking-out-loud the present that you are trying to act *differently* in.[24]

As often, in the hands of others your responsiveness to the present congeals into *method*, a protocol for repeatable research. I'm reminded of something Ian Hacking once wrote about Michel Foucault and his epigones: "Foucault carved numerous turns of phrase into ice sculptures, which had, for a moment, sharp contours. Then he walked away from them, insouciant, and let them melt, for he no longer needed them. His less gifted readers put the half-melted shapes in the freezer and, without thinking, reproduce these figures as if they still glistened in the midnight sun and meant something."[25] I've always thought, Stuart, that this profound reflection on Foucault's style applied equally to yours, and to the sort of conceptual work carried out by heuristic formulations like your "end of the innocent notion of the essential black subject." In any case, central though "New Ethnicities" is to your turn to identity, and catalytic though it has been in many discussions about black experience, for me easily the most compelling place to hear you thinking through this de-centered return of the problematic of identity is in the essay "Minimal Selves," published around the same time, the late 1980s. So I now want to spend some time using it to help me think about your intimacy with the experience-nearness of identity.

In 1986 the Institute of Contemporary Art in London organized a conference around the theme "The Real Me: Postmodernism and the Question of Identity." In the opening note to the volume of published essays, the editor Lisa Appignanesi gives an indication of the conceptual issues that shaped the context in which a number of participants—among them writers, philosophers, social theorists, historians—were asked to address the "will o' the wisp" (as she terms it) notion of the "real me." "Recent years have seen the all-but simultaneous emergence of a proliferation of 'discourses' which either efface the individual subject or reassert its gendered centrality," she writes, "only then to decentre the self into a variety of more or less minimal selves. The self-assertive 'I' finds its solidity and unity being eroded. At the same time it becomes the site for a feverish shoring-up operation."[26] The self is at once decentered *and* the site of an intense preoccupation, as though the new uncertainty about identity released a nervous pressure to normalize displacement. The provocation for the conference gathering, then, was "postmodern," in a sense perhaps particular to metropolitan theory of the 1980s and 1990s, and the volume presented a divergence of orientations and positions from Homi Bhabha at the beginning to Terry Eagleton at the end.[27]

Thus, as often, Stuart, there was a specific *occasion*, a specific "speech event," so to call it, a particular set of problems into which you were invited to think with others; and into which, in turn, you invited *us* to think with you. I don't know whether this was originally an extemporaneous talk or spoken from prepared notes (or a commingling of the two), but to my mind "Minimal Selves" (the title is one, I gather, you were given, not one you'd offered yourself) is an especially fertile essay with which, and through which, to consider your thinking around identity because its very *spoken* character eloquently captures the restless, responsive movement of your embodied and performed thinking-aloud, and therefore the sense in which the provisional process of your thinking mirrors the instability of the subject-matter itself, identity, *about which* you're speaking.[28] Indeed, very memorably, you literally begin by saying, "A few adjectival thoughts only . . ." (44)—with ellipses in the written version to mark what the resonant, perhaps ironic, silence in the spoken version would have indicated (supplemented, one can only imagine, with a significant glance in the direction of your audience), namely, the grammatical sense of provisionality and unfinishedness of the thinking-out-loud to follow, its openness toward a horizon that cannot be completely known in advance. And by opening your lecture with this remark, you immediately establish a certain authoritative "footing" (as Erving Goffman would have called this "form of talk" of the lecture) with your audience;

you issue them an invitation to hear you in *this* particular way and not in some other.[29] Specifically, you invite them to take your thoughts to be "adjectival" in the sense, perhaps, of offering something more in the way of *modifiers* than substantives, more in the way of processual "thinking" than of fully formulated "thoughts" that can stand forever.

But significantly, this won't be the only footing on which you proceed because your audience (and your readers) soon discover that these thoughts of yours on identity are not going to be *adjectival* only—*only* adjectival. They are also going to be, partly, autobiographical; that is, they are going to pass through the figuration of your own *personal* story of who you are—which brings us back to what I was saying earlier about the intimacy for you of the question of identity. You start off the essay by stating straightforwardly your realization that your sense of your own identity has been directly tied to "the fact of being a migrant," and therefore, you add somewhat polemically, "on the *difference* from the rest of you" (44)—referring in this way to your (presumably) largely white, British audience at the conference who are, in a profound sense, at *home* (certainly more so than you are). What is the rhetorical and conceptual move that you're performing here, Stuart, whereby you both *place* yourself as a subject of identity, and invite your audience to *not* misrecognize your difference from them? What is at stake in this mode of address that directly positions you at an *angle* to those who, perhaps within another domain of British Left politics, *thought they knew you*—who wouldn't have thought of *you* as a migrant, let alone black? What do they know of "displacement" and "dispersal" who *only* displacement and dispersal know (to give the question the nuance of a Jamesian phrasing)?[30] These—*displacement* and *dispersal*—the new terms lately being employed by postmodern thinkers to describe the experience of the decentered self are, you suggest, already familiar to *real*—as opposed to only metaphorical—migrants. (Indeed the tension, the nonidentical connection, between the real and the metaphorical, structures in a critical way the lecture as a whole.) So that in a paradoxical way, where once you and others found yourselves and your migrant experience in Britain marginal, perhaps invisible, certainly not exemplary, in this new atmosphere of postmodern fragmentation you now suddenly find yourself "centered"—indeed, strangely *defining* an emerging norm. "Welcome to migranthood," you say to your audience, with amused, even gleeful, cheek (44).

Now, of course, since this is *you* speaking, Stuart, one immediately suspects that you're offering your audience this seeming gesture of identification (this seeming footing) only to throw them off-guard, only to draw the carpet from under them, only to seduce them into a false sense of the security and contentment of sameness—the good night's rest they assume to be theirs by right. Little do they know that the point you are going to emphasize is about the *conceit*—their conceit—that erases difference in the rhetoric of migrancy-as-postmodern-chic. And yet at the same time, again paradoxically, it is this very postmodern conjuncture of theoretical attention to the instability of identity that enables *you* to find the conceptual idiom for what had hitherto seemed to escape naming. Isn't this one sense in which though you've never been exactly a postmodernist, you've never been exactly *not* one either?[31] Anyway, this simultaneous *distancing from* and *appreciation of* given theoretical turns, always implicated in them but never completely assimilated to them, we've come to see as characteristic of your style of a listening responsiveness.

You've been puzzling, you say, over a historical moment that suggests the uncertain emergence of a new conjuncture around migration and the figure of the migrant so crucial to postwar British social, political, and cultural history. Of course, the thing is that you yourself are part of the story of this conjuncture, having arrived in Britain from colonial Jamaica in 1951 to take up your Rhodes scholarship at Oxford. This was only three short years after the docking of the Empire *Windrush* in June 1948, carrying the first wave of West Indian migrants (nearly five hundred of them) to a then unknown destiny—to an "expectation," as George Lamming would famously put it in *The Pleasures of Exile*.[32] But a generation later something significant is changing, you urge, the scope and depth and complexity of which has not been fully understood. (We can see here the familiar, almost trademark, move in which you evoke the sense of a new, still inchoate, conjuncture, that will frame out the discursive space of a tentative, provisional intervention—again your *feeling* for contingency.) Young black British people, the second generation of West Indians in Britain (that is, the first generation born in Britain to West Indian parents), though every bit as marginalized and disadvantaged and disenfranchised as their immigrant parents, perhaps in some senses more so given the prevailing economic crisis in the 1980s, are no longer Samuel Selvon's lonely Londoners, lost and forlorn in the gray city.[33] Now they "look as if they own the territory" (44) of contemporary urban Britain. This is what impresses you—the insouciant confidence of these young Englanders.[34] They don't inhabit cities like London and Birmingham and Leeds with the same appeasing diffidence as their parents did. They don't carry themselves as though they were mere "guests" of the Mother Country's dubious hospitality. They're not in Britain on sufferance.

Now I know you've written about precisely this generational shift in the closing chapter of *Policing the Crisis*, published a decade before. There, as I noted earlier, in the context of situating the politics of "mugging" in terms of the structuring of racialization and the emerging law-and-order state, you and your cowriters had constructed a picture of the difficult coming-of-age of this generation.[35] But here in the later "Minimal Selves" lecture, by contrast, you have a different agenda, a different purpose, that turns partly on working through the affective phenomenology of your own experience of the unstable temporalities of identity. Can I put it that way? You can tell I'm trying to find my way toward an adequate language of description. You're clearly moved and inspired by these young people. Somehow or other you are yourself implicated in their story. You can recognize yourself in them—and also *not*, or you only partially, obliquely, recognize yourself in them. "I've wondered again and again," you write reflexively, "what it is about that long discovery-recovery of identity among blacks in this migrant situation, which allows them to lay a kind of claim to certain parts of the earth which aren't theirs with quite that certainty" (44). The uneven syntax here is salted by the warm if puzzled regard one can detect around the edges of your voice. I want to notice, partly as a way of underlining something I mentioned earlier and to which I'll return, namely, that for you identity is both *discovered* and *recovered*. And I wonder whether, in a certain respect, it isn't this younger generation's discovery-recovery of black identity that somehow opens the existential room for *your* own discovery-recovery of identity in Britain, whether these discoveries-recoveries (yours, theirs) don't happen together in an interconnected way, however uneven their generational temporalities. At any rate, this is the generation that is changing the politics of black identity in Britain—the generation that will inspire you to speak (as I mentioned before) of the "end of the innocent notion of the essential black subject." But I don't want to allow myself to be waylaid by this important direction; I want to return to the internal movement of "Minimal Selves."

One of the things you find curious about this younger generation, you say, is the way their conundrum of identity, a paradoxical kind of centered-decenteredness in contemporary Britain, has acquired a strange sort of cultural *allure* for others. Is that the right word—"allure"? These young black people are oddly envied by many of those very white people to whom you're speaking. You detect a strange and amusing play of desire and fantasy at work among them that has a share in motivating their postmodern romance with migrancy. "Envy is a very funny thing for the British to feel at this moment in time—to want to be black!" you say with mock—and slightly mocking—surprise. "Yet I feel some of you surreptitiously moving toward that marginal identity. I welcome you to that, too" (44). Recognizably, the *tease* is another footing at work in this lecture. Again, Stuart, in a performative way, you construct your own identification with this community of young black Britons in such a way that you can, on *their* behalf, and by a playful inversion of the immigrant experience, assume the role of welcoming host vis-à-vis white Britons who are themselves playing at inhabiting a marginal subject-position. The tone is clearly ironic, not offered with any hostility; but the intent is very *serious* indeed. One has the sense of you, here, in your legendary "easy-going Jamaican" manner, establishing a not-so-subtle line of tension between the contrasting perspectives from which a norm of experience (that is, migranthood) is identified and represented, on the one hand, by those for whom it is metaphorical and, on the other, by those for whom it is real. This inversion of roles you enact puts into play a whole range of colonial resonances concerning the politics and poetics of hospitality (who welcomes whom to what, when, and on what

THREE

—

terms) that we could spend some time talking about—that indeed we *have* spent some time talking about.[36]

Anyway, a shift is occurring that makes it possible for a new dialogue about identity to take place—including a dialogue about (and from the perspective of) your own identity. Or to put it differently, from another side, the postmodern metaphor of identity as migrancy and displacement allows you room to re-historicize, maybe even re-semanticize, the historical migrant experience that you know so intimately, precritically. And the skeptical question you want to pose is whether this "centering of marginality" is in fact "the representative postmodern experience" (44). For you, postmodern discourse may well be producing something of a sleight-of-hand, perhaps a characteristic one, disavowing itself as history. Your "experience," you say (and I think the word is deliberately chosen), is that what the discourse of the postmodern has produced is not something new but rather only "recognition" of where identity always was—that is, at odds with itself. Your aim in the talk, then, is to "redefine," and perhaps reposition, the "general feeling" many people (in your audience, for example) have that they are "recently migrated" (44).

The migrant experience of the colonized in Britain—your own personal story in particular—brings into view a concrete historicity of power obscured by the postmodernist celebration of migrancy as an inventive self-fashioning gesture. For the migrant (or anyway the black colonial migrant) is always obliged to respond to an interrogation that precisely objectifies and constructs her or him in a constricted place of identity—that demands an answer in the policing jargon of identity: Who are you? Why are you here? Where are your papers? When are you going back to where you came from? Identity here is *inflicted*; it is not a luxury. Therefore, identity for the migrant is not only always-already a question; this question is always-already inscribed in a relation to dominant, sometimes in fact, *repressive* state power. Your point, as I understand it, is that for the migrant identity is not merely a voluntary act of *self-naming*; it is often an experience of subjection to being named. And yet, disconcertingly, these questions coming from the sites and signifiers of power are often internalized, returned to the self in the form of an anxiously defining *self*-interrogation: Who am *I*? What am *I* doing here? Where do *I* belong? And sometimes the answers are surprising,

ATTUNEMENT TO IDENTITY

—

103

because sometimes the reasons for leaving one's homeland are not quite so elevated as might be expected from the official narratives of third-world economic need or self-improvement. They might at times be as corrosively and unsettlingly middle-class and personal as, in your story, Stuart—fleeing from one's mother and the symbolic order of moral-psychological and cultural value she represents. As you quip, this Jamaican middle-class familial dilemma may be a universal story, but it's not likely to be an existentially comfortable one, a story with which one can live explicitly, seamlessly; rather it invites a strange incommensurability and alienation. One might feel compelled, as you did, to continuously displace that entangled familial story so as to invent ever new ways of being yourself, of living, that is to say, with an imagined identity.

This oblique reference to your mother, though, Stuart, brings us a bit closer to the question of what it means to be aware of who one is—what that meant for you. For you say, somewhat obscurely, that long before you understood any of it theoretically, that is, in the contemporary language of social construction, you were "aware that identity is an invention" (44). What could you mean by this? I don't for a moment doubt you, but what would have given you this pretheoretical awareness of identity? What autobiographical experience could have made identity into a preconceptual problem for you? You're suggesting, I think, however indirectly, that you *found* yourself with an inchoate awareness of noncorrespondence that suggested to you that identity was not just implicitly there, comfortably invisible, the normal background against which subjectivity seamlessly, unproblematically unfolded. Is that a fair reading? What, though, are the sources of this decentered experience?

Identity is always constructed in displacement. Arguably, this is a psychoanalytic truism. Identity is never merely identical to itself—self-correspondent. Yet, for the colonized that identity is always constructed in a *double* displacement. Since the colonized subject lives in conditions of cultural appropriation, and historical erasure and denigration, and therefore in a constitutive state of alienation from some putative authentic self originating in a past that is now no longer directly—transparently—available, her or his identity is always experienced as twice displaced, always lived as doubly incommensurable with itself, or with some supposed "real me." For you, Stuart, this would be not merely

THREE

—

104

a psychoanalytic but a Fanonian truism. Indeed, this is the moment in "Minimal Selves" when you turn explicitly to Fanon's *Black Skin, White Masks*, precisely because you find there that he describes your experience of incommensurability in a vivid, phenomenologically attuned psychoanalytic idiom stretched to accommodate the figure of the black colonial migrant in the *métropole*. Fanon was not so far removed from you in age (you were about seven years his junior), so there is in his experience of late colonial France an echo of your own experience, at virtually the same time (the early 1950s), of late colonial Britain. You had both traveled from a West Indian city—he from Fort-de-France, you from Kingston—to a colonial fantasy. This is why you always found his unforgettable account of the alienated recognition and self-recognition of the colonized before the petrifying racializing gaze of the white European child so arresting, so haunting—so menacingly eloquent of the lived experience of the black colonized. Let's recall Fanon's voice here: "My body was returned to me displayed, disjointed, worn out, plunged into mourning on this white winter's day."[37] It was as though there was something in this appalling account that resonated with *you* intimately. Anyone listening to you talk some years later about Fanon in Isaac Julien's 1995 film *Frantz Fanon: Black Skin, White Mask* would immediately realize that in your familiar, warm, and measured sentences you're not only explicating Fanon's text but also talking about that text's concerns by talking *through* your embodied experience.[38] In *Black Skin, White Masks*, in other words, especially in his Hegelian formulation of the moral-political problem of colonial experience and identity, Fanon enables you to give a theoretical voice to a form of experience that you already know.

But even so, Stuart (and I know I'm straying here a bit), I've always been intrigued by your relation to this early text of Fanon's. If it was never a reified relation, it was never a *detailed* one either—you tended to *use* rather than read *Black Skin, White Masks* (if this is an intelligible distinction), a relation you often had, it is true, with texts that *meant* something to you, that you had absorbed, digested, in a profound way. So that, notably, the internal *structure* and discursive *movement* of Fanon's overall discussion seemed scarcely to concern you. I mean you seem not to have interested yourself over-much, for example, in the question of his handling of the negritude question. Think of Fanon's response to

Jean-Paul Sartre's Eurocentric misreading of it in *Black Orpheus*: "And when I tried to claim my negritude on the level of intellectual ideas and activity, they snatched it away from me. They proved to me that my reasoning was only a phase in the dialectic."[39] Or think of his equal doubts about Afrocentric renderings of it: "The discovery of the existence of a black civilization in the fifteenth century does not award me a certificate in humanity. Whether you like it or not, the past cannot in any way guide me in actuality."[40] Nor were you very interested in the text's specific relation to the work of Fanon's *maître*, Aimé Césaire, whose presence literally saturates it—Fanon's whole text unfolds under the sign of an epigraph from Césaire's *Discourse on Colonialism*.[41] Surely one of the important features of *Black Skin, White Masks* is the way it partakes of the larger ethos of a particular disjuncture in postwar French intellectual traditions—namely the relative displacement of the idiom of surrealism that so nourished Césaire's poems and essays, by the political language of existentialism associated with Sartre and his colleagues at *Les temps modernes*.[42] Or again, Stuart (and I hope I'm not pressing too hard on this), you never seemed very interested in the relation (or lack of one) between *Black Skin, White Masks* and Fanon's great 1961 manifesto of anticolonial revolution, *The Wretched of the Earth*.[43] For me, by contrast, growing up as I did in a politically volatile postcolonial Jamaica, it was this later, insurrectionary, work that most held my (and my generation's) attention—not identity, in other words, but third-world revolution. But this was not the case with you, speaking as you now were through a specifically *metropolitan* displacement.[44] And yet I'd always wanted to ask you whether one mightn't say that for Fanon the conundrum of colonial alienation, unresolvable as he well recognized as a matter of therapeutic technique, could *only* be overcome from within the politically oriented upheaval of anticolonial revolution (inverting the order of things by putting the last *first*, as he says)—that is, in the authorizing political direction of *les damnés de la terre*.

Anyway, as you explain in "Minimal Selves," these conditions of double displacement were the conditions of your own coming of age in 1930s and 1940s colonial Jamaica in a "brown" middle-class family aspiring to be what it was patently not, namely an English Victorian family. In such conditions, you say, "the notion of displacement as a place of 'identity' is a concept you learn to live with, long before you are able to spell it" (45).[45]

However, even as something is disclosed here, Stuart, in this brief and elliptical evocation of your familial origins, something is occluded or, if I may put it more strongly, something is *oversimplified* that might be worth exploring a bit more. There is something about your founding context in the moral-historical specificity of that brown middle class that is absolutely crucial for your experience of incommensurability and noncorrespondence. How can I describe it without traversing the whole social and cultural history of colonialism in Jamaica? I think that one shorthand way of making it intelligible is to remind ourselves that this brown middle class is the historical offspring of racial and sexual violence in the context of colonial plantation slavery, and that therefore its constitutive experience is one of racial *self-division* and *self-alienation*. Neither black nor white (neither fish nor fowl nor good red herring, as Richard Hart used to say), it could never quite correspond to being exactly one (racial) thing or another. If its cultural pretensions were driven by a white ideal from which it was excluded, its political unconscious was ever tormented by the visceral disavowal and embodied dread of its inescapable relation to blackness. It could never remove itself far enough from its corrupting racial past. It could never completely rid itself of the complicit meaning of the lingering trace of blackness.[46] What I'm trying to say, Stuart, merely as a way of elaborating what I take to be implicit in your remark about your intimacy with identity, is that for you noncorrespondence could never have been the mere artifice of postmodernism precisely because it ran across the painfully jagged edge of what Hacking might have called the "historical ontology" of your own raced and classed self.[47] For you noncorrespondence is founding, and inescapable—and therefore identity is founding and inescapable. Identity is the alchemical residue of your intractably lived difference. This is why you can say, almost unproblematically, that your *theoretical* idea of identity grew in significant measure out of a conundrum you knew precritically, prereflectively. For you were always-already "living with" and "living through" identity-difference, albeit a fundamentally alienated one in terms of your social-familial experience in colonial Jamaica.

It isn't surprising to me, given this background of privileged alienation, that your sense of being an "immigrant" in Britain didn't emerge straightforwardly out of living in the country for a decade, not even directly out of the 1958 Notting Hill riots by which, as you've said, you were not unaffected, personally or politically.[48] Rather, it emerged, you suggest, *relationally*, from your opposition to your mother's reactionary desire to separate you from your fellow West Indian migrants, the overwhelming majority of whom, unlike you, were black and working class—and therefore undoubtedly not the sort of people you were meant to associate with, even in the *translated* environment of racialized Britain. It is in the ambivalent fold constituted by your mother's ideological attempt to activate a familiar mode of brown-middle-class betrayal of black people, by returning you to your proper place of belonging, that—refusing this interpellation—you inscribe yourself as an act of rebellion into the subaltern identity "immigrant." (You say, "I remember the occasion when I returned to Jamaica on a visit sometime in the early 1960s, after the first wave of migration to England, my mother said to me: 'Hope they don't think you are one of those immigrants over there!' And of course, at that point I knew for the first time I was an immigrant" [45].) Living in proximity to a population with which you at least partially share the otherness of historical experience, and of cultural displacement and discrimination in racist Britain, you reject the privileged difference that your color/class allow you and you construct a political solidarity with people you can call your own—the people, as you've said many times, you saw streaming out of Paddington Station in the 1950s. Here, then, is one exemplary moment of your discovery-recovery of identity.

But this is not the end of the story. For no sooner are you "installed," as you would put it, in the identity of "immigrant" as a site of cultural-political self-understanding and self-fashioning (enjoying for the moment, perhaps, a good night's rest, safe now in the knowledge of who you finally *are*) than you begin to encounter its limitations, its own contradictions, and internal antinomies, and you begin, as you say, the long political education of thinking of yourself as "black." I'm sure there's a complicated story to be told here about the changing context of postcolonial Britain in the 1970s (the background context of *Policing the Crisis*), not to mention the changing context of postcolonial Jamaica in the

THREE

—

same period (the rise, for example, of Rastafari), that's relevant here.[49] I won't rehearse it though, so as not to further distract us. Your argument in a nutshell is that, initially, in one historical conjuncture, you learn to inhabit the identity "immigrant"; then, in an altered political-historical terrain, you learn to inhabit the identity "black":

> Constituting oneself as "black" is another recognition of self through difference: certain clear polarities and extremities against which one tries to define oneself. We constantly underestimate the importance, to certain crucial political things that have happened in the world, of this ability of people to constitute themselves, psychically, in the black identity. It has long been thought that this is really a simple process: a recognition—a resolution of irresolutions, a coming to rest in some place which was always there waiting for one. The "real me" at last! (45)

In short, black identity is *constructed*; and it is constructed in and through fissure and difference in relation to rival subject-positions. Black identity is not the mere expression of a submerged or latent subjectivity that was always *there* waiting to articulate its authenticity. It is historical, and therefore unstable, incomplete, contextual, and therefore transformable. And this construction is, moreover, also a psychological process, involving both desire and cognition. Black identity in this sense is always, as you would put it, underlining the dialogical relation, something "told, spoken, not simply found" (45).

And yet, of course, Stuart, paradoxically, though something not simply found, something not *arbitrarily* chosen either. Since you are so often taken to be a straightforward constructionist the fact that in your view identity is not a matter of pure choice is a dimension of your thinking that doesn't get a lot of attention. But part of what's interesting to me about "Minimal Selves" is precisely that this is a dimension very much at play. While identity is, as the postmodernists claim, invented, constructed, and therefore in a certain sense fictional, it is nevertheless not *merely* a fiction because it is always-already formed by, routed through, real pasts—not only metaphorical ones. We do, invariably, *find* ourselves already formed within determinate, authoritative, cultural-historical traditions and communities. We do not construct our identities out of nothing—out of pure imagination. Identity, as you say, is not simply a "journey of the mind" (45). Therefore, as I understand you, you're not saying that "migrant" or "black" are merely empty subject-positions that are simply and equally available to be occupied by *anyone*, or *everyone*, as and whenever they like. Identity is not a boundless possibility, a completely open frontier. We cannot *sovereignly* choose our identities—who we want to be—at random and at will. What I hear you saying, rather, is that our choices regarding what we can be are always partially oriented by what we are *given* through the historical powers that always-already shape us, by the world we are contingently *thrown* into and which we are obliged to navigate. And therefore in fact we always find ourselves living through a moral history to some extent already inscribed in us— inscribed, Fanon might have said, at the embodied or libidinal or psychic level of desire—and in relation to which we make what we can. Now, of course, I take it that in certain circumstances (depending, for example, upon who you're arguing with, what the stakes are) you might well formulate your cultural-political propositions about identity in such a way as to underscore possibility (what we can make) rather than constraint (what we have found); but such circumstances are presumably contingent, and therefore such formulations (at least in your hands) are presumably strategic.

Thus, Stuart, I'd say that the significant point of your autobiographical story in "Minimal Selves" about "constituting yourself as 'black,'" is *not* that "black" was an arbitrary choice you made as a personal or cultural-political identity. It wasn't. To the contrary, your recovery-discovery of yourself as black, while not inevitable, was nevertheless historically conditioned. As a branded contingency given to you through the historical experience of postslavery colonial racialization and lived in the ideological idiom of brown-Jamaican middle-class alienation and disavowal, black is a *possible* cultural-political identity to come to inhabit, to come to call your own, to come to self-consciously speak through, in a conjuncture (namely, the 1970s) in which it emerges as the name of a radical revaluation of the order of colonial value, a resignification of denigrated pasts, and the prospect of antiracist modes of political solidarity. Black,

THREE

—

therefore, is both the name of an always-already scripted experience of raced, racist marginalization and otherness, and of the self-conscious subversion of that script from within specific locations of reflexive identity formation and assertive solidarity.

Can I put it this way, Stuart? Am I stretching your formulations beyond recognition? I'm trying in this way to capture—and clarify—the way you seem to be *doing* at least three things at once in this vivid lecture: one, agreeing with the postmodernists in a limited way that identity is invented, made; two, suggesting to them, these postmodernists (who are, you take it, part of your audience), that this invention is not a mere theoretical privilege of postmodernism, but also the burden of real migrants, and therefore connected to powers not only of freedom but also of subjection; and three, that this invention has always to be understood in relation to the historical-political factors that condition and sometimes constrain its possibility.

———

But even this is not the whole point of "Minimal Selves," is it, Stuart? Something *else* is also at stake in all this that is oriented toward the normative or ethical question about the present as a political project— that is, the relationship between identity and futurity. For, as ever, your point is scarcely a philosophic reflection on identity but rather a meditation on the practical prospects for transformative politics.

Identities, you say, are evidently about contingent closures. We have already seen that, paradoxically, identities are not merely found, but also made, and at the same time made (partly) with what is found. Identities are the partial closures we make with the contingencies—contingent openings—in which we find ourselves. This is one important sense in which identity inhabits the continuous play of *finding* and *making*. But there is a second vital sense for you in which identity is about the closures by which we aim to hold contingency at bay. This is the sense in which political *action* in the present depends upon such partial, provisional, closures of self-conscious *identification*. As you argue, it is an important gain to recognize that identity is "constructed across difference" and thus to open the possibility of being able to live "with a politics of difference." But the recursive moment is also crucial when some determinate conception of identity takes hold (or, by articulation, is secured) however temporarily. For you, political action is not possible without that closure on a *specific* conception of identity. "Potentially," you say, employing a linguistic figure you've used elsewhere as well, "discourse is endless; the infinite semiosis of meaning."

> But to say anything at all in particular, you do have to stop talking. Of course every full stop is provisional. The next sentence will take nearly all of it back. So what's this "ending"? It's a kind of stake, a kind of wager. It says, "I need to say something, something . . . just now." It is not forever, not totally universally true. It is not underpinned by any infinite guarantees. But just now, this is what I mean; this is who I am. (45)

In various circumstances, depending upon the object in question, these "unfinished closures" might be called the self, politics, society, and so on.

This idea of identity transforms our idea of what politics is about—in a certain sense (though you would not put it quite this way) it attaches an "ethics" to politics inasmuch as it introduces the question of choice and risk and decision. Specifically, it transforms the idea and nature of political commitment. And commitment—identity-in-politics—is central to your idea of what politics is. "Is it possible," you ask, "acknowledging the discourse of self-reflexivity, to constitute a politics in the recognition of the necessarily fictional nature of the modern self, and the necessary arbitrariness of the closure around the imaginary communities in relation to which we are constantly in the process of becoming 'selves'?" This is a profound question: whether there can be a politics of difference, a politics, as you say, that is at one and the same time open to the vagaries of contingency and yet committed to the provisional decisions necessary for political action. A politics of infinite dispersal, of endless deferral, such as is often implied in the mercurial moods of postmodernism, is a "politics of no action at all." Thus you reject, rightly I think, what you call the "absolutist discourse" of *jouissance* that postmodernism seems to endorse. Difficult though it may be, you argue, it *should* be possible to conceive of a politics that accepts that there is "no necessary or essential correspondence" of "anything with anything" (45). This is a politics of *articulation*, the politics of a self-conscious hegemonic project. And this is the note on which you bring "Minimal Selves" to a close, not, I take it, because at this point thinking has failed you but, partly anyway, because constructing such a politics is *less* about thinking per se than about *acting*, figuring it out practically by actually trying it out in the plural world around you.

———

To my mind, Stuart, everything about this little essay (of not more than about thirty-five hundred words) is inimitably and invaluably *you*: in the tentative, questioning, exploratory but altogether concrete mode of the intervention; in the recursive voice one can hear thinking-out-loud in the immediacy of a still-evolving conjuncture; in the alertness to the listening even doubting presence of a certain audience; in the reflexive attunement to the plurality and ambiguity of the given situation—the unasked-for present—that nevertheless demands an attitude of sufficient openness to enable responsive negotiation. As ever, you are trying self-consciously to take your bearings, sounding out the new conventions, and wondering about their sustaining assumptions, what—and who—they leave out and why. Again characteristically, your aim is not to be dismissive, conclusive, but receptive, looking to build the conversation with what you find ready-to-hand, and with those you find ready-to-hear among your interlocutors. Your overall objective is to offer a strategic re-description of the given terms of the conjuncture that might have more productive ethical-political yield—the ever-present yes-*and*-no. The new sense of release and freedom experienced by the adoption of the postmodernist idea of the construction or invention of identity is neither to be simply celebrated nor dismissed, neither simply embraced nor overthrown—but receptively interrogated and clarified.

Moreover, the paradox that mobilizes you is not without a certain familiarity. For the very metaphor of "migrancy" that postmodernists often employ as the figure of their freedom betrays their inattention both to the historicity of the experience of the *real* migrants in their midst (yourself included, as you remind them), and, consequently, to the situatedness of their own white metropolitan desire for—or experience of—displacement. And yet, again characteristically, while being explicitly skeptical of the ahistorical celebration of displacement, your intention is not to simply criticize the idea of the construction of identity as such but to *reposition* it. By indicating that identities—insofar as they are identities at all, and not merely endlessly floating signifiers—are never merely invented but always invented and reinvented in relation to some sticky fracturing history, that your own personal arrival at the constructed identity "black" was itself the outcome of a historical learning in the context of a specific cultural-political conjuncture, you re-historicize the problem of identity formation but you do not thereby empty identity of its constructed character.

And still you do *more* than this, Stuart, as you so often do. The re-description and re-historicization of identity formation *point* us in the direction of new possibilities for a normative rethinking of politics, specifically a rethinking of the ethics of politics. This is what motivates you, animates you, though you've never called it that. For the idea of identity as endlessly open-ended, forever sliding across a blank field of possibilities, is not merely conceptually problematic, incoherent, but morally *bankrupt* and politically *disabling.* Politics *depends* upon identities, not necessarily permanent ones, it is true, but identities *nonetheless*. So in order to re-activate the prospect of a normative ethical-political subject it is necessary to be able to affirm, at one and the same time, an openness to the proliferation of difference, to the cunning of alterity, to the playful reinvention of selves, *and* the insistence that political claims always demand some working closure, a provisional full-stop, some determinate articulation of some avowable form or other of belonging-in-difference.

This, anyway, is how I've come to think with you, Stuart, and this is where I want to leave the matter of identity—for now.

With best wishes,
DAVID

THREE

—

114

Learning to Learn from Others

An Ethics of Receptive Generosity

DEAR STUART,

I'm coming now to the end of this long, imaginary, epistolary dialogue. This will be the last but one of these belated fictive letters to you. But it is also, perhaps, the most important for me, and the one toward which I've been *heading* all along, inasmuch as I will be trying here to capture more explicitly something of the *ethical* implications of your dialogical style—the ethics of your *voice*. Admittedly, you've never aspired to an explicit theory—I mean a *philosophic* theory—of ethics (or of anything else, for that matter). I keep repeating this. But I'd say, Stuart, that you are certainly a thinker whose ideas about culture, language, politics, and identity imply normative convictions about selves and others, and therefore disclose ethical underpinnings and ethical implications. While you never formally spoke in this (you might have said, lofty, high-minded) register, your particular style of criticism, the thinking-aloud you do with others that is both a mode of speaking *as well as* a mode of listening, suggests precisely an ethics of *responsiveness* to difference. You'd agree with this, *surely*. I'd say that what you've cultivated over the course of a long intellectual life is a distinctively ethical voice that is at the same time a distinctive ethics *of* and *through* voice: I mean by this, on the one hand, an embodied intellectual *presence* that is activated by the fully resonant call to speak out publicly against violations and harms and, on the other hand, an attunement to exclusions and disrespect and injustices that is generatively shaped by the relational register of voice. Yours, in short, Stuart, is a *dialogical* ethics. It is an ethics committed to the virtue of an ongoing, agonistic negotiation of belonging in identity and difference among plural voices. As such, it is an ethics founded not merely in the empirical facts of existing value-plurality (the mere ethnographic self-evidence of difference given once and for all), but in the discursive and nondiscursive processes and powers of historically constituted *pluralizations* (I'm thinking of some of William Connolly's work here).[1] In what follows, then, it will matter to me that the ethics embodied in—and disclosed by—your intellectual practice is not the abstract, rule-following ethics of the rationalist or Kantian sort (refracted these days in the work of neo-Kantian moral-political theorists such as Jürgen Habermas or John Rawls) in which what counts is mastery of the moral law as an a priori guarantee of unitary, stable, and sovereign identity. Rather, your ethics constitute a reciprocal responsiveness to varieties of otherness and marginalization. As I've come to understand you, listening to you at close quarters these last many years, your ethics is founded in and shaped by the agonistic compulsions of dialogical presence you've cultivated in the many kinds of community you've engaged and sustained. I'm suggesting that in your varied interventions over the sweep of your intellectual life there is a singular embodied voice you can hear thinking-out-loud together with singular embodied others in the conjunctures in which you've (contingently and deliberately) found yourself. As a social and cultural critic, you've rarely been far removed from what you're criticizing. Your targets are never mere formal abstractions. They're almost always concrete, near-at-hand: "within shouting distance," you'd say. Indeed, *proximity* is a virtue with you; it establishes the dialogical distances that give resonant measure to your ethics of vocal *presence*.[2]

More precisely, though, I want to describe this attitude of responsiveness in terms of a dialogical ethics of "receptive generosity." I borrow this felicitous and compelling idea from the political theorist Romand Coles, whose work I've been mulling over for some years now because of the unusually subtle self-consciousness I find there of the difficult challenges facing Western moral-political theorizing in its encounters with what lies culturally and morally beyond its normative—normalizing—comfort zones.[3] Again, Stuart, Coles is not a thinker who naturally pops up in your work, but I'm going to urge that you both share a great deal—a disposition toward the dialogical arts of listening, most especially—and that his idea of "receptive generosity" gives a fair description of an important aspect of your style. An ethics of receptive generosity, we will see, is an ethics that is committed not merely to giving to others, but to *receiving* from them as well. Such an ethics depends upon an attitude of vulnerable openness to learning from others, not merely masterfully teaching them—indeed, it is an ethics in which the former (learning) might be more important than the latter (teaching), or in which teaching is *itself* a way of learning, and learning a way of teaching. An ethics of receptive generosity, therefore, is *not* an ethics of tolerance or cosmopolitan hospitality—the sort of passive "making-room" for destitute or needy others that has recently become so de rigueur in contemporary theory.[4] What's more, in later work Coles connects this idea of receptive generosity to a *tragic* sensibility, or a tragic disposition, in thinking about liberalism and democracy, an orientation toward moral-political reflection that honors the role of chance and paradox and contingency, and conflict and resentments and ambiguity and finitude, that seems to me to comport very much with the modest sense of willing dispossession and the modulated alertness to the conceits of hubris—to what reasons rationally, relentlessly, conceal—I believe you to have cultivated in an exemplary way.[5] An ethics of receptive generosity is a dimension of a tragic ethics, that is, an ethics alert to human action's frailty and plurality, and vulnerability to time and the collision of irreconcilable or incommensurable ends. I will argue then, Stuart, that what particularly marks your style is that you are not only a generous intellectual gift-giver but also an active receiver of the intellectual gifts of others—*this is what your legendary openness to chance and change is all about.* And in the respectful mode in which you embody it, this tragic ethics of receptive generosity is usefully conceived of in terms of the dialogical and relational register of *voice* (in an earlier letter, we've already become acquainted with the community of voice and the tragic). An ethics of receptive generosity is, above all, a tragic ethics disposed as much to speaking as to *listening*—that most difficult of virtues. Indeed, Coles has a keenly perceptive sense of the specifically *dialogical* imperative that shapes the charity involved in receptive generosity that underlines exactly this point. "Yet receptive generosity itself," he says, "is not to be a new regulative currency. Its articulations emerge from locations that are wide and deep in their differences, and the substance of these positions draws them to difficult listening as well as speaking to those who endorse visions that are neither generous nor receptive."[6]

In my view, then, Stuart, Coles is especially pertinent to think with here in relation to you because there are promising points of contact *as well as* tension in the moral-political motivations and the conceptual sensibilities that drive and shape your respective preoccupations. And reflecting on these will help me to put my finger more suggestively, and more tangibly and explicitly on the implications of voice for your particular ethical stance and style. In what follows, I want to talk about these first in rough outline, and then go on to elaborate Coles's admirable idea of receptive generosity, saying something of the way it resonates with ideas about voice and listening and finitude, and how therefore it comports solicitously with the notion of a tragic sensibility. I will at certain points, you will see, express a doubt about aspects of Coles's formulations, but only in the spirit of pushing them in the direction I believe them already to be heading, and in the spirit, as well, of thinking in your company.

———

So to begin with, Stuart, I note that like you Coles is a theorist who takes *real* politics seriously. Unlike many (academic) moral-political theorists writing today, Coles is expressly interested in the realities of contemporary politics. Both of you are trying to clarify the concrete situation (the "contradictory, stony ground," as you might say), of the present conjuncture, and not simply or exclusively as a *philosophic* or *theoretical* exercise, but more pertinently so as to determine the best intellectual-political way of *intervening* in it, of reorganizing our collective thinking about the relationship between the *given* and the *possible*.[7] Not surprisingly, then, you both think of "theory"—its constitution and its function—in remarkably similar ways. Like you, Coles urges that theory should develop in relation to social struggles, and not in abstraction from them. A "risky proximity" between the two, he says, is what we should aim for. As he puts it, for example, in a passage I imagine you'd agree with, "democratic theory ought to develop significantly (but by no means exhaustively) in dialogical and more receptive encounters with democratic struggles in ways that might allow the emerging practices and purposes of democratic associational life to call into question and possibly alter our core assumptions."[8] What do you think of this formulation? Like you, Coles has an intuitive ability to capture the give-and-take of contingent relationality.

I've earlier talked about how for you a theory has the sense of what Aristotle called *phronesis*, or practical thinking, a sort of Deleuzian toolbox: it consists of the practical wisdoms or prudential reasonings generated out of the discursive histories we contentiously inhabit and that enable us to orient ourselves toward, not truth as such but, thoughtfully, the best truths possible in a given moment. Might one imagine, then, Stuart, a kind of *hermeneutic* loop between *political* work and *theoretical* work such that, while never reducible to each other, never eclipsed by the other, are nevertheless constantly—dialectically, dialogically—being shaped and reoriented and supplemented by each other?[9] Again, not surprisingly, for you both a serious measure of political activism has been a central aspect of your political identities.[10] *Doing* something, not merely thinking something. For both of you, therefore, thinking-speaking-acting forms a dynamic, unstable, ongoing, and always interconnected triadic structure of purposeful, relational movement.

Moreover, Stuart, both you and Coles are concerned with the normative relation between the given and the possible—that is to say, you both want to intervene in such a way as to advance an agenda of *Left* progressive politics. Both of you see yourselves as trying to think in the *wake* of the collapse of the traditional Left idea of the guaranteed privilege of a single political subject (the proletariat), and are interested in exploring modes of political *solidarity* that have been called (for better or worse) "coalition politics." Coles, then, is also interested in thinking imaginatively, innovatively, about what concepts of the self and identity—or, as he puts it, "what sort of self, what type of ethical opening to oneself and to others"—might be capable of assembling and articulating, animating and sustaining, a contingent politics of coalition-building, in effect, what you would call a politics *without guarantees*.[11] In particular this is a politics sensitively—sometimes *sensuously*—attuned to what Coles felicitously calls "the pregnancy of edges."[12] Do you like that turn of phrase, Stuart, "the pregnancy of edges"? Doesn't it suggestively evoke something important about the sort of ethos of critical engagement you've aspired to as well? In other words, it's not at the overconfident legislating or state-authorized center that one should look for creative possibilities or cooperative oppositional energies, Coles suggests (as would you); rather, it is at the vulnerable, marginal, and dispersed borders of identity and practice that a fertile "tension-laden dwelling" and learning can take place. In fact I think you'd find particularly intriguing the dialogue that Coles is attempting to develop between certain edges of radical democratic political theory and certain edges of Christian ethics.[13] Not, of course, because you have been drawn to anything specifically to do with Christianity (though you have spoken eloquently about a Rastafari reading of the Bible against the received grain of a white supremacist Christian ethos) but because I think you'd immediately recognize the virtue of trying to work with the progressive edges of whatever conceptual and political sources we have ready-to-hand. In my view, Stuart, you too are a "tension-laden dweller," a tightrope walker, looking always to produce or to incite a generative "edge-effect" in any particular conjuncture—this is the way I think of you in the moment of the early New Left, for example.[14] Your inclination has always been to patiently work the edges where various agonistic forces intersect, collide, without presuming that a harmonious relationship will be—*should* be—the logical outcome.

And yet this business of thinking and acting politically from the concrete present toward a Left project as the *horizon* of possibility, while importantly something you two share, is nevertheless something you share *differently*. So far as I can tell, Coles would conceive of that horizon under the general description of "radical democracy," in the post-Marxist sense given to it famously by Ernesto Laclau and Chantal Mouffe in *Hegemony and Socialist Strategy*.[15] I've already remarked (in the previous letter) on aspects of the contrast between your style and

Laclau's, and this is not the place to talk about your complex relation to this influential book. But my impression, Stuart, is that though you also might call yourself (or at least *allow* yourself to be called) a radical democrat, you would insist on the proviso that your post-Marxism grows out of a never-ending—and never-endingly *agonistic*—engagement with Marx *and* Marxism. For you, that Left project in which the theoretical problematic of "hegemony" came to function as an inescapable conceptual tool was always—at least up until very near the end, if I am not mistaken—a concrete political question of *socialist* (not merely radical democratic) strategy. The *heritage* of socialism (and therefore of Marxism, one way or the other) was one of almost inextinguishable resonance and relevance for you. This is true for Laclau as well, certainly—again, at least until very near the end. This is why, as we have already seen, the thought of Antonio Gramsci remained for you (and again, for Laclau too) so generative to think with, to learn from. Gramsci wasn't merely a "radical democrat." That's somehow easily forgotten these days. He was a communist. Isn't that important? I've always thought that the ground of this socialist heritage marks an interesting—perhaps even tension-making—contrast between yourself and thinkers like Coles and other North American radical democrats such as William Connolly or James Tully, on whom Marx and the Marxist tradition seem to have no strong— at least no formal or *explicit*—material claim. What's interesting to me, Stuart, is that while you were forever arguing with and against *liberalism* (and more lately, neoliberalism), largely if not only with conceptual tools generated from within an enlarged Marxist tradition, Coles (perhaps in his later, more so than his earlier, work) is often arguing out from *within* liberal political *theory*. I don't mean this to be a pejorative characterization. But, for example, John Rawls, as the foremost liberal theorist of liberalism in the late twentieth century (since the reorienting event of *A Theory of Justice*), has little bearing on your thinking. You don't feel obliged to get to grips with his work, to discern in detail its yields and its limits, whereas for Coles something crucial is at stake in feeling his way in and around and through Rawls. You both acknowledge the liberal hegemony of the present, but you come at it from an intellectual tradition *outside* of—or at least in *political* opposition to—it. For you, in other words, the route to post-Marxism is *through* Marxism and its internal debates. What difference does this make, do you think? What are the implications? I've been puzzling over this contrast for a while.

Anyway, part of what is attractive about Coles's style of dialogical engagement is his subtle, nonreductive way of reading those thinkers he thinks he can *learn* from without necessarily agreeing with everything (indeed anything) they say. Learning, I'd offer, is a big thing with Coles, especially learning to think *anew*, learning to think *differently*. How do we learn from others? Or how do we learn *by* learning from others? In essence, these are his questions. I believe they are *your* questions too, Stuart. Coles answers them something like this: one learns—and learns to learn—from others by reading sympathetically for what is *most* generative in a thinker's thinking, not what is *least*. He reads, therefore, less to find *fault* in others than to mobilize those energies, dispositions, inclinations, and insights in their work that might teach him something he doesn't already know, and thereby to expand and deepen his conceptual range and moral horizons. This often entails *pressing* texts, *nudging* them, to yield what they are, on their own terms, sometimes reluctant to disclose. I find this aptitude in your style too, Stuart, this way of provoking or inciting a text to say more than it typically or conventionally appears to say. The classic instance, of course, is your reading of the introduction to Marx's *Grundrisse*, practicing there what your former Centre for Contemporary Cultural Studies colleague Richard Johnson would later call "reading for the best Marx."[16] As Coles suggests, this means that thinkers are often stretched, even slightly distended, so as to bring the generative tensions in their work "into engagement with the movement of [his] own thinking."[17] What motivates him, then, in reading the work of others, is not the truth of their discourse but whether that discourse can offer him any clarifying illumination for his own path. Reading for Coles is a mode of clarification. To my mind something both profound and subtle is at work here.

Take, for example, the way he reads Alasdair MacIntyre, on the one hand, and Jacques Derrida, on the other, and then *both* together—thinkers so seemingly diametrically opposed to each other that it's hard to imagine them in the same discursive space, as neighbors, interlocutors. But that's what Coles wants us to do. I think it will interest you, Stuart, and it will give you a fair sense of the receptive sensibilities Coles brings to his consideration of what a nondismissive dialogical listening-thinking-with-others—a practice of hearkening, perhaps—amounts to. MacIntyre and Derrida, Coles says, share the "dubious fortune of having a large readership that—in celebration or dismissal—tends to register only one dimension of [their] thinking."[18] Where most readers of MacIntyre ignore the play of difference, conflict, contestation, and vulnerability in his work, so most readers of Derrida are hard-pressed to discern in his writing the tropes of context, tradition, determinacy, and historicity. For Coles, however, these are impoverished, impoverishing, readings that ignore the edges, that recoil from practicing a little "tension-dwelling" with these thinkers. In his generous view, no writer worth reading can be merely one-dimensional. It would be foolish *not* to acknowledge the centrality to MacIntyre's work of a deep notion of community and tradition, of the idea that we are "traditioned beings" whose "powers of rationality and judgment flourish in dialogue with inherited modes of being and vision"; and it may be necessary to recognize, moreover, that given certain inflections or emphases, these can offer unattractive and even politically dangerous "paths of reassurance."[19] But Coles urges that such readings of MacIntyre, if inflexible, can miss his recursive attunement to the generative role of narrative and poetics, and argument and heterogeneity, *within* traditions, and thus neglect how these subtleties animate traditions with life-giving dynamism and vitality. Reading for what is "wisest" in MacIntyre, Coles says, we find him articulating a project that is both traditioned in teleological directions, as well as vulnerable in non-teleological ones to the traditions of others. Tradition in MacIntyre does not preclude genealogy or deconstruction in some form, and is therefore not entirely incompatible with Derrida's thinking. Similarly, Coles reads Derrida, unfashionably, and against the conventional idea that his philosophy is one of sheer indeterminacy and undecidability, of an endlessly floating signifier or an inescapable textuality. For Coles, these readings are facile inasmuch as they too easily overlook the senses in which Derrida is, above all, a philosopher of *paradox*. The creativity of Derrida's thinking, he suggests, does not exclusively lie in his exuberant antimetaphysical posture of subversion, but *also* in his less-attended-to "calls to cultivate ethical and political judgment in the animating tensions between themes of radically unanticipatable otherness and radical dialectical democratic traditioning."[20] The paradox, Coles would say, is *everything*. Thus he takes up Derrida's early engagement with Edmund Husserl's phenomenology and finds there suggestive—and some might say, surprising—affirmations of historical sensibility, tradition, teleology, and responsibility. Moreover, these are themes Coles finds sustained and indeed elaborated in later work such as *The Other Heading* in which Derrida reflects on the "modern heritage" that an unexamined "we" is said to need not only to place in question but also to shoulder responsibility for. Read in this way, Coles suggests, Derrida's work depends upon a generative if sometimes-concealed notion of inheritance or stability not so far removed from the direction of MacIntyre's thinking.

You will agree with me, Stuart, I think, that this practice of reading generously and nonreductively around the edges is a potentially productive way of putting seemingly antithetical thinkers into contentious dialogue with each other. And yet, curiously, perhaps startlingly, Coles soon adds that, in the end, Derrida's position is to be *preferred* to MacIntyre's: "As I read the encounter I stage here, Derrida gets the upper hand."[21] How odd! Was that really necessary? Quite apart from the disturbing *disciplining* implications of this metaphor (the "upper hand"), it's hard to see how Coles arrives at this conclusion (offered in advance of the discussion, I might add), or just what motivations drive, or what purposes are served by, reinscribing this *rivalry* between them. And in any case, I would have thought that on Coles's own nonreductive dialogical terms, who gets the "upper hand" couldn't be straightforwardly decidable—certainly not as a *general*, overall matter but only, if at all, in this or that case of intervention in which they are comparatively mobilized. It is a dispiriting, perplexing moment in the essay, and I am not so sure that it isn't a deliberate *choice* he's making, though I can't myself discern the *internal* justifying grounds for it. And yet I wonder, Stuart, whether *you* wouldn't agree with Coles on this—whether too, in the end, if you were obliged to *choose* between their contrasting dispositions, you wouldn't find Derrida perhaps affording you more revisionary room than MacIntyre for the sorts of unsettling, interventionist theory-work and identity-work you find important. I suspect that, like Coles, while you fully acknowledge the grounding claim of community, of history (as indeed we've seen), you are *temperamentally* more drawn to that moment in the tension-dwelling dialectic when the tendency to closure is disturbed, disrupted, than to that moment when the displacement solidifies and seeks to name and sustain itself. Can one ever find an absolute, unshakable, irreversible, once-and-for-all balance between these tendencies, do you think? Perhaps not, you might say. I'd say that this constitutive impossibility points in the direction of the tragic. But where does that leave us? What's the nature of the impasse here? I am going to return to this a little later, Stuart, but I hope you can see now why for me Coles is so suggestive a thinker to draw alongside you. His style and preoccupations disclose a resonant but nonidentical connection that helps to illuminate something of your own distinctive dialogical style.

———

For some time, but most explicitly in his second book, *Rethinking Generosity*, Coles has been exploring the idea of a refigured ethics of *caritas*, of giving, of generosity, trying to see how it might be made a more central virtue of a specifically *dialogical* ethics. On his view, only a self that is animated by the excellences of gift giving can make coalition politics at once *tenable* and *desirable*. However, the cultivation of this virtue depends upon rethinking generosity. Coles argues that dominant modes of imagining and interpreting generosity in Western history—whether inspired by Christianity or by modern secular subjectivity—are limited by the fact that they begin from the premise of a self-originating, self-identical, and self-sufficient subject who is the source of being and truth, and moral virtue and beauty. In this imagination, the self is often pictured as a fount of benevolent, sometimes munificent giving. Generosity is avowed to be a valued good, indeed a sustaining ideal. But notably, in this picture of the magnanimous Western self, though gifts emanate from it and flow toward deprived others—the disadvantaged, the underprivileged, the disregarded, and disrespected—nothing *returns* to it reciprocally. This self is a giver but not a *receiver*. The reason for this is not that there is nothing to receive from others—that others have nothing to give worthy of receiving. Nor is it necessarily that this nonreceptive self is, at bottom, merely an *insincere* or *inauthentic* giver. Rather, it is, more fundamentally, that the picture of generosity that constitutes the self of such a giver systematically *precludes* a robust notion of receptivity.

Take, for example, as Coles suggests, the modern subject of rational will and sovereign autonomy, certainly among the highest ideals of the Western self since the age of Enlightenment. As Immanuel Kant famously conceives it in, for example, *Groundwork of the Metaphysics of Morals*, this is a self that asserts a claim to be the author of its own moral law as the generative guide to its duty toward others. Self-determining self-authorship, therefore, is the self's supreme accomplishment and guarded virtue. This is not to say, of course, that this self lacks respect for others. To the contrary, the Kantian self is pronouncedly a respectful self. But its genuine practice of respect for, and goodwill toward, others is generated out of, and guaranteed by, a prior attitude, indeed a grounding principle, of individual *self*-respect. Kant, as is well known, had high esteem for the worth of persons as ends in themselves and was keen to warn against humiliating others, treating them differently than one would expect to be treated oneself. Thus, as a single-minded principle, the Kantian self gives generously without instrumental *expectation* of return. But, notably, what is missing here is an equal duty (indeed an equal moral incentive) to cultivate an attitude or disposition of respectful and noninstrumental *receptivity* toward others. This means that the Kantian self generally has nothing to *receive* from presumably the passive others to whom, as willing moral agents, it extends its own respectful benevolence and generosity. In a frank posture of upright certainty, the Kantian self remains unchanged in its social interaction with the others to whom it selflessly gives. Indeed, it is *immune* to change; in a certain sense it has inoculated itself *against* change precisely by the doctrinal assertion of its principled autonomy and masterful self-governance. In this picture, then, the self is *monological* in being and identity. Its vigilant, prideful sense of itself as impervious and independent is such that the *otherness* of the other is perceived less as a gift of humanity to be learned from, than an irritation or a lack, or worse, a threatening danger to be kept at a distance if not repressed or even, sometimes, eliminated.

FOUR

—

As you can see, Stuart, Coles is motivated by an understandable worry about what happens to generosity when it is separated from receptivity, as it is in the heritage of Kant. Well, what happens, as we know only too well historically, is that generosity doesn't necessarily disappear but tends one-sidedly toward paternalism, arrogance, and varieties of imperialism. Coles's worry therefore concerns a very prevalent, self-congratulatory manner of practicing generosity in the modern West, in which the giving self is complacently confident in advance of (or in spite of) any encounter with difference, with otherness, of the singular benefits of its own resplendent gifts—whether of God, or Freedom, or Enlightenment, or Democracy. It activates an expressly monological—as opposed to a dialogical—ethics of generosity. Receptivity, one might say, then, is the side of generosity that is harder to cultivate. Paradoxically, receiving is more difficult than giving. It takes less (of the self) to give than to receive. And yet, receiving is as important as giving. Indeed, sometimes, even often, it is *more* important to be able to receive than to be able to give, more important to be able to accept the gifts of others (the gifts of their otherness) than to oblige them to accept one's own. An ethics of receptive generosity requires the cultivation of the capacity and the willingness to relinquish the desire for masterful giving. And it depends equally upon the cultivation of the corresponding capacity and willingness to make oneself open to a reception of the other not merely as a passive receiver but as an active giver, a giver whose gift of otherness moreover might not be so easy to digest or assimilate, and might potentially unsettle the stable conceits of one's identity. In short, receptive generosity entails a willing vulnerability to influences that may be hard to predict or control, or indeed comprehend.

As I think should now be clear, Stuart, unlike most contemporary Western moral-political theorists that I know of, even those who acknowledge the warrant of the problem of difference in some form, Coles goes a far way in taking on board the recognition that his own theory might have something substantive to learn from the historical traditions of others. For Coles, admirably, this learning from others is not a matter of being merely passively (or smugly) tolerant of differences, in the cosmopolitan mode of Richard Rorty or Thomas McCarthy—the familiar contemporary posture that Clifford Geertz memorably referred to as the "desperate tolerance of UNESCO cosmopolitanism."[22] Rather, it is a matter of actively cultivating the uncomfortable openness to the ways and thinking of others, cultivating receptivity to unlearning the privileges of historical power and the knowledge presumptions that accompany it. In this you can see, Stuart, that Coles has much in common with David Levin, whose work on the idea of a "listening self" I referred to in an earlier letter.[23] Indeed, too, not surprisingly, oriented as he is to the register of voice and voicing, Coles is a protagonist of a hermeneutics of *listening*, or, as he calls it, the "difficult arts of listening."[24] Although Martin Heidegger doesn't much appear among his favored interlocutors (so far as I can tell, anyway), I think that Coles would appreciate Levin's Heideggerian attempt to develop the promise of "hearkening" as the principal virtue of a "listening self"—an especially attuned mode of attending to what in others—in otherness—we might otherwise remain inattentively, unreceptively deaf to. Thus we see that the dialogical conception of receptive generosity has—or *can* have—a suggestively *aural* modulation. Also notable is that Coles, like Levin (though interestingly without the latter's engagement with Freud, and thus missing the dissonances of desire), understands that whereas listening is a potentiality we commonly possess, it requires for its *realization* a patient labor of cultivation—a never-ending work not only upon the varied concepts that constitute Western moral-political theory but also upon the thinking-feeling-embodied *selves* who mobilize and employ those concepts. This sensitivity to changing *oneself* as well as changing one's ideas in dialogue with others is an attitude you would applaud, Stuart—characteristically, it was one of the virtues you (sensitive to Freud for many reasons) cultivated in yourself.

Even more interesting to my mind is that (as I indicated earlier) Coles links the idea of the listening aptitudes of receptive generosity, the ethos, in other words of the listening self, to a *tragic* sensibility—a sensibility, as he puts it, "that stretches its listeners between calls to the importance of articulating, mediating, and striving toward the highest values of a community, on the one hand, and painful evocations of the unacknowledged suffering often wrought by a community's ideals . . . and the inextinguishable need to be transformed through receptive engagements

FOUR

—

with those a community marginalizes and subjugates, on the other."[25] Coles is especially concerned with the tragic in reference to the resources with which political liberalism, in the representative work, say, of John Rawls and Donald Moon, seeks to formulate the problem of tolerance and equality and respect in relation to political order.[26] He rightly believes that these resources are impoverished, and diminish—"vitiate"— our ability to respond appropriately to difference. Coles thinks that the sensibility for tragic paradox is consistently betrayed by political liberalism, even where, as in Rawls and particularly Moon, there is a deliberate attempt to take conflict and contradiction more fully into account. These attempts, he maintains, are, in the end, anemic and counterproductive, because political liberalism "misconstrues the tragic in ways that exaggerate our self-assurance, reinforce certain closures in public discourse, and de-energize political practice."[27] Tending to treat conflict and contradiction in largely reconciliatory and assimilative ways, political liberalism remains deaf to the radical implications of dwelling at the noisy, vulnerable edges of encounters with difference where one's ability to hold oneself masterfully *away* from what one cannot control, what one cannot shut out, avoid, or repress, frays and breaks down, and leaves one helplessly overtaken by unbidden otherness. I'm reminded, Stuart, that Raymond Williams too was familiar with this recuperative drive in the moral imagination of liberalism—he spoke, for example, of the domestication of conflict that takes place in the "liberal tragedies" of Henrik Ibsen and Arthur Miller.[28]

And you too were familiar with this tendency, though, true enough, you might not have called it "tragic." At any rate, at least as I read it, your famous "without guarantees" is a formulation meant precisely to *let open* a tragic vulnerability, a tragic exposure, to what can't be known entirely in advance, *not*, as many understand it, to license the conceit of pure constructionist agency: it is meant to dwell in the tension between what we are given and what we can be, what we can make of what we have found. Contingency and the tragic are not enemies; they are next of kin, as I suggested in an earlier letter. Moreover, as you will remember, Stuart, Adriana Cavarero urged in her critique of ocularcentrism that this disposition toward the tragic can be linked to the whole arena of sound and voice. As she reminded us, our sense of hearing—from which our capacity to listen attentively is cultivated—is a more open, vulnerable sense than that of sight. We cannot as simply close our ears as we can our eyes because our ears have no shield. We cannot easily choose *not* to hear. Sound comes to us, temporally, relationally, and contingently. Consequently, speaking-listening exposes us to chance, to ends that are never fully within our control, and in this sense voice has a close kinship both with contingency and with the tragic.

———

Still, Stuart, there are doubtful moments in Coles's conceptualization of receptive generosity that are worth considering. The crucial question here is, I think, the following: What is entailed in listening to, and learning from, the traditions of others, not in a patronizing, superficial way, but in a way sufficient to intelligently engage the deep structure of assumptions that motivate what these traditions formulate as problems and horizons? In a quite remarkable chapter of his third book, *Beyond Gated Politics*, Coles inquires into the trope of "common currency" involved in shaping or orienting the idea of a cosmopolitan and multicultural political morality. As usual Coles is critically attuned to the sleights-of-hand by which liberal accounts of "public reason" seek to present themselves as offering a common currency on the basis of which people with conflicting conceptions of the good (rival or irreconcilable "comprehensive doctrines") might be able to arrive, deliberatively, at agreements concerning matters of common concern. And since John Locke is an originary interlocutor here for liberal theory, the whole question of modernity, colonialism, and non-Western difference is unavoidable. In a series of exploratory readings, Coles shows us that liberal thinkers like John Rawls (in *The Law of Peoples*) and Martha Nussbaum (in *Cultivating Humanity*), exemplary thinkers who in different ways are striving to articulate a more "postcolonial" cosmopolitan self-consciousness than liberalism typically avows, turn out nevertheless to be inheritors of Locke's colonial liberalism inasmuch as there remains in their conceptions of public reason a strong echo of the "colonialist's immodest forgetfulness" of the deep implication of humanist universalism with colonial despotism.[29]

So, of course, Stuart, as you can well imagine, opening up the question of colonial difference in this way, there is much to expect from the "radically dialogical and critical cosmopolitanism" that Coles is putting on offer for our consideration. Modesty and attunement are precisely what we have come to admire in his invariably provocative interventions. Neither Rawls nor Nussbaum take the writings of non-Western thinkers seriously, and Coles aims to correct the Western conceit embodied in this persistent neglect, this "immodest forgetfulness." In particular, he does this by drawing on Gloria Anzaldúa's suggestive idea of *nepantla*, or nepantilism, developed in her influential book *Borderlands/ La Frontera*.[30] Nepantla is an Aztec word meaning "to be between" or "torn between ways," and Anzaldúa uses it to shape the sense of a liminal space, an unpredictable, imperfect, provisional, precarious zone where transformations can potentially take place. For Coles, nepantilism is significant because it discloses, he says, "an ethical mode of thinking and democratic engagement that responds to the problems and possibilities of cosmopolitanism in the context of colonialism and global capitalism." It resists, he argues, any simple celebration of hybridity. It's very easy to see why this idea of nepantilism, fertile with a provocative sense of generative paradox, is attractive to Coles, and how it helps him formulate his idea of a "nepantilist generosity," that is "a generosity that elaborates itself—internally and in community with others—in dialogues torn between different sensibilities and visions of the future."[31] Partly of course, Stuart, Coles is here in search of a non-Western idiom of cultural-political discourse, and from Anzaldúa he is led to further suggest that a variety of other thinkers—among them, Abdelkebir Khatibi (1938–2009), W. E. B. Du Bois (1868–1963), and Edouard Glissant (1928–2011)—similarly offer modes of paradoxical thinking alert to the "tension-laden borders between people(s)."[32] It's not expressly said, but the suggestion seems to be that as a theoretical domain "postcolonialism" distinguishes itself from the pieties of liberal universalism through its preoccupation with learning from the voices and visions of peoples engaged in specific struggles.

Now, I fully applaud the move being executed here, but I confess to not being perfectly persuaded by it. As I've said elsewhere, in reference to the equally anti-Eurocentric work of James Tully, I appreciate the evocation of the relevance to contemporary moral political theory of the critique of colonialist power and colonialist discourse, and agree, wholeheartedly, that Western political theorists would do well to take "postcolonialism" (however conceived) more seriously than they do.[33] But what is notable though, is that, as with Coles here, what one gets is typically no more than a list of putatively relevant non-Western think-ers who have suggestive concepts that seem, on the face of it, useful for the advance or complication of *Western* theory. What we don't generally get is a genealogy of the intellectual tradition (or traditions) *in relation to which* these non-Western thinkers are arguing, and *out of which* their seemingly radical concepts emerge. Thus, for example, it is interesting to note that Anzaldúa's *Borderlands/La Frontera* is not read against the backdrop of her theory tradition in the way that Rawls's or Nussbaum's texts are read, implicitly or explicitly, against the backdrop of the liberal theory tradition in which they are variously embedded, and that in some relevant sense Coles more or less shares. Her idea of nepantla is rather *picked out* from the cultural-intellectual tradition as a concept useful to *his* theory-purposes. Coles sees no reason to describe, thickly or otherwise, that tradition, the precise location within it of the concept of nepantla, its semantic range, its perhaps contested or conflicted status, its modes of authorization, and so on. In some way, this sort of reading appears justifiable because all Coles is doing is looking for vantage points from which to expose the deficiencies of *Western* moral-political theory, to resist the normativity of his own cultural-theoretical worlds. This is the extent of its usefulness. But for me, something is amiss here. It seems the sort of gesture familiar at least since Montaigne's essay "On Canni-bals," in which he famously invoked those Brazilians in order to criticize Europe's conceits about itself.[34] You will remember that Montaigne's critique did not entail his learning very much about Brazilian moral-cultural traditions; and similarly Coles does not feel obliged to learn very much about the non-Western intellectual tradition from which he borrows his subversive concept. So we don't know what really enables its extraction from its background context, its language game, and what makes its availability for deployment elsewhere possible.

My doubt, Stuart, has principally to do with the *asymmetry* that is, in-advertently, reproduced here. Obviously enough we are *all* limited by the kinds of cultural knowledge we possess or can reasonably acquire in any

FOUR

—

given lifetime. But it should be obvious enough also that some people have been, and still are, historically obliged—as conscripts of modernity, so to call them—to learn the West's intellectual traditions *almost* as if they were their own, from a sort of ambiguous inside-outside that enables or constrains them to speak more or less *intelligibly*, more or less *intelligently*, as modern subjects, or anyway as *naturalized* moderns. I take it that Anzaldúa is one such embattled conscript of modernity, embodying the collision of unequally competing traditions. By contrast, those Euro-American moderns who are—admirably—critical of the hegemony (or worse) of their own moral and political traditions and seek to cultivate dialogical openness to the lives and thinking of others, are generally not concerned (certainly not *required* as a matter of their own intellectual, let alone individual or social, thriving) to learn the intellectual traditions of others from the *inside*, that is to say, to learn to grasp not this or that concept or phrase but the *background* discursive contexts in which these concepts and phrases are constituted and embedded.

There is a crucial politics of translation at stake here, I believe. I wonder, therefore, Stuart, whether something far more profound isn't required of receptive generosity than Coles seems willing to allow—something that, indeed, lies in the *direction* he urges, but that demands a different effort of unlearning and learning than he presupposes. And this, in a sense, takes us back to the tension Coles constructs between Derrida and MacIntyre. For remember that Coles tells us that in the end Derrida *bests* MacIntyre in the dialogical joust he stages between them. But one aspect of MacIntyre's conception of a tradition that Coles curiously overlooks, and one that unsurprisingly is altogether absent from Derrida's evocation of the idea of a European "heritage," concerns not only the idea that concepts within a tradition form an interconnected web (and this is no less the case for Anzaldúa's nepantilism than for, say, Rawls's "veil of ignorance"), but that to understand one tradition's concepts from the standpoint of another's entails a practice of *internal* learning of the language-game that supports these concepts—an internal learning that in an ideal situation amounts to a kind of *dialogue between traditions*.

Of course I don't want to seem churlish here, Stuart; I don't want to seem stingy, or unduly ungenerous or unappreciative. That would be so contrary to everything I'm trying to embrace in your style. Moreover,

I've learned too much from Coles's work (and from that of allied political theorists I've mentioned before like Tully and Connolly) for anything
so graceless and ungrateful. Still, I think there's something deeper and
more resonant in MacIntyre's idea of a tradition than Coles allows us to
recognize, and that seems to me to warrant a bit more reflection. I want
to see specifically whether his idea of communication *across* traditions
offers any resources with which to extend and perhaps enrich the idea
of a dialogical ethics of receptive generosity; and I want to see, more
dubiously you might say, whether in so doing I can't draw *your* ethos of
responsiveness more within its orbit than you would easily admit.

———

I know, Stuart, that you didn't closely follow Alasdair MacIntyre's work
since when you knew him as a fellow socialist back in the late 1950s. You
mentioned him once or twice in our conversations about those years but
not, as far as I remember, in great detail, not to suggest any particular
relationship, any particular quality of interest or affinity or friendship.
There's no natural reason of course that you should have said more than
you did. After all, though sympathetic to the New Left, defending its
project against some of its detractors, publishing in its journals, and so
on, his political sympathies leaned more in the direction of Trotskyism (indeed an admiration for Leon Trotsky would remain an important element
in his moral thinking long after his break with Marxism).[35] But MacIntyre
traveled an interesting road to arrive at the formulation, beginning in the
late 1970s, of his idea of a tradition, of tradition-constituted rationality,
and tradition-oriented moral inquiry, and some would argue that there are
significant overall *continuities* as well as discontinuities between his late
work and his earlier socialist ideas and ethical-political engagements.[36]

I'm not sure if you'll remember, Stuart, that in the early 1950s when
he thought of himself as a Marxist *and* an Anglican Christian philosopher the young MacIntyre published a short book called *Marxism: An
Interpretation*. It's an unusual, and unusually prescient, essay, shaped
by MacIntyre's familiarity with Marx's critical reading of Hegel and

Feuerbach, and in which one can discern his gathering disillusionment with the forms of community exemplified in both the Church and in the communist party.[37] I wonder whether your close comrade of these years, Charles Taylor, himself then a socialist and Catholic philosopher, would have pondered this work with you.[38] But in any case I'm sure you'll have some memory, however uncertain, of that evocatively titled two-part essay "Notes from the Moral Wilderness," published in 1958 and 1959 in the last issues of *The New Reasoner* before the merger with *Universities and Left Review*.[39] As more and more of MacIntyre's readers are coming to recognize, this is an essay of enormous importance for understanding the relation between his earlier and later work. In it MacIntyre is joining a debate initiated by E. P. Thompson's seminal essay "Socialist Humanism: An Epistle to the Philistines," published in the inaugural (1957) issue of *The New Reasoner*, and thus part of the whole response to the crisis of 1956 that you constantly invoke as your political *point d'origine*.[40] This was certainly one of the first overt and systematic criticisms of Stalinism by an avowed British communist. There, in his characteristically pugnacious style, Thompson both attacked, rebuked, condemned the distorting, stultifying orthodoxy—Stalinism, Zhdanovism—of the British communist party (with which he and several of his comrades had just broken), *and* simultaneously appealed for a renewal of a socialist-humanist Marxism that recognized the role and potentiality of human values, human agency, human creativity. Of course this argument became familiar Thompson fare for many years to come—not least in his famous later critique of Althusserian antihumanism.[41] But one of the implications of his intervention in this "epistle to the philistines" was to place within a framework for discussion the whole question of the *moral* values by which right and wrong action (among communists as well as noncommunists) was to be credibly and effectively judged.[42] What was the difference between the "proletarian morality" of the Stalinists and the "bourgeois morality" of the liberal-capitalist West, and how was this to be determined? In a sense it was this moral ambiguity—or seeming moral undecidability— that troubled MacIntyre and to which he sought to respond in the tentative, exploratory, outline of "Notes from the Moral Wilderness."[43] As I understand it, Stuart, and I'm surely simplifying here, MacIntyre's principal concern was to suggest that the moral criticism of Stalinism that the humanist Left felt obliged—or "tempted," as he put it—to embrace is a doubtful one inasmuch as it is grounded in no shared moral principles that they could identify much less specify as having *authority* over us. "They repudiate Stalinist crimes in the name of moral principle; but the fragility of their appeal to moral principle lies in the apparently arbitrary nature of that appeal," MacIntyre wrote.[44] In rejecting the historically reductionist "ought" from "is" of Stalinism the newly minted anticommunist critic saw her or his moral stance as independent of anything historically happening around them. In other words, the criticism of Stalinism, which many confidently asserted, remained just as subjectivist (or "emotivist," as MacIntyre would later term it) as the moral individualism of the liberals from whom they were equally trying to distance themselves. Indeed, here MacIntyre articulated an insight he would later develop to significant effect, namely the deep indebtedness of Marxism to the same Enlightenment sources as liberalism.[45]

But MacIntyre came to think of the work of this period as largely a philosophic failure, and in the decade that followed he endured what one commentator has called an "epistemological crisis," during which he broke with both his Christianity and his Marxism (though, interestingly, it appears he remained on the editorial board of the Trotskyist theoretical journal *International Socialism*, at least until 1968).[46] In the 1970s, however, MacIntyre began to move in the direction of a reconstructed, or revisionary—or some would even say, "revolutionary"—Aristotelianism and it is this work that came to be realized in *After Virtue* and, in adjusted and elaborated form, the books that followed.[47] You knew, I think, Stuart, that this work interested me a great deal and that I'd tried to use it here and there in my own work. Pity therefore that we couldn't have spoken more directly about *why* I found MacIntyre's work so suggestive for its ability to take seriously some of the trenchant problems concerning the *standpoint* from which one seeks to understand the traditions of historical others. Anyway, I don't intend to oppress you unduly with the details of MacIntyre's often involved philosophic arguments; what I want to talk to you briefly about here (bearing in mind the question Coles raises) is his idea of a tradition, and what might be entailed in the possible *relation* or exchange between different—perhaps rival—moral-historical traditions.

Doubtlessly, Stuart, MacIntyre would have to be one of the last thinkers anyone would draw alongside you. Perhaps that's true, though Peter Sedgwick has written something of MacIntyre's style (about its robust multiplicity and public address) that to my mind could easily have been written of yours.[48] In any case, the thing is that, much like you (and beyond the shared attachment to concepts like narrative, practice, history, contingency), MacIntyre has been an intellectual itinerant, restless, continually questioning in his effort to find and re-find his way, responsively open to the conflicts and conundrums and contradictions confronting him. But more than this, part of what's intriguing about the dilemma MacIntyre has been worrying through since his Marxist days is that, in a crucial way, it is connected to, if not necessarily derived from, his personal experience of *divided* inheritance—an experience very familiar to us conscripts of modernity. In an autobiographical interview conducted more than two decades ago, MacIntyre talked about having the "philosophical good fortune" of being brought up in "two antagonistic systems of belief and attitude."[49] On one side, Gaelic oral culture whose "concepts were conveyed through its histories" rather than through theories. This was an increasingly devalued and world-historically decaying and superseded way of life and knowledge. On the other side, the English-language bourgeois culture of modern life—a culture, notably, of "theories rather than stories." Empowered, hegemonic, it presented itself not as one rationality and morality among others, but as rationality and morality *as such*, as the abstract realization of universal humanity. This side of MacIntyre's inheritance presented itself as having defeated and transcended the tradition-bound narratives and ritual practices of his Gaelic world. Sound familiar, Stuart? I think that we can both profoundly appreciate the conflict and incoherence that results from this lopsided tension. It is part of our own inheritance of growing up in the divided cultural world of colonial and postcolonial Jamaica.

In a sense, in *After Virtue* and its philosophic sequels (especially *Whose Justice? Which Rationality?* and *Three Rival Versions of Moral*

Inquiry) MacIntyre's project has been to show how the Enlightenment, far from transcending or defeating tradition as such, has only obscured its own dependence upon and embeddedness within a specific tradition, or specific interconnected traditions (however antitraditionist it may be, and however attenuated its traditionist resources have become). Now, a living tradition, MacIntyre compactly wrote in a defining chapter of *After Virtue*, should be understood as a "historically extended, socially embodied argument, and an argument precisely in part about the goods which constitute that tradition."[50] Traditions are self-reflexive and constructive, and temporal and practice-oriented. Important, therefore, for MacIntyre, is the relation between historically constituted social practices and the narratives that, over the course of generations, lend these practices authoritative point and purpose and orientation. In this way traditions are about persuasively connecting pasts to presents and to possible futures in such a way that the lives lived within their purview, in quest of the virtues internal to them, acquire a certain unity, however differentiated and provisional and unfinished. I know, Stuart, that, put this way, these are not emphases that are instinctively yours. But I wonder whether we aren't in fact not so very far away from a formulation with which you *were*, indeed, inclined to identify, namely, Raymond Williams's formulation in *Culture and Society* of culture as a "whole way of life."[51] MacIntyre, you may remember, was an admirer of at least this book of Williams's, if not others.[52] But with a little bit of stretching here and there, couldn't we say that what MacIntyre is aiming to do with the idea of a tradition is to describe the internal coherence of the rationalities and sensibilities and moralities that constitute such a whole way of life?

Unfortunately, given that scholarly habit of reductive or one-sided reading that Coles warns us against, it has to be repeated endlessly that, contrary to his Enlightenment-inspired critics, MacIntyre does not presuppose that such traditions are solipsistic, closed entities—that traditions are somehow hostile to difference.[53] What he *does* presuppose, though, is that traditions are not self-evidently mutually transparent to each other, that the languages in which their rationalities and moralities are constituted and articulated are not self-evidently mutually intelligible, translatable, or commensurable. The conceit of Enlightenment-

FOUR

—

oriented or Enlightenment-derived knowledge-practices—theories, so-called—is that they have privileged access to the knowledge-practices embodied in concrete historical traditions. Theory takes it that no real *learning* of the traditions of others is required in order to evaluate them, make use of them, dismiss them, or merely pronounce on them. Theory's presumption is that, being itself context-free, tradition-free, it has unfettered access to the contexts and traditions of others. Thus it seems to me that the challenge for Western theory, or anyway for such Western theory as wishes to fruitfully hearken to the worlds of others, is to *learn* to properly take itself to be no more than one tradition among others; and to learn to practice doing so by, first, systematically *unlearning* its conceit of omniscient privilege, and, second, by seeking to listen to, and learn *from the inside*, ethnographically perhaps, the traditions of others.[54] Note that what is involved here is not a matter of the translation of words or concepts from one tradition's language into another's, but rather the translation of *whole* discursive contexts that enable one to grasp the problem-space of relations and powers that organize the semantic and rhetorical range of interconnected words and concepts, and their *uses*.

My wager here, Stuart, such as it is, is that we might think of this process as making certain tentative, provisional steps toward a dialogue *among* traditions—or at least a modest contribution to identifying the conditions without which such a dialogue would be impossible. Clearly, given the world in which we live, basic to any such dialogue is recognition of the global asymmetry in the power relations among traditions (including the asymmetrical power relations among languages, that Talal Asad has urged us to be mindful of).[55] Part of what is entailed is a transformation of these relations such that hegemonic traditions accustomed to giving to (not to say imposing on) the traditions of others are encouraged to practice a more *receptive* openness to these others. Of course, Stuart, you would remind us that recognition of a need for egalitarian responsiveness is no guarantee of commensurability, let alone harmony or reconciliation—for nothing finally seals us off from the possibility of failure or disaster. This is a tragic truth. But without taking the risk, I can hear you say, little of any real generosity, and therefore genuine learning, is possible.

LEARNING TO LEARN FROM OTHERS

—

Still, I want to repeat here that all this is not to imply any deep disagreement with the spirit of Coles's intervention, only to look for where and how his poetics of receptive generosity might be extended and deepened in directions I want to associate with your social style of speaking and listening, the hearkening stance you urge us to learn, and learn with. Thus, in our quest for the best way to think the entwining of receiving and giving, I'm not persuaded (as Coles is) that Nietzsche would be our most receptive guide.[56] You may remember that *Thus Spoke Zarathustra* is said to have returned the question of generosity to Western philosophy after a long hiatus. Famously, Zarathustra urges on his disciples the idea that the "gift-giving virtue" is the highest of all virtues; it is the virtue that defines the splendor of the self-sacrificing soul. But is his honorable giving matched by an open receptivity? There are those who have suspicions that perhaps not. As some have asked in response to Zarathustra's elevated pronouncements, if only giving is the real sign of moral (and manly) greatness, is receiving then its *reverse*, a sign of servitude and debt? *Receiving* in Nietzsche does appear to be more a mark of the *loss* of autonomy than an affirmation of it (even though, ironically, Zarathustra's whole discourse is in fact prompted by his *receipt*, and not his giving, of a gift).[57] So here again we have a conception of generosity that—however joyful and excessive—remains *unidirectional*, without an attunement to reception, and *therefore*, I believe, attenuated and impoverished. I'm more inclined to think that MacIntyre's idea of a potential dialogue among traditions (however agonistic) gives us more to work with, obliges us to think harder about what dialogue should entail, and therefore what the conditions are of receptively receiving from others.

———

This is a direction you didn't quite take yourself, Stuart. But my suggestion is that the *opening* into what an ethics of receptive generosity might look like is already there in your particular practice of thinking aloud with others, your style of speaking that is simultaneously a hermeneutics of listening. To my mind, you are an exemplary receptive giver insofar as you strive to practice a mode of effecting change among others that is, at the same time, a mode of changing *yourself* through the influence of others. This is part of the lesson you draw from the dialogical story of identity, or the story of the dialogical process of *identification*. On your view, as we have seen, identity, including of course your own, is an unstable structure of *co-dependence*. As an ongoing, unfinished, conversation, therefore, identity ought to depend upon a willing exposure to the agonism of otherness (in its varied expressions), a willing openness to changing oneself by unlearning the normalized presuppositions of what one has *so far* taken for granted, the conceits by which one has *so far* organized one's commitments. What Terry Eagleton disparages as your attunement to intellectual fashions is really this virtue of receptivity *at work*, this readiness to hear that one might have been mistaken, or that there are different and better ways of thinking about—thinking within—the present-as-conjuncture.

I don't think anyone would need much persuading, Stuart, that you were a generous self in exactly this sense of a *receptive* giver. You were never merely a privatized intellectual self, but also a *builder* and *sustainer* of intellectual community. And as such you were never-not sharing yourself with those around you, enabling, shouldering, bolstering, and supporting them in the common endeavors in which you were together engaged. All of your work with the varied communities of which you were a generative participant—whether with the first New Left, with the Birmingham center, with black artists and curators, with the *Marxism Today* group—was of this kind, a practice of engaged and selfless giving of a significant part of yourself. But at the same time you would have been the first to tell me that all of this giving was also, reciprocally, a paradoxical kind of receiving as well. You, Stuart, were an *insatiable* learner. You were a *congenital* borrower of the ideas of others. You were never so closed or so proud as to be unable to gain something from others. You had no false conceit about originality. You had no misplaced fear of recycling. And this I think liberated you into a kind of modesty, and courtesy, a sense of proportion really, that was your true gift. Some will remember, as I do, your retirement conference at the Open University in Milton Keynes in 1997. Many people spoke, former students and close associates from the many parts of your wide circle of social, political, and cultural engagements. They spoke, as was appropriate, about what you had meant to them, what you had *given* to them. And then you spoke, Stuart. And with a deft and self-effacing grace and gratitude, very unlike that of Zarathustra, it seems to me, you spoke in turn of what *you* had *received* from each of these mainly younger speakers, and from many others as well, who had contributed, you said, to making you *who* and *what* you were. It was, I thought then, and think now, a remarkable illustration of the character—and measure—of your dialogical ethos of receptive generosity.

Therefore, to me, in contrast to the meager charity of many contemporary moral theorists, we find in you, Stuart, the elements of an ethics of the self-and-other attuned precisely to the edges, the margins, where identity scarcely holds with certainty and where ambiguity, otherness, finitude, the outside, have a tendency to decenter and undermine its fables of stable self-presence. We find in you a listening-speaking self. What you propose is that we take seriously that there is something altogether reductive and therefore morally *impoverished* about the picture of human selves and human interaction that emerges from the one-sided Enlightenment admiration for a sovereign, autonomous self (however critical), legislating the single good for us all but unable or unwilling to *unlearn* its habitus of raced or gendered or cultural dominance, its disposition toward supremacy. We stand a better chance of flourishing, you modestly but audibly suggest, the more open we can *make* ourselves to our own vulnerability—our own fragile, exposed, receptivity—to unassimilable, unabsorbable difference. This is not easy. This is not multicultural sentimentality, you would say. With Levin and MacIntyre you would agree that a real ethical labor of continuous learning and unlearning and relearning is required. And in this process you would say, with people like Coles and Tully and Connolly, that such recursive receptivity entails an ongoing and dissonant practice of working on the self that resists two foreclosing pressures at once: the normalizing pressure to repress and subjugate otherness, including that contingently disruptive otherness within the self, *and* the vindicationist pressure to transform historical infringements and marginalized dispositions into the ground of a poetics of revenge and a political reversal of subjugations.

With my best wishes,
DAVID

FOUR

—

Adieu

Walk Good

———

DEAR STUART,

So here we are. I've taken you far and wide, and it's now perhaps time
to simply bring the consoling fiction of this long epistolary farewell to a
modest close. It is one of the stranger experiences of aftermaths, of awak-
ening to irreversible finitude, that suddenly there is so much to say—
all the things that might have been talked about, but weren't, when we
enjoyed the illusion of an infinity of conjunctures-to-come, the illusion,
you might have said, of a good night's rest. Only after the last goodbye—
and with craving urgency—do you realize what you should have said but
didn't, what you should have asked but didn't. Is this what friendship
does with time? Is this the price friends pay for the hazard of contingency? I don't know. But it feels like it.

 These letters to you are slightly involved, but they are meant only
to clarify what often lay in the interstices of our many conversations,
around their untidy, unfinished edges. They make no deep claim of any
proper analytical sort. Indeed, they *abjure* the privilege of the analytic.
They even seek to evade what conventionally goes by the name of *criticism*. They honor thinking, I hope, but they make no *argument*, properly
speaking, at least of any sustainable sort. They want something else,

Stuart, something more ordinary, more common, more unrefined, more unexceptional, but no less important, I believe—namely, to reflect on *learning* in a context of intellectual friendship. They ask with humility: What do we owe intellectually to those we call our friends, to those whose work we know and value, not only in itself, as work, but as the work of our friends whom we know and value? And they answer: we owe respectful *listening*. That is what these letters aim to do. They aim to listen. They aim to adopt the receptive temper and orientation of a listening self. They have no telos beyond that. I'm reminded once again of Ralph Waldo Emerson, who sagely remarked that "the only reward of virtue is virtue; the only way to have a friend is to be one."[1] Perhaps in a modest way these letters will have enacted one of the paths toward the realization of this Emersonian dictum.

The thing I've learned most from you, Stuart—beyond the disjuncture between encoding and decoding, beyond the problem of a Marxism without guarantees, beyond the methodological innovations of cultural studies, beyond the subversions of racial essence, beyond the call of diaspora and the unfinished conversation of identity, beyond the endless ruses of representation and the powers of hegemony—is about *voice*. I've learned it, of course, by way of *your* voice—the singular way, with its familiar rhythms and tonalities, its invitations and provocations, your voice *salted* the agonistic intimacy of an intellectual style at the generative center of which moved a scarcely foregrounded dialogical ethics of receptive generosity. Contingency and identity, as I've tried to elaborate them here, have always been bound up in, always disclosed by, always projected through, the provisional recursivity of your spoken voice. Its granular resonance, so inimitably the "stony ground" of your intellectual presence, seasoned an embodied way of speaking with others that has always also been an embodied way of *listening* to them. I'm saying that this, in effect, is your organic, homemade hermeneutic, the endless— and endlessly improvised—cultivation of a *learning* self for whom learning-unlearning was a *relation* with concrete others (not only with the other in yourself). And this is at once a personal and political and pedagogical form of sociality. For you, in short, the activity of hermeneutic has been more an *attitude*—an outlook—than a method. And part of what the lineaments that thread this relational attitude of listening and learning have offered you specifically is a way of thinking *change*. This is always your cultural-political horizon: change, the recovery-discovery of the possibility of new directions. What else is there? Indeed, attunement to change (not merely commitment to it; *attunement*)—including that difficult attentiveness involved in changing *yourself* in relation to others—names the radical ethos of your intellectual vocation. At least, so it has seemed to me.

I've plainly taken a selfish liberty with you in these letters, Stuart. I hope you won't think I've misused you beyond repair, beyond the measure of what friendship can properly support. I fully acknowledge the presumption involved in invoking you in this way. The pathos of elegy can sometimes—understandably—seem an indulgence. I hope not a purely sentimental or unseemly one. For the pathos of elegy can look for elation too. It can look for a muted commemoration, a path toward giving thanks. These are of course not your words. They are inescapably mine. And, alas, you will not read them—except in the degree to which, in your own uncannily receptive way, you already have. I sincerely hope, though, that even in their hesitations and missteps they have at least honored something lasting in the spirit of our friendship, something that will, in the end, survive us both.

I won't write to you again, Stuart, though maybe I will write *of* you for another occasion—about which we also spoke.

In the meantime, as we like to say where you and I come from, walk good, my friend.

DAVID

ACKNOWLEDGMENTS

This book grows directly out of a series of three lectures I delivered at the Centre for Humanities Research at the University of the Western Cape, South Africa, in November and December 2013, under the general title "Stuart Hall's Voice." The occasion offered me an opportunity to develop an intuition about Stuart Hall's way of being an engaged intellectual that I'd been mulling over for a number of years: the role of voice in the ethos of his style. For that lecture invitation, and for their generosity and indulgence during my visit, I thank Suren Pillay and Premesh Lalu. I learned a lot during my three weeks in their stimulating company; I learned a lot about learning. The students and faculty who attended the lectures, and who offered me their reservations and misgivings and occasionally their approval, encouraged me to try harder to formulate better what I was hesitantly trying to do.

The present form of the book, as I've also already indicated, the reinvention of the lectures as letters, took shape in the wake of Stuart Hall's death in February 2014, when I was beginning to doubt my original intention. It has not been an easy book to reconceive and rewrite. All the more reason, then, to be grateful and more to those who read the revised manuscript and made suggestions for further revision, elaboration, and clarification. Talal Asad read with his usual perspicuous care, especially drawing to my attention certain unresolved tensions he discerned at play across the letters. To Julian Henriques, I owe a very special debt, for tuning me in to the work on voice and sound that he too was reading and absorbing for his own writing on music. Without his direction and gentle nudging, I would not have ventured along this path. As with others of my books, Ritty Lukose brought a discerning and sympathetic sensibility to her approach to the manuscript, shaped in part by her warm awareness of the larger personal and intellectual context out of which it grew, the manifest as well as the latent currents that recursively seasoned its preoccupations. I count myself lucky to have readers such as these who could tacitly recognize that the duty to which they had committed themselves in reading me like this involved less a prescriptive or evaluative attitude than a responsive, listening one, an attunement to the project they understood me to have undertaken. This is why each of them at various points could see better than I could what I was trying to do, and *not* do. All were aware of my desire to blur genres in order to try to capture some otherwise elusive dimensions of the obligations and pleasures of intellectual friendship. I would also like to thank Catherine Hall specially, for giving the manuscript her attention and for sharing with me, in a searching conversation, her critical sense of the concerns that drive it.

In addition, I would like to thank Kelly Martin, my *Small Axe* production manager and copyeditor, for being at once firm and charitable with my writing, here as elsewhere. Over the years I have grown to depend upon her advice, and sometimes her interdiction.

Finally, obviously, this book could not have been written without the vibe and texture of my friendship with Stuart Hall. I believe I have now said enough to indicate a small measure at least of what I owe to his example—even where (perhaps the more so where) what I have taken from that example is not exactly, or not always, what he might have urged or hoped for in me. This, I take it, though, is only one of the many liberties friendship allows, not soon to be yielded.

NOTES

Apology

1. These lectures were given under the auspices of the Centre for Humanities Research, University of the Western Cape, Bellville, South Africa, on 22 November 2013, 29 November 2013, and 4 December 2013. I would once again like to express my thanks to Suren Pillay and Premesh Lalu for extending to me their invitation and surrounding me with their warm hospitality. I hope they won't mind too much the changes this work has undergone since those splendid weeks in their company.

2. David Scott, "Stuart Hall's Ethics," *Small Axe*, no. 17 (March 2005): 1–16. The conference took place in Kingston, Jamaica, in June 2004. The presentations from that occasion (not including my own) were published in Brian Meeks, ed., *Culture, Politics, Race, and Diaspora: The Thought of Stuart Hall* (Kingston, Jamaica: Ian Randle, 2007). This volume also includes Hall's closing reflections from that occasion, "Through the Prism of an Intellectual Life" (269–91).

3. See David Scott, "Stuart Hall at Eighty," *Small Axe*, no. 38 (July 2012): vii–x; and "The Last Conjuncture," *Small Axe*, no. 44 (July 2014): vii–x.

4. See David Scott, "Politics, Contingency, Strategy: An Interview with Stuart Hall," *Small Axe*, no. 1 (March 1997): 141–59.

5. I have in mind here Rita Felski's recent book, *The Limits of Critique* (Chicago: University of Chicago Press, 2015).

6. See David Scott, "The Temporality of Generations: Dialogue, Tradition, Criticism," *New Literary History* 45, no. 2 (2014): 172–73.

7. Scott, "Temporality of Generations," 159–60.

8. See Georg Lukács, "On the Nature and Form of the Essay: A Letter to Leo Popper," in *Soul and Form*, trans. Anna Bostock (Cambridge, MA: MIT Press, 1978), 1–18; and Françoise Sagan, "Lettre d'amour à Jean-Paul Sartre," in *Avec mon meilleur souvenir* (Paris: Gallimard, 1984), 126–35.

9. See Karl Marx and Friedrich Engels, *The Marx-Engels Correspondence: The Personal Letters, 1844–1877*, ed. Fritz J. Raddatz, trans. Ewald Osers (London: Weidenfeld and Nicolson, 1980). The correspondence, writes Raddatz, "may confidently be described as one of the most tremendous historical and human documents of the nineteenth century, testimony to a friendship of rare intensity" (1). No one who reads the letters can doubt this.

10. See Lotte Kohler and Hans Saner, eds., *Hannah Arendt and Karl Jaspers: Correspondence, 1926–1969*, trans. Robert Kimber and Rita Kimber (New York: Harcourt Brace Jovanovich, 1992), especially the editors' introduction, vii–xxv; and Carol Brightman, ed., *Between Friends: The Correspondence between Hannah Arendt and Mary McCarthy* (New York: Harcourt Brace, 1995), especially Carol Brightman, "Introduction: An Epistolary Romance," vii–xxx. For a marvelous evocation of McCarthy's sense of Arendt and their friendship, see Mary McCarthy, "Saying Good-by to Hannah," *New York Times Review of Books*, 22 January 1976, www.nybooks.com /articles/archives/1976/jan/22/saying-good-by-to-hannah/?pagination =false&printpage=true. For her sense of what duty followed from that friendship after Arendt's death, see Mary McCarthy, "Editor's Postface," in *The Life of the Mind*, by Hannah Arendt (New York: Harcourt Brace, 1978), 241–54. For an account of one famous break in a once-inseparable friendship, see Ronald Aronson, *Camus and Sartre: The Story of a Friendship and the Quarrel That Ended It* (Chicago: University of Chicago Press, 2005).

11. For a recent and thoughtful discussion of Arendt's idea of, and commitment to, friendship, as well as its relationship to her wider political theory, see Jon Nixon, *Hannah Arendt and the Politics of Friendship* (London: Bloomsbury Academic, 2015). "She made no grand claims for friendship," Nixon writes of Arendt, "but the friendships she formed held out the promise of continuity and stability in a world of discontinuity and instability. As such, they played into her thinking about the nature of power and politics and her understanding of the human condition" (46). I agree. But whether this amounts to a "politics of friendship," as the title of Nixon's book suggests, I'm not sure. See also Daniel Maier-Katkin, *Stranger from Abroad: Hannah Arendt, Martin Heidegger, Friendship, and Forgiveness* (New York: W. W. Norton, 2010), in which he writes, "Circles of friends were continuing features of Hannah's life from the earliest days in Konigsberg to the last days in New York. That space of love, which is wholly or largely occupied in some lives by children, was occupied, for Hannah, by friendships" (85).

12. For the ancients, I am thinking of Plato's "Lysis, or Friendship," in *Lysis, Phaedrus, and Symposium: Plato on Homosexuality* (Amherst, MA: Prometheus, 1991), 15–41; books 8 and 9 of Aristotle's *Nicomachean Ethics*, ed. Roger Crisp (New York: Cambridge University Press, 2000); and Cicero's "Laelius: On Friendship," in *On the Good Life* (New York: Penguin Classics, 1971), 172–227. For the moderns, see Michel de Montaigne, "Of Friendship," in *Essays* (New York: Penguin, 1958); Immanuel Kant, *The Metaphysics of Morals* (1797; New York: Cambridge University Press, 1996), 215–17; Ralph Waldo Emerson, "Friendship," in *The Essential Writings of Ralph Waldo Emerson*, ed. Brooks Atkinson (New York: Modern Classics, 2000), 201–14; Maurice Blanchot, "Friendship," in *Friendship*, trans. Elizabeth Rottenberg (Stanford, CA: Stanford University Press, 1997), 289–92; Michel Foucault, "Friendship as a Way of Life," in *Ethics: Subjectivity and Truth*, ed. Paul Rabinow (New York: New Press, 1998), 135–40; and Derek Walcott, "On Robert Lowell," *New York Review of Books* 31, no. 1 (1984): 25–31.

13. See Foucault, "Friendship as a Way of Life," 138–39. In *Friendship as a Way of Life: Foucault, AIDS, and the Politics of Shared Estrangement* (Albany: State University of New York Press, 2012), Tom Roach takes up what he thinks of as the ethical implications of Foucault's suggestive remarks about friendship. That the friendship debate has been almost exclusively male has not gone without critical comment. See A. C. Grayling, *Friendship* (New Haven, CT: Yale University Press, 2013), 12–14. For a discussion of women and friendship, see Janet Todd, *Women's Friendship in Literature* (New York: Columbia University Press, 1980); and Sharon Marcus, *Between Women: Friendship, Desire, and Marriage in Victorian England* (Princeton, NJ: Princeton University Press, 2007).

14. Neera Kapur Badhwar dates the resurgence of interest in friendship to the publication of Elizabeth Telfer's essay "Friendship," *Proceedings of the Aristotelian Society* 71, no. 1 (1971): 223–41. See Neera Kapur Badhwar, "Introduction: The Nature and Significance of Friendship," in *Friendship: A Philosophical Reader*, ed. Neera Kapur Badhwar (Ithaca, NY: Cornell University Press, 1993), 2. Lawrence Blum's *Friendship, Altruism, and Morality* (London: Routledge, 1980) also made an important contribution to the emerging discussion.

15. See Kant, *Metaphysics of Morals*, 215–17; and John Stuart Mill, *The Subjection of Women* (1869; Indianapolis: Hackett, 1988), chap. 4.

16. See Badhwar, "Introduction," in which she writes instructively, "The problem of reconciling friendship with total devotion to God has interesting counterparts in the two chief rival theories in contemporary ethics, Kantianism and consequentialism. Each theory in its own way commands total devotion to morality, and each sees friendship as an intrinsically

nonethical good in need of justification by the supreme principle of morality. More generally, each sees morality as a system of external constraints
on our pursuit of personal, partial, nonmoral goods. Hence, within these
traditions, friendship is an intrinsically nonethical good that is *subject* to
moral principles, but does not *embody* them" (20; emphasis in original). On
virtue-ethics as a significant trend in recent ethical theory, see Rosalind
Hursthouse, *On Virtue Ethics* (New York: Oxford University Press, 1999);
and Daniel C. Russell, ed., *The Cambridge Companion to Virtue Ethics* (New
York: Cambridge University Press, 2013).

17. "End friendship" is Badhwar's term; see her "Introduction," 4.

18. For helpful discussions of the conundrum of the doctrine of the friend as
"another self," see Paul Schollmeier, *Other Selves: Aristotle on Personal and
Political Friendship* (Albany: State University of New York Press, 1994), chap. 3;
and Lorraine Smith Pangle, *Aristotle and the Philosophy of Friendship* (New
York: Cambridge University Press, 2003), chap. 7.

19. Paul Ricoeur also takes up this theme, in *Oneself as Another*, trans. Kathleen
Blamey (Chicago: University of Chicago Press, 1992), 181–83.

20. Arendt, *Life of the Mind*, 179–93.

21. There is a certain ambiguity in Aristotle. In the well-known opening chapter
of the first book on friendship, he begins, "After this [that is, after the earlier discussion of self-control and incontinence, and pleasure and pain], the
next step would be a discussion of friendship, since it is a virtue, or involves
virtue, and is an absolute necessity in life" (*Nicomachean Ethics*, 143).

22. Aristotle has a wonderful passage in which he says, "Naturally, such friendships are rare, because people of this kind are few. Besides, they require
time and familiarity. As the saying goes, they cannot know each other until
they have eaten the proverbial salt together; nor can they accept each other
or be friends until each has shown himself to be worthy of love and gained
the other's confidence" (*Nicomachean Ethics*, 147). C. S. Lewis's remark can
be found in *The Four Loves: An Exploration of the Nature of Love* (New York:
Mariner, 2012), 58.

23. See Telfer, "Friendship," in which both the "passions" and the "duties" of
friendship are discussed.

24. See, for example, Aristotle's discussion of "concord" and political friendship, in *Nicomachean Ethics*, 172; see also Schollmeier, *Other Selves*, chap. 7.
In the essay "Socrates," in her collection *The Promise of Politics* (New York:
Schocken, 2005), Arendt suggestively writes, "The political element in
friendship is that in the truthful dialogue each of the friends can understand the truth inherent in the other's opinion. More than his friend as a
person, one friend understands how and in what specific articulateness the
world appears to the other, who as a person is forever unequal or different.
This kind of understanding—seeing the world (as we rather tritely say)

from the other fellow's point of view—is the political kind of insight par excellence" (17–18). But is this the same as speaking of a "politics of friendship" in the way that, for example, Jacques Derrida does in *The Politics of Friendship*, trans. George Collins (New York: Verso, 1997)?

25. See Scott, "Temporality of Generations."

26. Stuart Hall, "Cultural Studies and the Centre: Some Problematics and Problems," in *Culture, Media, Language*, ed. Stuart Hall, Dorothy Hobson, Andrew Lowe, and Paul Willis (1980; New York: Routledge, 1992), 15.

27. Stuart Hall, "New Ethnicities," in *Black Film, British Cinema*, ed. Kobena Mercer, ICA Documents 7 (London: Institute of Contemporary Arts, 1988), 27.

28. Scott, "Temporality of Generations," 160.

29. See Stuart Hall, introduction to *Representation: Cultural Representations and Signifying Practices*, ed. Stuart Hall (London: Sage, 1997), 3.

30. Ludwig Wittgenstein, *Philosophical Investigations*, trans. G. E. M. Anscombe (London: Macmillan, 1953); *Culture and Value*, ed. G. H. Von Wright, trans. Peter Winch (Chicago: University of Chicago Press, 1984); *On Certainty*, ed. G. E. M. Anscombe and G. H. Von Wright, trans. Denis Paul and G. E. M. Anscombe (New York: Harper and Row, 1972). For a discussion of Wittgenstein's "ethics of clarification," see J. Jeremy Wisnewski, *Wittgenstein and Ethical Inquiry: A Defense of Ethics as Clarification* (London: Continuum, 2007); and for the connection of this to Wittgenstein's approach to learning, see Patrick Quinn, *Wittgenstein on Thinking, Learning, and Teaching* (Oxford: Peter Lang, 2015). For a useful discussion of Wittgenstein's later turn, see Ray Monk, *Ludwig Wittgenstein: The Duty of Genius* (London: Jonathan Cape, 1990). One way of connecting Wittgenstein's style of thinking to Hall might be to take up some of the issues raised by James Tully in "Situated Creatively: Wittgenstein and Political Philosophy," in *Public Philosophy in New Key*, vol. 1, *Democracy and Civic Freedom* (New York: Cambridge University Press, 2008), 39–70. More generally, see Cressida Heyes, ed., *The Grammar of Politics: Wittgenstein and Political Philosophy* (Ithaca, NY: Cornell University Press, 2003), in which, also, an earlier version of Tully's essay appeared.

31. See Susan Sontag, "The Aesthetics of Silence," in *Styles of Radical Will* (New York: Picador, 1969), 6.

32. It is not irrelevant that Wittgenstein himself wrote a number of letters to friends aimed precisely at clarifying his thinking on various topics. See Paul Engelmann, *Letters from Ludwig Wittgenstein with a Memoir* (Oxford: Blackwell, 1967). And in Emerson we find a sensibility for the letter-form in relation to friendship: "To my friend I write a letter and from him I receive a letter. That seems to you a little. It suffices me. It is a spiritual gift, worthy of him to give and of me to receive. It profanes nobody. In these warm lines the heart will trust itself, as it will not to the tongue, and pour out the

prophecy of a godlier existence than all the annals of heroism have yet made good" ("Friendship," 211).

33. Adriana Cavarero, *For More Than One Voice: Toward a Philosophy of Vocal Expression* (Stanford, CA: Stanford University Press, 2005).

34. See Gemma Corradi Fiumara, *The Other Side of Language: A Philosophy of Listening*, trans. Charles Lambert (New York: Routledge, 1990); and David Michael Levin, *The Listening Self: Personal Growth, Social Change, and the Closure of Metaphysics* (New York: Routledge, 1989).

35. See W. B. Gallie, "Essentially Contested Concepts," in *Philosophy and the Historical Understanding*, 2nd ed. (New York: Schocken, 1968), 157–91.

36. Romand Coles, *Rethinking Generosity: Critical Theory and the Politics of Caritas* (Ithaca, NY: Cornell University Press, 1997).

ONE. *A Listening Self*

1. Terry Eagleton, "The Hippest," *London Review of Books* 18, no. 5 (1996), 3; hereafter cited in the text. The essay was reprinted as "Stuart Hall," in Terry Eagleton, *Figures of Dissent* (London: Verso, 2003), 207–15. See David Morley and Kuan-Hsing Chen, eds., *Stuart Hall: Critical Dialogues in Cultural Studies* (London: Routledge, 1996).

2. Isaac Julien, dir., *The Attendant* (London, 1993). For an interesting discussion of the making of the eight-minute film, see Isaac Julien, "Confessions of a Snow Queen: Notes on the Making of *The Attendant*," *Critical Quarterly* 36, no. 1 (1994): 120–26. See also the exchange on Hall's appearance in *The Attendant* in Mark Nash and Isaac Julien, "Dialogues with Stuart Hall," in Morley and Chen, *Stuart Hall*, 479.

3. Eagleton offers a more measured, less patronizing, less tongue-in-cheek assessment of Stuart Hall's influence and style in a BBC Radio 3 interview with Philip Dodd, 12 February 2014. See www.bbc.co.uk/programmes/p01s55wv (accessed 10 June 2014).

4. See Stuart Hall, "What Is This 'Black' in Black Popular Culture?," in *Black Popular Culture*, ed. Gina Dent (Seattle, WA: Bay Press, 1992), in which he writes, "I ask you to note how, within the black repertoire, *style*—which mainstream cultural critics often believe to be the mere husk, the wrapping, the sugar coating on the pill—has become *itself* the subject of what is going on" (27; emphasis in original).

5. The inscription is quoted in a number of Fanon biographies, including Peter Geismar, *Fanon: A Biography* (New York: Dial, 1971), 11; and David Macey, *Frantz Fanon: A Biography* (New York: Picador, 2001), 139.

6. I'm alluding, of course, to Susan Sontag's famous essay "On Style" (1965), collected in her first volume of essays, *Against Interpretation* (New York: Picador, 1966). I'm grateful to my friend Julian Henriques for reminding me

of the value of Sontag's discussion of style for thinking about Stuart Hall, and much else.

7. Sontag, *Against Interpretation*, 17.
8. The allusion is to the title of Susan Sontag's second collection of essays, *Styles of Radical Will* (New York: Picador, 1969).
9. See David Scott, "The Vocation of a Caribbean Intellectual: An Interview with Lloyd Best," *Small Axe*, no. 1 (March 1997): 135.
10. See George Lamming, "But Alas Edgar," Guyana Independence issue, *New World Quarterly* 2, no. 3 (1966): 18–19. On Lamming's relationship to Mittelholzer and his death, see David Scott, "The Sovereignty of the Imagination: An Interview with George Lamming," *Small Axe*, no. 12 (September 2002): 72–200.
11. Roland Barthes, "The Grain of the Voice," in *Image, Music, Text*, trans. Stephen Heath (New York: Noonday, 1977), 188. Of course, one can catch something of his own embodied voice in the large number of interviews collected in Barthes, *The Grain of the Voice: Interviews, 1962–1980*, trans. Linda Coverdale (New York: Hill and Wang, 1985).
12. See the excellent collection of essays in Erving Goffman, *Forms of Talk* (Philadelphia: University of Pennsylvania Press, 1981).
13. See Mike Dibb, dir., *Personally Speaking: A Long Conversation with Stuart Hall*, interview conducted by Maya Jaggi (Dibb Directions, UK, 2009).
14. See John Akomfrah, dir., *The Unfinished Conversation* (Autograph, London, 2012); and *The Stuart Hall Project* (Smoking Dogs Films, London, 2013).
15. See Stuart Hall and Tony Jefferson, eds., *Resistance through Rituals: Youth Sub-cultures in Post-war Britain* (London: Hutchinson, 1976); and Stuart Hall, Chas Critcher, Tony Jefferson, John Clarke, and Brian Roberts, *Policing the Crisis: Mugging, the State, and Law and Order* (London: Macmillan, 1978). In the introduction to *Policing the Crisis*, there is a useful discussion of this practice (ix). For a discussion of the pedagogical practice at the center, see Stuart Hall, "Cultural Studies at the Centre: Some Problematics and Problems," in *Culture, Media, Language: Working Papers in Cultural Studies, 1972–79*, ed. Stuart Hall, Dorothy Hobson, Andrew Lowe, and Paul Willis (1980; New York: Routledge, 1992), 42–45; and Stuart Hall, "The Emergence of Cultural Studies and the Crisis of the Humanities," *October*, no. 53 (Summer 1990): 11–23.
16. Readers of the cowritten work by Stuart Hall and Paddy Whannel, *The Popular Arts* (London: Hutchinson, 1964), will recognize that the idea of teaching was, from very early on, a central element in Hall's idea of what it means to be an intellectual—in particular, the idea (only later formulated in this way) of forming or cultivating "organic" intellectuals as agents of change.
17. Roland Barthes, "Writers, Intellectuals, Teachers," in *Image, Music, Text*, 190, 191.

NOTES TO LETTER ONE

—

18. Barthes, "Writers, Intellectuals, Teachers," 190.

19. See Don Ihde, *Listening and Voice: Phenomenologies of Sound*, 2nd ed. (Albany: State University of New York Press, 2007); and Jonathan Rée, *I See a Voice: A Philosophical History of Language, Deafness, and the Senses* (London: HarperCollins, 1999). The latter is an enormously sensitive and insightful book. For a discussion of it that seems to me, nevertheless, not to capture its full implications, see Ian Hacking, "Gabble, Twitter, and Hoot," *London Review of Books* 21, no. 13 (1999): 15–16.

20. See Mladen Dolar, *A Voice and Nothing More* (Cambridge, MA: MIT Press, 2006), 22.

21. Dolar, *A Voice and Nothing More*, 15. The reference here to Wittgenstein is very suggestive. See also Marjorie Perloff, *Wittgenstein's Ladder: Poetic Language and the Strangeness of the Ordinary* (Chicago: University of Chicago Press, 1996).

22. Adriana Cavarero, *For More Than One Voice: Towards a Philosophy of Vocal Expression* (Stanford, CA: Stanford University Press, 2005). I am enormously grateful to my friend Julian Henriques for suggesting this work to me.

23. Not the least interesting facet of this book to me is the chapter that considers Kamau Brathwaite's seminal work *History of the Voice: The Development of Nation Language in Anglophone Caribbean Poetry* (London: New Beacon, 1984). See Cavarero, *More Than One Voice*, 146–51.

24. See Jean-Luc Nancy, *Being Singular Plural*, trans. Robert D. Richardson and Anne E. O'Byrne (Stanford, CA: Stanford University Press, 2000); Emmanuel Levinas, *Infinity and Totality: An Essay on Exteriority*, trans. Alphonso Lingis (Pittsburgh, PA: Duquesne University Press, 1969); and Hannah Arendt, *The Human Condition* (Chicago: University of Chicago Press, 1958), and, more pronouncedly, its sequel, *The Life of the Mind* (New York: Harcourt Brace, 1978). In an important appendix, Cavarero engages Derrida's well-known critique of logocentrism in his *Of Grammatology*, trans. Gayatri Chakravorty Spivak (Chicago: University of Chicago Press, 1976).

25. See Walter Ong, *Ramus, Method, and the Decay of Dialogue: From the Art of Discourse to the Art of Reason* (1958; Chicago: University of Chicago Press, 2004). In his perceptive foreword to this edition, Adrian Johns writes, "Ramism was oriented entirely to sight, not sound. As a movement it was by and large anti-dialogic, anti-dramatic, anti-poetic, and anti-symbolic. It implied that conversation was not creative; novelty should be sought instead in the practices of visual juxtaposition and comparison" (ix). I am very grateful to Talal Asad for bringing this book to my attention.

26. Hans Jonas, "The Nobility of Sight: A Study in the Phenomenology of the Senses," in *The Phenomenon of Life: Toward a Philosophical Biology* (New York: Harper and Row, 1966), 135–56.

27. See Rée, "Listening with the Voice," in *I See a Voice*, 51–57. He writes of himself as a child: "I had no real control over my ears, for a start. They could not be closed or swiveled, and though I might block them with my fingers, I could not shut out external sound completely; in any case there was the ceaseless internal concert of my breathing and swallowing, and the eerie continuo of my beating heart" (51).

28. Rée uses the phrase "ocular moderns" (*I See a Voice*, 4). In his magisterial book *Downcast Eyes: The Denigration of Vision in Twentieth-Century French Thought* (Berkeley: University of California Press, 1993), Martin Jay maps the attempts, from Henri Bergson to Jean-François Lyotard, to dismantle the totalizing hegemony of vision in French thought since the Enlightenment. Not surprisingly, Jay has his doubts about the mere counter-evocation of voice and listening in the hermeneutic tradition and urges instead a more balanced approach to the appreciation of the senses and their relation to knowing.

29. See Cavarero, *More Than One Voice*, 8. Cavarero is inspired by Italo Calvino's story "A King Listens," in *Under the Jaguar Sun*, trans. William Weaver (New York: Harcourt Brace, 1988).

30. Cavarero, *More Than One Voice*, 14 (emphasis added).

31. See Dmitri Nikulin, *On Dialogue* (Lanham, MD: Lexington, 2005).

32. Cavarero, *More Than One Voice*, 13.

33. Rée, *I See A Voice*, 33.

34. Cavarero, *More Than One Voice*, 173.

35. Cavarero, *More Than One Voice*, 175.

36. Arendt, *Life of the Mind*, 110–25.

37. "It is this duality of myself with myself that makes thinking a true activity, in which I am both the one who asks and the one who answers." Arendt, *Life of the Mind*, 185.

38. See Hannah Arendt, "Karl Jaspers: A Laudatio," in *Men in Dark Times* (New York: Harcourt Brace Jovanovich, 1968), 71–80.

39. For a lucid discussion that takes a different perspective, see Richard Bernstein, "Arendt on Thinking," in *The Cambridge Companion to Hannah Arendt*, ed. Dana Villa (Cambridge: Cambridge University Press, 2000), 277–92.

40. Jean-Luc Nancy, *À l'écoute* (Paris: Galilée, 2002), 1; translated by Charlotte Mandell as *Listening* (New York: Fordham University Press, 2007), 1 (emphasis in original).

41. Gemma Corradi Fiumara, *The Other Side of Language: A Philosophy of Listening*, trans. Charles Lambert (New York: Routledge, 1990), 16.

42. Fiumara, *Other Side of Language*, 28; the quote is from Hans-Georg Gadamer, *Truth and Method*, trans. Joel Weinsheimer and Donald G.

Marshall, 2nd rev. ed. (New York: Continuum, 2004), 324 (emphasis added by Fiumara).

43. Fiumara, *Other Side of Language*, 29.

44. David Levin, *The Listening Self: Personal Growth, Social Change, and the Closure of Metaphysics* (New York: Routledge, 1989). For a somewhat different approach, one based on an "experimental" phenomenology, see Ihde, *Listening and Voice*.

45. See Lisbeth Lipari, *Listening, Thinking, Being: Toward an Ethics of Attunement* (University Park: Pennsylvania State University Press, 2014).

46. See, for example, Martin Heidegger, *Being and Time*, trans. Joan Stambaugh (Albany: State University of New York Press, 2010), 155–61. The phrase "the ear of our thinking" comes from Heidegger's "The Word of Nietzsche: 'God Is Dead,'" in *The Question Concerning Technology, and Other Essays* (New York: Harper and Row, 1977). Heidegger closes the essay in this suggestive way: "And the ear of our thinking, does it still not hear the cry? It will refuse to hear it so long as it does not begin to think. Thinking begins only when we have come to know that reason, glorified for centuries, is the most stiff-necked adversary of thought" (112). See also Levin, introduction to *Listening Self*, 1–8.

47. See Jennifer L. Heuson, "Heidegger's Ears: Hearing, Attunement, and the Acoustic Shaping of *Being and Time*," *Contemporary Music Review* 31, nos. 5–6 (2012): 411–23; and Jacques Derrida, "Heidegger's Ear: Philopolemology (Geschlect IV)," in *Reading Heidegger: Commemorations*, ed. John Sallis (Bloomington: Indiana University Press, 1993), 163–218.

48. I am thinking, for example, of the following important reconstructive biographical works: Hugo Ott, *Martin Heidegger: A Political Life*, trans. Allan Blunden (New York: Basic Books, 1993); and Rüdiger Safranski, *Martin Heidegger: Between Good and Evil*, trans. Ewald Osers (Cambridge, MA: Harvard University Press, 1998). Still, the question George Steiner worries over in *Martin Heidegger* (Chicago: University of Chicago Press, 1991) regarding Heidegger's adamant silence is hard not to dismiss. Steiner writes, "Once more: the disabling fact is Heidegger's silence after 1945. This appalling abstention is contemporaneous with some of his most far-reaching work in reference to the nature of planetary-ecological crises, in reference to language and of the arts. Martin Heidegger is working and lecturing at the peak of his powers during the very years in which he refuses all response to question of the true quality of Hitlerism and of the Auschwitz consequence" (xxvii).

49. Levin, *Listening Self*, 1.

50. Heidegger, *Being and Time*, 153.

51. Heidegger, *Being and Time*, 159.

52. Heidegger, *Being and Time*, 158. See also his discussion of Herder in *On the Essence of Language: The Metaphysics of Language and the Essencing of the Word*, trans. Wanda Torres Gregory and Yvonne Unna (Albany: State University of New York Press, 2004), 93–108.

53. See Diane P. Michelfelder and Richard E. Palmer, eds., *Dialogue and Deconstruction: The Gadamer-Derrida Encounter* (Albany: State University of New York Press, 1989); and Richard Bernstein, "The Conversation That Never Happened (Gadamer/Derrida)," *Review of Metaphysics* 61, no. 3 (2008): 577–603.

54. Gadamer, *Truth and Method*, 304, 336.

55. Gadamer writes, "When you look at something, you can also look away from it by looking in another direction, but you cannot 'hear away.' This difference between seeing and hearing is important for us because the primacy of hearing is the basis of the hermeneutical phenomenon, as Aristotle saw. There is nothing that is not available to hearing through the medium of language. Whereas all the other senses have no immediate share in the universality of the verbal experience of the world, but only offer the key to their own specific fields, hearing is an avenue to the whole because it is able to listen to the logos." *Truth and Method*, 358.

56. See Martin Jay, "The Rise of Hermeneutics and the Crisis of Ocularcentrism," in *Force Fields: Between Intellectual History and Cultural Critique* (New York: Routledge, 1993), 99–113.

57. See Bernstein, "Conversation That Never Happened."

58. Gadamer's contribution was called "Text and Interpretation." See Michelfelder and Palmer, *Dialogue and Deconstruction*, 21–51.

59. Derrida's main contribution was called "Interpreting Signatures (Nietzsche/Heidegger): Two Questions," collected in Michelfelder and Palmer, *Dialogue and Deconstruction*, 58–71.

60. On "arbitrary closure," see, for example, Stuart Hall, "Cultural Studies and Its Theoretical Legacies," in *Cultural Studies*, ed. Lawrence Grossberg, Cary Nelson, and Paula Treichler (New York: Routledge, 1992), 278.

TWO. *Responsiveness to the Present*

1. The quotation is taken from Stuart Hall, "Through the Prism of an Intellectual Life," in *Culture, Politics, Race, and Diaspora: The Thought of Stuart Hall*, ed. Brian Meeks (Kingston, Jamaica: Ian Randle, 2007), 280.

2. Michael Oakeshott, "Present, Future, and Past," in *On History, and Other Essays* (Indianapolis: Liberty Fund, 1999), 8.

3. See Stuart Hall, "The New Conservatism and the Old," *Universities and Left Review* 1, no. 1 (1957): 23.

4. See, for example, Lawrence Grossberg, "Stuart Hall on Race and Racism: Cultural Studies and the Practice of Contextualism," in Meeks, *Culture, Politics*, 98–119.

5. Hall, "Through the Prism," 278–79. My suggestion is articulated in my lecture "Stuart Hall's Ethics," *Small Axe*, no. 17 (March 2005): 1–16.

6. Michel Foucault, *Discipline and Punish: The Birth of the Prison*, trans. Alan Sheridan (New York: Vintage, 1979).

7. See Louis Althusser, *For Marx*, trans. Ben Brewster (London: Verso, 1977), esp. chap. 3, "Contradiction and Overdetermination"; and the section "Analysis of Situations: Relations of Force," in Antonio Gramsci, "The Modern Prince," in *Selections from the Prison Notebooks*, trans. Quintin Hoare and Geoffrey Nowell Smith (New York: International Publishers, 1971), 177–80.

8. Stuart Hall, Chas Critcher, Tony Jefferson, John Clarke, and Brian Roberts, *Policing the Crisis: Mugging, the State, and Law and Order* (London: Macmillan, 1978).

9. Stuart Hall, Chas Critcher, Tony Jefferson, John Clarke, and Brian Roberts, preface to *Policing the Crisis*, 2nd ed. (London: Palgrave Macmillan, 2013), xv. The figure is taken from Althusser, "Contradiction and Overdetermination" in *For Marx*, 99.

10. Hall, "Through the Prism," 277.

11. Remember that after Marx set it aside unfinished in 1858, the *Grundrisse* remained unpublished until 1939. It was translated into English only in 1973, when it became a central text for understanding Marx's method at the Centre for Contemporary Cultural Studies. See Stuart Hall, "Marx's Notes on Method: A 'Reading' of the '1857 Introduction,'" *Working Papers in Cultural Studies* 6 (1974): 132–71. For a helpful discussion, see also J. Macgregor Wise, "Reading Hall Reading Marx," *Cultural Studies* 17, no. 2 (2003): 105–12.

12. Hall, "Through the Prism," 279.

13. Hall, "Through the Prism," 279.

14. As far as I can tell, Hall begins using this phrase—"without guarantees"—in the late 1970s, but its most famous instance is in the essay "The Problem of Ideology: Marxism without Guarantees," in *Marx: One Hundred Years On*, ed. Betty Matthews (London: Lawrence and Wishart, 1983).

15. Kenneth Burke writes, "Imagine that you enter a parlor. You come late. When you arrive, others have long preceded you, and they are engaged in a heated discussion, a discussion too heated for them to pause and tell you exactly what it is about. In fact, the discussion had already begun long before any of them got there, so that no one present is qualified to retrace for you all the steps that had gone before. You listen for a while, until you decide that you have caught the tenor of the argument; then you put in your oar. Someone answers; you answer him; another comes to your defense; another

aligns himself against you, to either the embarrassment or gratification of your opponent, depending upon the quality of your ally's assistance. However, the discussion is interminable. The hour grows late, you must depart. And you do depart, with the discussion still vigorously in progress." See Kenneth Burke, *The Philosophy of Literary Form* (1941; Berkeley: University of California Press, 1974), 110–11.

16. Stuart Hall and Paddy Whannel, *The Popular Arts* (London: Hutchinson, 1964); Hall et al., *Policing the Crisis*.

17. See David Scott, "The Last Conjuncture," *Small Axe*, no. 44 (July 2014): v–x.

18. Georg Lukács, "The Nature and Form of the Essay: A Letter to Leo Popper," in *Soul and Form*, trans. Anna Bostock (Cambridge, MA: MIT Press, 1978).

19. Lukács, "Nature and Form of the Essay," 18.

20. Theodor W. Adorno, "The Essay as Form," *New German Critique*, no. 32 (Spring–Summer 1984): 151–71.

21. Adorno, "Essay as Form," 168, 170.

22. Stuart Hall, "The Great Moving Right Show," *Marxism Today*, January 1979, 14–20. *Marxism Today* was, in many respects, a unique formation, certainly under the editorship of Jacques, and was arguably one of the most influential political magazines in Britain between 1978 and 1991. For some discussion of this institution, see Francis Beckett, *Enemy Within: The Rise and Fall of the British Communist Party* (London: John Murray, 1995), 149, 170, 194–95, 197, 228.

23. From Martin Jacques, "Appreciation: Stuart Hall, 1932–2014," *Observer*, 16 February 2014, www.martinjacques.com/articles/articles-geopolitics -globalisation/appreciation-stuart-hall-1932-2014. Jacques repeated the story in his wonderful remarks at the Stuart Hall Memorial; see www .stuarthallmemorial.org/the-memorial.

24. In November 1998, *Marxism Today*, seven years after the magazine had formally closed, came out with a special issue to engage the "Blair project." The issue included Hall's essay "The Great Moving Nowhere Show" (9–14).

25. See Stuart Hall, *The Hard Road to Renewal: Thatcherism and the Crisis of the Left* (London: Verso, 1988).

26. Hall was very fond of this Althusserian image of "bending the stick," and, given his strategic, political sensibility, it isn't hard to see why. Louis Althusser borrowed it from Lenin and, it has been argued, used it in his post-1968 period of revisionism (for some discussion, see "On the Subject of Theoretical Practice: William S. Lewis in Dialogue with David McInerney" in *borderlands*, available at www.borderlands.net.au/vol4no2_2005/lewis _interview.htm). See Althusser, "Marx in His Limits," in *Philosophy of the Encounter: Later Writings, 1978–1987*, trans. G. M. Goshgarian (London: Verso, 2006), 23, 88, in which he quotes Lenin using the figure in reply to his

critics regarding the character of the 1902 polemic *What Is to Be Done?* See also Robert Service, *Lenin: A Biography* (London: Macmillan, 2000), 154.

27. Hall, "Great Moving Right Show," 14.
28. Hall, "Great Moving Right Show," 14.
29. Hall, "Great Moving Right Show," 20.
30. See David Scott, *Refashioning Futures: Criticism after Postcoloniality* (Princeton, NJ: Princeton University Press, 1999), 5–10; and *Conscripts of Modernity: The Tragedy of Colonial Enlightenment* (Durham: Duke University Press, 2004), 4–6. The inspiration, of course, is R. G. Collingwood, *An Autobiography* (Oxford: Oxford University Press, 1939), chap. 5.
31. Hall has reflected on what the connections might be between the idea of a conjuncture and the idea of a "problem-space." See Hall, "Through the Prism," 278.
32. On the New Left and its rise and internal conundrums, see Lin Chun, *The British New Left* (Edinburgh: Edinburgh University Press, 1993); Michael Kenny, *The First New Left: British Intellectuals after Stalin* (London: Lawrence and Wishart, 1995); and Dennis Dworkin, *Cultural Marxism in Postwar Britain: History, the New Left, and the Origins of Cultural Studies* (Durham: Duke University Press, 1997). See also Keith Flett, ed., *1956 and All That* (Newcastle, UK: Cambridge Scholars, 2007).
33. Stuart Hall, "A Sense of Classlessness," *Universities and Left Review*, no. 5 (Autumn 1958): 26–32.
34. Hall, "Sense of Classlessness," 26.
35. Hall, "Sense of Classlessness," 26. See Richard Hoggart, *The Uses of Literacy: Aspects of Working Class Life* (London: Pelican, 1957); and Raymond Williams, *Culture and Society, 1780–1950* (London: Chatto and Windus, 1958). These are books that remained enormously important to Hall, even when he distanced himself from their specific formulations of the culture problem. The beleaguered sense of "apathy" was, of course, a trope of the moment of youth discontent, often drawn from such literary work as John Osborne's 1956 play *Look Back in Anger*. It would also become the title of a book edited by E. P. Thompson, *Out of Apathy* (London: New Left, 1960).
36. David Riesman, *The Lonely Crowd: A Study of the Changing American Character* (New York: Doubleday, 1950); C. Wright Mills, *The Power Elite* (Oxford: Oxford University Press, 1956); William Whyte, *The Organization Man* (New York: Simon and Schuster, 1956); John Kenneth Galbraith, *The Affluent Society: The Economics of the Age of Opulence* (New York: Houghton, 1958).
37. Hall, "Sense of Classlessness," 27.
38. Hall, "Sense of Classlessness," 27. Gramsci, interestingly, knew this letter; he refers to it at various points in *Selections from the Prison Notebooks* (427, 437).
39. Hall, "Sense of Classlessness," 27. Famously it was Charles Taylor who brought the French translation of *Economic and Philosophical Manuscripts*

from Paris to Oxford in 1958 and translated portions into English. See Chun, *British New Left*, 34.

40. Stuart Hall, "The Big Swipe," *Universities and Left Review*, no. 7 (Autumn 1959): 50–52.

41. For some discussion, see Chun, *British New Left*, chap. 1.

42. Hall, "Big Swipe," 50.

43. Hall, "Big Swipe," 50 (emphasis in original).

44. Ralph Samuel, "Class and Classlessness," *Universities and Left Review*, no. 6 (Spring 1959): 44–50.

45. E. P. Thompson, "Commitment in Politics," *Universities and Left Review*, no. 6 (Spring 1959): 50–55.

46. Thompson, "Commitment in Politics," 50. On Thompson's attitude to Hall, see Kenny, *First New Left*, 27–28; and Dworkin, *Cultural Marxism*, 68. Thompson was of course not an easy person to get along with person-ally and intellectually, even for people closer to him generationally and politically, such as John Saville and Ralph Miliband, his *New Reasoner* comrades. See Scott Hamilton, *The Crisis of Theory: E. P. Thompson, the New Left, and Postwar British Politics* (Manchester, UK: Manchester University Press, 2011), 105–9; and Michael Newman, "Thompson and the Early New Left," in *E. P. Thompson and English Radicalism*, ed. Roger Fieldhouse and Richard Taylor (Manchester, UK: Manchester University Press, 2013), 158–80.

47. Thompson, "Commitment in Politics," 51.

48. Thompson, "Commitment in Politics," 51 (emphasis in original).

49. Thompson, "Commitment in Politics," 53–54. Interestingly, Thompson does not mention Williams by name in the essay, and he speaks of a "mis-use" of Hoggart.

50. Hall, "Big Swipe," 51 (emphasis in original).

51. See Kenny, *First New Left*, 202–5.

52. Stuart Hall, "Authoritarian Populism: A Reply," *New Left Review*, no. 151 (May–June 1985): 115–24. This was a reply to Bob Jessop, Kevin Bonnett, Simon Bromley, and Tom Ling, "Authoritarian Populism, Two Nations, and Thatcherism," *New Left Review*, no. 147 (September–October 1984): 32–60.

53. See Stuart Hall and Alan Hunt, "Interview with Nicos Poulantzas," *Marx-ism Today* (July 1979): 194–201. Jessop's book *Nicos Poulantzas: State, Class, and Strategy* (London: Palgrave, 1985) would appear a few years later. Poulantzas of course had come to the attention of British Marx-ists in his earlier debate with Ralph Miliband. See, for example, Ernesto Laclau, "The Specificity of the Political: The Poulantzas-Miliband Debate," *Economy and Society* 4 (1975): 87–110; and, more recently, Bob Jessop, "Dialogue of the Deaf: Some Reflections on the Poulantzas-Miliband Debate," in *Class, Power, and the State in Capitalist Society: Essays on Ralph*

Miliband, ed. P. Wetherly, C. W. Barrow, and P. Burnham (Basingstoke, UK: Palgrave, 2007), 132–57.

54. Stuart Hall, "Nicos Poulantzas: State, Power, Socialism," *New Left Review*, no. 119 (January–February 1980): 68.

55. Hall, "Nicos Poulantzas," 68–69.

56. Hall, "Authoritarian Populism: A Reply," 118.

57. Hall, "Authoritarian Populism: A Reply," 118.

58. Hall, "Authoritarian Populism: A Reply," 118. For a superb extended discussion of Gramsci's styles of concept formation along these lines in which Hall could just as well be talking about his own, see Stuart Hall, "Gramsci's Relevance for the Study of Race and Ethnicity," in *Stuart Hall: Critical Dialogues in Cultural Studies*, ed. David Morley and Kuan-Hsing Chen (New York: Routledge, 1996), 411–15.

59. Jessop et al., "Authoritarian Populism," 37.

60. Hall, "Authoritarian Populism: A Reply," 121.

61. As one instance, see Judith Butler, Ernesto Laclau, and Slavoj Žižek, *Contingency, Hegemony, Universality: Contemporary Dialogues on the Left* (New York: Verso, 2000).

62. See Rorty's responses to Critchley, Laclau, and Derrida in Chantal Mouffe, ed., *Deconstruction and Pragmatism: Simon Critchley, Jacques Derrida, Ernesto Laclau, and Richard Rorty* (New York: Routledge, 1996).

63. See Lawrence Grossberg, "On Postmodernism and Articulation: An Interview with Stuart Hall," in Morley and Chen, *Stuart Hall*, 150.

64. See Richard Rorty, *Contingency, Irony, and Solidarity* (New York: Cambridge University Press, 1989).

65. William Connolly, *Identity | Difference: Democratic Negotiations of Political Paradox* (Ithaca, NY: Cornell University Press, 1991).

66. Scott, "Last Conjuncture," viii.

67. See David Scott, *Omens of Diversity: Tragedy, Time, Memory, Justice* (Durham: Duke University Press, 2014).

68. I'm thinking, of course, of Hannah Arendt, *The Human Condition* (Chicago: University of Chicago Press, 1958), chap. 5.

69. For the direction of this thinking, I am profoundly indebted to David Cooper, *The Measure of Things: Humanism, Humility, and Mystery* (New York: Oxford University Press, 2002), which in virtually every sentence has stimulated me.

THREE. *Attunement to Identity*

1. See Jonathan Rutherford, *After Identity* (London: Lawrence and Wishart, 2007). More than a decade and a half before, Rutherford had edited an important volume titled *Identity: Community, Culture, Difference* (London:

Lawrence and Wishart, 1990), in which Stuart Hall's essay "Cultural Identity and Diaspora" (222–37) appeared.

2. Stuart Hall, Chas Critcher, Tony Jefferson, John Clarke, and Brian Roberts, *Policing the Crisis: Mugging, the State, and Law and Order* (London: Macmillan, 1978).

3. I am thinking, for example, of Bernard Williams, *Problems of the Self* (Cambridge: Cambridge University Press, 1973); Derek Parfit, *Reasons and Persons* (New York: Oxford University Press, 1986); Charles Taylor, *Sources of the Self: The Making of Modern Identity* (Cambridge: Cambridge University Press, 1989); and Paul Ricoeur, *Oneself as Another*, trans. Kathleen Blamey (Chicago: University of Chicago Press, 1992).

4. See Stuart Hall and Martin Jacques, eds., *New Times: The Changing Face of Politics in the 1990s* (London: Verso, 1990).

5. See, for example, Ross McKibbin, "The Way We Live Now," *London Review of Books* (11 January 1990): 3–5.

6. See, interestingly, Alex Callinicos, "Stuart Hall in Perspective," *International Socialism*, no. 142 (posted 2 April 2014). Callinicos seeks to inquire into the factors "that might have immunised Hall to the absurdities of *Marxism Today*'s cult of 'New Times'" and that made it easy for him to "drift into fellow-travelling with the Eurocommunist wing of the CPGB [Communist Party of Great Britain]." Part of the problem, Callinicos ventures, is that Hall's theoretical explorations of Marxism were "carried out without any organised connection to British working class life—from which Hall may well have felt alienated because of his own black, Jamaican identity." See isj.org.uk/stuart-hall-in-perspective.

7. Stuart Hall and Martin Jacques, introduction to Hall and Jacques, *New Times*, 11.

8. Hall and Jacques, introduction to *New Times*, 12.

9. Stuart Hall, "The Great Moving Right Show," *Marxism Today* (January 1979): 17. Here, the passage reads, "'Thatcherism' has given this traditional arena of conservative philosophy expansive play," whereas in *Hard Road to Renewal* it reads, "'Thatcherism' has given these elements of neo-liberal doctrine within conservative 'philosophy' an extensive rejuvenation." Stuart Hall, *The Hard Road to Renewal: Thatcherism and the Crisis of the Left* (London: Verso, 1988), 46.

10. See Stuart Hall, "The March of the Neoliberals," *Guardian*, 12 September 2011; and Stuart Hall, "The Neo-liberal Revolution," *Cultural Studies* 25, no. 6 (2011): 705–28, a shorter version of which first appeared in *Soundings* 48 (Summer 2011): 9–27. See also Isaac Julien's film installation *Playtime* (2014), in which Hall makes an appearance in an exchange with David Harvey on contemporary capitalism.

11. Hall, "Meaning of New Times," 119–20, 130; Hall and Jacques, introduction to *New Times*, 17–18.

12. See in particular the 1992 special issue of *Ten.8* (vol. 2, no. 3) edited by Stuart Hall and David A. Bailey and organized around the theme "The Critical Decade: Black Photography in the 80s." See also Stuart Hall, "Assembling the 1980s: The Deluge—and After," in *Shades of Black: Assembling Black Arts in 1980s Britain*, ed. David A. Bailey, Ian Baucom, and Sonya Boyce (Durham: Duke University Press, 1993), 1–19; and "Vanley Burke and the 'Desire for Blackness,'" in *Vanley Burke: A Retrospective*, ed. Mark Sealy (London: Lawrence and Wishart, 1993), 12–15. For one contextualizing history, see Stuart Hall, "Black Diaspora Artists in Britain: Three 'Moments' in Post-war History," *History Workshop Journal* 61, no. 1 (2006): 1–24; and Stuart Hall and Mark Sealy, *Different: Contemporary Photography and Black Identity* (London: Phaidon, 2001).

13. See, for example, Stuart Hall, "Introduction: Who Needs 'Identity,'" in *Questions of Cultural Identity*, ed. Stuart Hall and Paul du Gay (London: Sage, 1996), 1–17; and Stuart Hall, "The Question of Cultural Identity," in *Modernity and Its Futures*, ed. Stuart Hall, David Held, and Tony McGrew (Cambridge: Polity, 1992), 273–326.

14. See Ernesto Laclau and Chantal Mouffe, *Hegemony and Socialist Strategy: Toward a Radical Democratic Politics* (London: Verso, 1985). On identity, specifically, see Ernesto Laclau, "Universalism, Particularism, and the Question of Identity," *October* 61 (Summer 1992): 83–90; and Ernesto Laclau, ed., *The Making of Political Identities* (London: Verso, 1994), especially his introduction.

15. In some sense this was Hall's view of Laclau. See also David Scott, "Politics, Contingency, Strategy: An Interview with Stuart Hall," *Small Axe*, no. 1 (March 1997): 157. For a defense of Laclau against "theoreticism," see Oliver Marchart, "Politics and Ontological Difference: On the 'Strictly Philosophical' in Laclau's Work," in *Laclau: A Critical Reader*, ed. Simon Critchley and Oliver Marchart (New York: Routledge, 2004), 54–72.

16. Interestingly, Laclau understood himself to have an oblique (at best) relation to the project of cultural studies. In an interview with Paul Bowman, and in response to a question about the relation of his work to cultural studies, Laclau says, "Cultural Studies, in the way they were propagated by Stuart Hall, have become one of the most exciting developments in the Anglo-Saxon cultural scene. I never worked within a cultural studies matrix, but have taken full advantage of the intellectual stimulus that it provided. Some of the essays in *The Making of Political Identities* have been more influenced by cultural studies than others, but I would say that, on the whole, they belong to a different intellectual universe. The orientation of both the Programme of Discourse Analysis and the Centre for Theoreti-

cal Studies in the Humanities and Social Sciences at Essex belong, I would say, more to a terrain created by the cross-fertilisation between Continental Philosophy, Lacanian Psychoanalysis and the theory of hegemony, than to cultural studies in the usual sense of the term." See Ernesto Laclau, "Politics, Polemics, and Academics: An Interview by Paul Bowman," *Parallax* 5, no 2 (1999): 94–95.

17. See Fanon's remark about the anomaly of method in the introduction to *Peau noire, masques blancs* (Paris: Éditions de Seuil, 1952), 9: "Il est de bon ton de faire précéder un ouvrage de psychologie d'un point de vue méthodologique. Nous faillirons à l'usage. Nous laissons les méthodes aux botanistes et aux mathématiciens. Il y a un point où les méthodes se réabsorbent" (It is considered good form to preface a work of psychology with a methodological perspective. We will break with this custom. Let us leave methods to botanists and mathematicians. There comes a point at which methods are reabsorbed). I have altered slightly the Richard Philcox translation in Frantz Fanon, *Black Skin, White Masks* (New York: Grove, 2008), xvi. It is in fact a curious phrasing I think, *se réabsorber*, to be reabsorbed, as it were, into themselves, as though they had become irrelevant. Fanon is brusquely separating himself from a certain ethos of work, which for him has no bearing on his preoccupations. (I am very grateful to Michel Chevalier for a discussion on this point.) See also Richard Rorty, "Response to Ernesto Laclau," in *Deconstruction and Pragmatism: Simon Critchley, Jacques Derrida, Ernesto Laclau, and Richard Rorty*, ed. Chantal Mouffe (New York: Routledge, 1996), 49–70.

18. See Heinz Kohut, *The Analysis of the Self: A Systematic Approach to the Psychoanalytic Treatment of Narcissistic Personality Disorders* (Chicago: University of Chicago Press, 1971). Clifford Geertz mobilizes the distinction in his well-known essay "'From the Native's Point of View': On the Nature of Anthropological Understanding," in *Local Knowledge: Further Essays in Interpretive Anthropology* (New York: Basic Books, 1983), 57–58.

19. Stuart Hall, "Old and New Identities, Old and New Ethnicities," in *Culture, Globalization, and the World System*, ed. Anthony King (Minneapolis: University of Minnesota Press, 1997), 42. Hereafter, references to this essay are given parenthetically in the text.

20. Stuart Hall, "New Ethnicities," in "Black Film, British Cinema," ed. Kobena Mercer, ICA *Documents* 7 (London: Institute of Contemporary Arts, 1988), 27–31.

21. See David Scott, "Stuart Hall's Ethics," *Small Axe*, no. 17 (March 2005): 10–12. Hall refers to "New Ethnicities" as "somewhat notorious" in "What Is This 'Black' in Black Popular Culture?," in *Black Popular Culture*, ed. Gina Dent (Seattle, WA: Bay Press, 1992), 21.

22. Hall, "New Ethnicities," 28.

23. Indeed, Hall opens the essay with his characteristically provisional description of a conjuncture that cannot be thought of in terms of "two clearly discernible phases" that are definitive. See Hall, "New Ethnicities," 27.

24. Hall, "What Is This 'Black,'" 32.

25. Ian Hacking, *Mad Travelers: Reflections on the Reality of Transient Mental Illness* (Charlottesville: University of Virginia Press, 1998), 85.

26. Lisa Appignanesi, "Editor's Note," in "Identity: The Real Me," ed. Lisa Appignanesi, ICA *Documents* 6 (London: Institute of Contemporary Arts, 1987), 2.

27. Homi K. Bhabha's contribution, which forms a kind of introduction, is called "The Commitment to Theory" (5–11); Terry Eagleton's, which appears as the concluding essay, is called "The Politics of Subjectivity" (47–48)— both in Appignanesi, "Identity: The Real Me."

28. Stuart Hall, "Minimal Selves," in Appignanesi, "Identity: The Real Me," 44–46. Hereafter, references to this essay are given parenthetically in the text.

29. See Erving Goffman, "The Lecture," in *Forms of Talk* (Philadelphia: University of Pennsylvania Press, 1981), 173–74.

30. The allusion of course is to the unpaginated preface to C. L. R. James, *Beyond a Boundary* (London: Hutchinson, 1963), in which James famously writes, "This book is neither cricket reminiscences nor autobiography. It poses the question *What do they know of cricket who only cricket know?* To answer involves ideas as well as facts" (italics in the original).

31. See Lawrence Grossberg, "On Postmodernism and Articulation: An Interview with Stuart Hall," in *Stuart Hall: Critical Dialogues in Cultural Studies*, ed. David Morley and Kuan-Hsing Chen (New York: Routledge, 1996), 131–34.

32. "Journey to an Expectation" is the final chapter of George Lamming's memoir of his generation's journey to England in the 1950s to make writers of themselves. See *The Pleasures of Exile* (London: Michael Joseph, 1960), 211–29. The story of this first wave of migrants and their impact on the remaking of post–World War II Britain is told in Mike Phillips and Trevor Phillips, *"Windrush": The Irresistible Rise of Multi-Racial Britain* (New York: HarperCollins, 1999).

33. Samuel Selvon's *The Lonely Londoners* (London: Alan Wingate, 1956) is the classic novel of West Indian migration in the 1950s.

34. Stuart Hall, *The Young Englanders* (London: National Committee for Commonwealth Immigrants, 1967). In the conclusion to this prescient lecture of the late 1960s, Hall observes, "I have noticed that the young immigrants I have met in the last year or two are falling back on their own

reserves. They are closing-in their lines of contact, re-discovering their own racial and national identities and stereotyping their white counterparts. In itself, this may not be a bad thing—if integration means the enforced loss and rejection of their own identity, then it is too high a price to pay. Most people want recognition by their peers, but it must be recognition on equal and honorable terms" (14).

35. See Hall, Critcher, Jefferson, Clarke, and Roberts, "The Politics of 'Mugging,'" in *Policing the Crisis*, 328–97.

36. Stuart Hall and David Scott, "Hospitality's Others: A Conversation," in *The Unexpected Guest: Art, Writing, and Thinking on Hospitality*, ed. Sally Tallant and Paul Domela (London: Art Books, 2012), 291–304.

37. "Mon corps me revenait étalé, disjoint, rétamé, tout endeuillé dans ce jour blanc d'hiver." Fanon, *Peau noire, masques blancs*, 91. I have altered somewhat the Philcox translation in Fanon, *Black Skin, White Masks*, 93.

38. Isaac Julien, dir., *Frantz Fanon: Black Skin, White Mask* (1995).

39. Fanon, *Black Skin, White Masks*, 111; I have altered the Philcox translation of "Et quand j'essayais, sur le plan de l'idée et de l'activité intellectuelle, de revendiquer ma négritude, on me l'arrachait. On me démontrait que ma démarche n'était qu'un terme dans la dialectique" (Fanon, *Peau noire, masques blancs*, 107).

40. Fanon, *Black Skin, White Masks*, 199–200; I have altered the Philcox translation of "Le découverte de l'existence d'une civilisation nègre au XVe siècle ne me décerne pas un brevet d'humanité. Qu'on le veuille ou non, le passé ne peut pas en aucune façon me guider dans l'actualité" (Fanon, *Peau noire, masques blancs*, 182).

41. The epigraph at the beginning of the introduction to Fanon's *Peau noire, masques blancs*, reads, "Je parle de millions d'hommes à qui on a inculqué savamment la peur, le complexe d'infériorité, le tremblement, l'agenouillement, le désespoir, le larbinisme" (5) (I am talking about millions of men in whom fear, an inferiority complex, trembling, kneeling, despair, slavishness, has been knowingly inculcated). It is taken of course from Aimé Césaire, *Discours sur le colonialisme* (Paris: Présence Africaine, 1955), 24. For the Philcox translation, see Fanon, *Black Skin, White Masks*, xi.

42. For a discussion of Fanon's relation to Sartre, see David Macey, *Frantz Fanon: A Biography* (New York: Picador, 2000), 452–68. And on Fanon's relation to *Les temps modernes*, see Howard Davis, *Sartre and "Les temps modernes"* (Cambridge: Cambridge University Press, 2009), 85–89.

43. Fanon, *Les damnés de la terre* (Paris: Maspero, 1961); translated as *The Wretched of the Earth* by Constance Farrington (New York: Grove, 1967) and by Richard Philcox (New York: Grove, 2004).

NOTES TO LETTER THREE

—

44. See Stuart Hall, "The After-life of Frantz Fanon: Why Fanon? Why Now? Why *Black Skin, White Masks?*," in *The Fact of Blackness: Frantz Fanon and Visual Representation*, ed. Alan Reed (Seattle, WA: Bay Press, 1996), 12–37.

45. For Hall's analysis of the Jamaican social structure, see Stuart Hall, "Pluralism, Race, and Class in Caribbean Society," in *Race and Class in Post-colonial Society: A Study of Ethnic Group Relations in the English-Speaking Caribbean, Bolivia, Chile, and Mexico* (Paris: UNESCO, 1977), 150–82.

46. Oddly, there are only two histories of this social formation. See Mavis Campbell, *The Dynamics of Change in a Slave Society: A Sociopolitical History of the Free Coloreds of Jamaica, 1800–1865* (Rutherford, NJ: Associated Universities Press, 1976); and Gad Heuman, *Between Black and White: Race, Politics, and the Free Coloreds in Jamaica, 1792–1865* (Westport, CT: Greenwood, 1981).

47. See Ian Hacking, *Historical Ontology* (Cambridge, MA: Harvard University Press, 2004).

48. On the events in Notting Hill in late August and early September 1958, see Edward Pilkington, *Beyond the Mother Country: West Indians and the Notting Hill White Riots* (London: I. B. Tauris, 1990). For Stuart Hall's remarks, see *Young Englanders*, 3–4.

49. See also the interview "A Conversation with Stuart Hall," in which Hall talks about the term *black* being made available to him "by Rastafarianism and by the civil rights movement." *Journal of the International Institute* 7, no. 1 (1999), quod.lib.umich.edu/j/jii/4750978.0007.107/—conversation-with-stuart-hall?rgn=main;view=fulltext, para. 5 under "On Theories and Experiences of the Subject."

FOUR. *Learning to Learn from Others*

1. See, especially, William Connolly, *The Ethos of Pluralization* (Minneapolis: University of Minnesota Press, 1995), a book that has always seemed to me of enormous theoretical subtlety.

2. "A little to the side, but not outside," Michael Walzer writes, "critical distance is measured in inches." *Interpretation and Social Criticism* (Cambridge, MA: Harvard University Press, 1987), 61.

3. See Romand Coles, "Liberty, Equality, Receptive Generosity: Neo-Nietzschean Reflections on the Ethics and Politics of Coalition," *American Political Science Review* 90, no. 2 (1996): 375–88; *Self/Power/Other: Political Theory and Dialogical Ethics* (Ithaca, NY: Cornell University Press, 1992); *Rethinking Generosity: Critical Theory and the Politics of Caritas* (Ithaca, NY: Cornell University Press, 1997); and, most recently, *Beyond Gated Politics: Reflections for the Possibility of Democracy* (Minneapolis: University of Minnesota Press, 2005).

4. Stuart Hall and David Scott, "Hospitality's Others," in *The Unexpected Guest*, ed. Sally Tallant and Paul Domela (London: Art/Books, 2012).

5. See Romand Coles, "Tragedy's Tragedy: Political Liberalism and Its Others," in *Beyond Gated Politics*, 1–41.

6. Coles, "Tragedy's Tragedy," 35.

7. Hall's phrase occurs, among other places, in his contribution to "Then and Now: A Re-evaluation of the New Left," a discussion among three of the founding editors of *Universities and Left Review*—Hall, Charles Taylor, and Raphael Samuel—at a conference revisiting the first New Left and published in *Out of Apathy: Voices of the New Left Thirty Years On*, ed. Oxford University Socialist Group (London: Verso, 1989), 151.

8. Romand Coles, "Moving Democracy: The Political Arts of Listening, Traveling, and Tabling," in *Beyond Gated Politics*, 214.

9. Relevant here too is the thinking of James Tully, who develops what he calls a "reciprocal relation" between philosophy and political practice. See *Public Philosophy in a New Key*, vol. 1 (Cambridge: Cambridge University Press, 2008), 17.

10. Coles talks about his involvement with the Industrial Areas Foundation in *Beyond Gated Politics*, xxxiv–xxxv, and chap. 7.

11. Coles, "Liberty, Equality, Receptive Generosity," 375.

12. Coles, *Self/Power/Other*, 1.

13. See, for example, Stanley Hauerwas and Romand Coles, *Christianity, Democracy, and the Radical Ordinary: Conversations between a Radical Democrat and a Christian* (Eugene, OR: Cascade, 2008), especially the introduction. Interesting to me, of course, in the context of this book, is that the "conversation" between Hauerwas and Coles is partly conducted through letters.

14. See Coles, *Self/Power/Other*, 1.

15. Ernesto Laclau and Chantal Mouffe, *Hegemony and Socialist Strategy: Towards a Radical Democratic Politics* (London: Verso, 1985). On the career of the idea of "radical democracy," see David Trent, ed., *Radical Democracy: Identity, Citizenship, and the State* (New York: Routledge, 1995).

16. See Richard Johnson, "Reading for the Best Marx: History-Writing and Historical Abstraction," in *Making Histories: Studies in History-Writing and Politics*, ed. Richard Johnson, G. McLennan, Bill Schwarz, and D. Sutton (London: Hutchinson, 1982), 153–201. Johnson succeeded Hall as director of the Centre for Contemporary Cultural Studies in 1979.

17. Romand Coles, "MacIntyre and the Confidence Trickster of Rivalish Tradition," in *Beyond Gated Politics*, 80.

18. Romand Coles, "Derrida and the Promise of Democracy," in *Beyond Gated Politics*, 139.

19. Coles, "MacIntyre," 89, 103.

20. Coles, "MacIntyre," 103.

21. Coles, "Derrida," 140.

22. See, for example, my discussion of Richard Rorty, in David Scott, "Culture and Criticism: Theory and Postcolonial Claims on Anthropological Disciplinarity," *Critique of Anthropology* 12, no. 4 (1992): 371–94; and of Thomas McCarthy's *Race, Empire, and the Idea of Human Development* (Cambridge: Cambridge University Press, 2009), in David Scott, "The Traditions of Historical Others," *Symposium on Gender Race and Philosophy* 8, no. 1 (2012), sgrp.typepad.com/sgrp/winter-2012-symposium-mccarthy -2009.html. Clifford Geertz used the phrase in his 1985 Tanner Lecture "The Uses of Diversity." See *Available Light: Anthropological Reflections on Philosophical Topics* (Princeton, NJ: Princeton University Press, 2000), 72.

23. David Michael Levin, *The Listening Self: Personal Growth, Social Change, and the Closure of Metaphysics* (New York: Routledge, 1989).

24. See Coles, "Moving Democracy," 213–37.

25. Coles, "Moving Democracy," 2.

26. Coles is thinking here of John Rawls, *A Theory of Justice* (Cambridge, MA: Harvard University Press, 1971); and Donald Moon, *Constructing Community: Moral Pluralism and Tragic Conflicts* (Princeton, NJ: Princeton University Press, 1993).

27. Coles, "Tragedy's Tragedy," 2.

28. Raymond Williams, *Modern Tragedy* (London: Chatto and Windus, 1966), pt. 2, chap. 1.

29. See John Rawls, *The Law of Peoples* (Cambridge, MA: Harvard University Press, 1999); and Martha Nussbaum, *Cultivating Humanity* (Cambridge, MA: Harvard University Press, 1997). See the discussion in Romand Coles, "Contesting Cosmopolitan Currency," in *Beyond Gated Politics*, 55–64.

30. See Gloria Anzaldúa, *Borderlands/La Frontera: The New Mestiza* (San Francisco: Aunt Lute, 1987). She writes, "In a constant state of mental nepantilism, an Aztec word meaning torn between ways, la mestiza is a product of the transfer of the cultural and spiritual values of one group to another. Being tricultural, monolingual, bilingual, or multilingual, speaking a patois, and in a state of perpetual transition, the mestiza faces a dilemma of the mixed breed: which collectivity does the daughter of a darkskinned mother listen to?" (100).

31. Coles, "Contesting Cosmopolitan Currency," 66.

32. Coles, "Contesting Cosmopolitan Currency," 68.

33. See David Scott, "The Moral Justification of Reparation for New World Slavery," in *Freedom and Democracy in an Imperial Context: Dialogues with James Tully*, ed. Robert Nichols and Jakeet Singh (New York: Routledge, 2014), 100–120.

34. See Montaigne, "On Cannibals," in *Essays* (New York: Penguin, 1958), 105–19.

35. For an instructive defense of the New Left against some of his Trotskyist comrades, see Alasdair MacIntyre, "The 'New Left,'" *Labour Review* 4, no. 3 (1959): 98–100, reprinted in *Alasdair MacIntyre's Engagement with Marxism*, ed. Paul Blackledge and Neil Davidson (London: Haymarket, 2009), 87–93. MacIntyre also contributed to the New Left volume *Out of Apathy*, ed. E. P. Thompson (London: New Left, 1960), 195–240; Hall was also a contributor, with an essay titled "The Supply of Demand" (56–97). On MacIntyre's relation to Trotskyism, see Neil Davidson, "Alasdair MacIntyre and Trotskyism," in *Virtue and Politics: Alasdair MacIntyre's Revolutionary Aristotelianism*, ed. Paul Blackledge and Kelvin Knight (Notre Dame, IN: University of Notre Dame Press, 2011), 152–76. Notably, the final chapter of *After Virtue: A Study in Moral Theory* (Notre Dame, IN: University of Notre Dame Press, 1981) is titled "After Virtue: Nietzsche or Aristotle, Trotsky and St. Benedict" (256–63).

36. See Neil Davidson, "Alasdair MacIntyre as a Marxist," in *1956 and All That*, ed. Keith Flett (Newcastle, UK: Cambridge Scholars, 2007); Paul Blackledge and Neil Davidson, "Introduction: The Unknown Alasdair MacIntyre," in Blackledge and Davidson, *Alasdair MacIntyre's Engagement with Marxism*, xiii–l; Kelvin Knight, *Aristotelian Philosophy: Ethics and Politics from Aristotle to MacIntyre* (Cambridge, UK: Polity, 2007), esp. chap. 4; Neil Davidson, "Alasdair MacIntyre as a Marxist," in *Holding Fast to an Image of the Past: Explorations in the Marxist Tradition* (Chicago: Haymarket, 2014), 129–81; and Christopher Lutz, *Reading Alasdair MacIntyre's "After Virtue"* (London: Bloomsbury Academic, 2012).

37. Alasdair MacIntyre, *Marxism: An Interpretation* (London: SCM, 1953). He laments toward the end, for example, "So that one is finally brought to the point where one must ask how the themes of the gospel and of Marx can be made relevant at all in the light of the corruption of the Church and of the Communist Party" (121). Still, MacIntyre doesn't refrain from going on to point in the directions he sees important. One intriguing feature of the book is the pair of epigraphs that stand at its entrance (on the unpaginated title page). The first, from Oswald Spengler, reads, "Christianity is the grandmother of Bolshevism"; the second, from R. H. Tawney, reads, "The true descendant of the doctrines of Aquinas is the labour theory of value. The last of the Schoolmen was Karl Marx."

38. Indeed, it would be interesting to ponder the connections and contrasts between these two now-towering contemporary philosophers who are very often mentioned together, for example, as "communitarians." Taylor has commented on MacIntyre's *After Virtue*, "Aristotle or Nietzsche," *Partisan Review* 51, no. 2 (1984): 301–6; and MacIntyre has commented on Taylor's *Sources of the Self: The Making of Modern Identity* (New York: Cambridge

University Press, 1992), in "Critical Remarks on *The Sources of the Self* by Charles Taylor," *Philosophy and Phenomenological Research* 54, no. 1 (1994): 187–90.

39. Alasdair MacIntyre, "Notes from the Moral Wilderness I," *New Reasoner*, no. 7 (Winter 1958–59): 90–100; and "Notes from the Moral Wilderness II," *New Reasoner*, no. 8 (Spring 1959): 89–97.

40. E. P. Thompson, "Socialist Humanism: An Epistle to the Philistines," *New Reasoner*, no. 1 (Summer 1957): 105–23 and 124–43. For a discussion, see Paul Blackledge, "Socialist Humanism and Revolutionary Politics in the British Left," in Flett, *1956 and All That*.

41. See E. P. Thompson, *The Poverty of Theory* (London: Merlin, 1978).

42. There were a number of responses to Thompson in the pages of *The New Reasoner* in 1957 and 1958. Among the most often discussed are those of Harry Hanson, "An Open Letter to Edward Thompson," *New Reasoner*, no. 2 (Autumn 1957): 79–91; and Charles Taylor, "Socialism and Humanism," *New Reasoner*, no. 2 (Autumn 1957): 92–98. For a useful discussion of Thompson's essay and Taylor's response to it, including the fact that Thompson's essay was in part made possible by the Marx manuscripts that Taylor brought back from Paris in 1957, see Freddy Foks, "E. P. Thompson, Charles Taylor, and the Turn to Socialist Humanism, 1957–1959," www.academia.edu /3152399/E.P._Thompson_Charles_Taylor_and_the_turn_to_Socialist _Humanism_1957-1959 (accessed 30 April 2015). Foks helpfully situates Taylor's critique of Thompson in relation to not only the French postwar debates on humanism involving Jean-Paul Sartre and Maurice Merleau-Ponty but also those involving the Catholic philosopher Jacques Maritain.

43. See MacIntyre, "Notes I," 90.

44. MacIntyre, "Notes I," 90.

45. In the preface to *After Virtue*, MacIntyre writes of his intellectual journey, "The conclusion I reached and which is embodied in this book—although Marxism itself is only a marginal preoccupation—is that Marxism's moral defects and failures arise from the extent to which it, like liberal individualism, embodies the ethos of the distinctively modern and modernizing world, and that nothing less than a rejection of a large part of that ethos will provide us with a rationally and morally defensible standpoint from which to judge and act—and in terms of which to evaluate various rival and heterogeneous schemes which compete for our allegiance" (x).

46. See Blackledge and Davidson, "Introduction: The Unknown Alasdair MacIntyre," xliii; and Davidson, "Alasdair MacIntyre as a Marxist," 161–66.

47. See especially MacIntyre, *After Virtue*; "Epistemological Crises, Dramatic Narrative, and the Philosophy of Science," *Monist* 60, no. 4 (1977): 453–72;

Whose Justice, Which Rationality? (Notre Dame, IN: University of Notre Dame Press, 1988); *Three Rival Versions of Moral Inquiry* (Notre Dame, IN: University of Notre Dame Press, 1990); and *Dependent Rational Animals: Why Human Beings Need the Virtues* (Peru, IL: Open Court, 1999). For the idea of MacIntyre as a revolutionary Aristotelian, see Blackledge and Knight, *Virtue and Politics*. Interestingly, MacIntyre has himself endorsed the term "revolutionary Aristotelianism." See Alasdair MacIntyre, "Politics, Philosophy, and the Common Good," in *The MacIntyre Reader*, ed. Kelvin Knight (Notre Dame, IN: University of Notre Dame Press, 1998), 235.

48. Sedgwick wrote, in an early review of his friend's book, *After Virtue*, "I write of Alasdair MacIntyre as an intellectual rather than solely as an academic: and would justify this characterisation partly by observing that, while his style of argument draws much of its force from a particular professional training (analytic philosophy in the British tradition of enquiry), its strengths are hard to locate as proceeding from any one academic area. There are elements of sociological theory here, and some attention to historical or anthropological enquiry. . . . There are also many references to the social organisation of literature (the saga and epic as well as the novel) as well as of other arts, musical and visual, which are often seen as less social. While MacIntyre's philosophical identity is securely anchored in his long, often polemical involvement with the great ethical works of the past (and with modern systematic writers on moral questions), the power of his writings derives largely from his enviable capacity to take selected themes from the technical, professionalised debates among philosophers and social scientists and re-fashion them as material for the urgent attention of a non-specialised public, often using dramatic, poetic and prophetic devices in the casting of his arguments." See Peter Sedgwick, "The Ethical Dance: A Review of Alasdair MacIntyre's *After Virtue*," *Socialist Register*, no. 19 (1982): 259–60. Also referred to in Blackledge and Davidson, "Introduction: The Unknown Alasdair MacIntyre," xix.

49. See the interview by Giovanna Borradori, "Nietzsche or Aristotle? Alasdair MacIntyre," in her collection *The American Philosopher: Conversations with Quine, Davidson, Putnam, Nozick, Danto, Rorty, Cavell, MacIntyre*, trans. Rosanna Crocitto (Chicago: University of Chicago Press, 1994), 139–40.

50. MacIntyre, *After Virtue*, 222.

51. See, for example, Raymond Williams, *Culture and Society, 1750–1980*, 2nd ed. (New York: Columbia University Press, 1983), viii, xviii, 18, 29.

52. See Alasdair MacIntyre, "Culture and Revolution," *International Socialism*, 1st ser., no. 5 (Summer 1961): 28. Reprinted in Blackledge and Davidson,

Alasdair MacIntyre's Engagement with Marxism, 175–78. MacIntyre writes admiringly of Williams's quality of thinking and writing, that it liberates us from the "sterility and frustration" of much of the socialist theorizing of his day. However, though positively sympathetic toward *Culture and Society* (1958), MacIntyre was critical of its sequel, *The Long Revolution* (1961). Part of his assessment is worth quoting in full (from the Blackledge and Davidson edition): "Although Williams is not a Marxist, he escapes imprisonment by the present in *Culture and Society* because he brings together such a host of conflicting witnesses that no one conceptual scheme dominates us. Cobbett, Mill, Disraeli, Gissing, Lawrence, Tawney and many others all contribute to a growing, if contradictory, consciousness of the possibility of a common culture. But, in *The Long Revolution*, where the question is asked how far that possibility has in fact been realised, the situation is much worse. Put briefly, Williams accepts as authentic the unity of our society and his long revolution is a revolution against nothing except the inertia of the past. The false consciousness of gradualism is allowed to be judged in its own terms" (177).

53. For MacIntyre's response to criticisms of the thesis of *After Virtue*, see Alasdair MacIntyre, "Postscript to the Second Edition," in *After Virtue*, 264–78. For a far-ranging discussion of MacIntyre's work, see the essays collected in Blackledge and Knight, *Virtue and Politics*, and MacIntyre's response there, in "Where We Were, Where We Are, Where We Need to Be" (307–34).

54. It is an interesting feature of MacIntyre's thinking that it has been suggestively informed and inflected by anthropology. Indeed, MacIntyre has spoken of being influenced in particular by the work of Franz Steiner (1909–52), whose book *Taboo* (New York: Philosophical Library, 1956) is too little read these days, even in anthropology departments. MacIntyre says, "Most happily for me, when I was a student in London I met the anthropologist Franz Steiner, who pointed me toward ways of understanding moralities that avoided both the reductionism of presenting morality as a mere secondary expression of something else, and the abstractionism that detaches principles from socially embodied practice." See Borradori, "Nietzsche or Aristotle? Alasdair MacIntyre," 258–59.

55. See the well-known essay by Talal Asad, "The Concept of Cultural Translation in British Social Anthropology," in *Writing Culture: The Poetics and Politics of Ethnography*, ed. James Clifford and George E. Marcus (Berkeley: University of California Press, 1986), 141–64.

56. Coles develops his Nietzschean direction in "Liberty, Equality, Receptive Generosity," and again in "Introduction: Questioning *Caritas*," in *Rethinking Generosity*, 15–23. See also the very suggestive argument in Rosalyn Diprose,

Corporeal Generosity: On Giving with Nietzsche, Merleau-Ponty, and Levinas (Albany: State University of New York Press, 2002).

57. See Friedrich Nietzsche, "On the Gift-Giving Virtue," in *Thus Spoke Zarathustra*, trans. Walter Kaufman (New York: Penguin, 1978), 74–79.

Adieu

1. Ralph Waldo Emerson, "Friendship," in *The Essential Writings of Ralph Emerson*, ed. Brooks Atkinson (New York: Modern Classics, 2000), 211.

NOTE TO ADIEU

—

INDEX

Engels, Friedrich, 71–72, 150n9
epistemology, 57–58, 79–80
epistolary form, 1, 3–8, 12, 17–18, 21–22, 40, 150n9, 153n32
"The Essay as Form" (Adorno), 63
essay form, 5–6, 61–64
essentialists, 11–12, 53–55, 96–106, 144
ethics: contingency and, 53–55, 81–84; deontology and, 9, 126–27; friendship and, 9–10; politics and, 80–81; receptive generosity and, 116–18, 125–40; style and, 23–27, 29–30; utilitarianism and, 9; virtue and, 9–10; voice and, 18–21, 23–28, 30–36, 46–48, 54, 115–18
ethnicity, 89. *See also* "New Ethnicities" (Hall); race
Eurocentrism, 48–49, 106, 131–33
event, the, 56
examples, 30, 140–42
experiences (near and distant), 91–93, 113–14

Fanon, Frantz, 27–29, 91, 105–6, 167n17, 169nn39–40
Felski, Rita, 5
feminism, 94–95
finding, 109–13
finitude, 3, 55, 60, 63, 82–84, 117, 143
Fiumara, Gemma, 19, 42–43, 47, 74
form (content of the form), 2, 4, 29, 35, 61–64. *See also* epistolary form; essay form
For Marx (Althusser), 57
For More Than One Voice (Cavarero), 35
Foucault, Michel, 8, 56–58, 76–77, 97
fragments, 62
Frantz Fanon (Julien), 105
Freud, Sigmund, 95, 128
Friedman, Milton, 88
friendship, 7–18, 45–51, 143–45, 150n9, 153n32
"Friendship" (Telfer), 151n14

Gadamer, Hans-Georg, 42, 45–49, 159n55
Galbraith, John Kenneth, 71
Gallie, W. B., 20
Geertz, Clifford, 91–92, 128
gender, 88, 94–95, 97–98
generosity, 125–30, 140
Glissant, Edouard, 131
Goffman, Erving, 31, 98–99
grain, the, 30–31, 85
Gramsci, Antonio, 57, 74, 77, 80, 87, 121
"The Great Moving Right Show" (Hall), 64–71, 74, 76, 78–81, 83, 87
Groundwork of the Metaphysics of Morals (Kant), 126
Grundrisse (Marx), 59, 122, 160n11

Habermas, Jürgen, 116
Hacking, Ian, 97, 107
Hall, Stuart: cultural studies and, 4, 21, 31–32, 166n16; death of, 2–5, 7; ethics of, 2, 21, 23–27, 30–34, 140–42; intellectual style of, 1–2, 4, 13–19, 23–34, 50–51, 53–56, 113–18, 120–21, 140–42; writings of, 14, 61, 64–81, 93–113, 155n16, 160n14, 168n23, 168n34. *See also specific writings*
Hannah Arendt and the Politics of Friendship (Nixon), 150n11
Hanson, Harry, 174n42
The Hard Road to Renewal (volume), 65, 87–88
Hart, Richard, 107
Hayek, Friedrich, 88
hearing, 34–42, 49, 129–30, 159n55
hearkening, 44–45, 49, 128, 158n46
Hegel, G. W. F., 134–35
Hegemony and Socialist Strategy (Laclau and Mouffe), 90, 120
Hegemony Group, 74
Heidegger, Martin, 40, 43–46, 48, 128, 158n46, 158n48
Henriques, Julian, 154n6, 156n22